Talking Diversity
with **Teachers**
and **Teacher Educators**

Talking Diversity
with **Teachers**
and **Teacher Educators**

Exercises and
Critical Conversations
Across the Curriculum

Edited by
Bárbara C. Cruz
Cheryl R. Ellerbrock
Anete Vásquez
Elaine V. Howes

Foreword by
Geneva Gay

Teachers College
Columbia University
New York and London

Published by Teachers College Press, 1234 Amsterdam Avenue, New York, NY 10027

Library of Congress Cataloging-in-Publication Data

Talking diversity with teachers and teacher educators : exercises and critical conversations across the curriculum / edited by Barbara C. Cruz, Cheryl R. Ellerbrock, Anete Vasquez, Elaine V. Howes ; foreword by Geneva Gay.
        pages cm
    Includes index.
    ISBN 978-0-8077-5537-2 (pbk. : alk. paper) —
    ISBN 978-0-8077-7291-1 (e-book)
        1. Multicultural education—Study and teaching (Higher)—United States. 2. Culturally relevant pedagogy—United States. 3. Teachers—Training of—United States. I. Cruz, Bárbara, editor of compilation. II. Ellerbrock, Cheryl R., editor of compilation. III. Vásquez, Anete, editor of compilation. IV. Howes, Elaine V., editor of compilation.
    LC1099.3.T35 2014
    370.117—dc23   2014004970

ISBN 978-0-8077-5537-2 (paper)
ISBN 978-0-8077-7291-1 (ebook)

Printed on acid-free paper
Manufactured in the United States of America

21   20   19   18   17   16   15   14   8   7   6   5   4   3   2   1

For those faculty and students—
present and past—
who inspired us to write this book

Contents

Foreword

There is no shortage of scholarship on the need for knowledge acquisition about and pedagogical skill development for ethnic, racial, cultural, social, and linguistic diversity in teacher preparation programs. Moreover, there is a significant amount of agreement about what prompts these needs and what should be essential components of their development even though different scholars use different approaches and emphases of analysis. For example, many scholars agree that teachers need to be more critically cognizant and analytical about how their own cultural orientations affect their teaching as well as how the cultural socialization of students from different ethnic backgrounds affects the students' learning. As Nieto and Bode (2012) and Gay (2003, 2010) suggest, multicultural education competence requires both personal and professional development. In other words, one cannot become an effective multicultural teacher without simultaneously becoming a multicultural *person*, even though proposals for when this transformation should begin and how it should proceed vary. Other points of agreement include teachers' learning how to scaffold the funds of knowledge of diverse students in classroom instruction; being caring advocates for diverse students; and teaching for cultural competence, social justice, and sociopolitical transformation, along with heightened academic achievement.

The implied logic of these proposals is that teacher educators must have the skills and commitments to assist teacher candidates in acquiring these competencies. Yet, explicitly *educating teacher educators for teaching diversity* is still a rare occurrence in scholarship about ethnic, racial, cultural, economic, and linguistic diversity. Some authors do address this need broadly and rather sketchily, but their explanations do not provide descriptive specificity and extensive details about what this preparation looks like in actual practice. Instead, the focus tends to be on the knowledge and skill development of teacher candidates. Sleeter's (2001) review of 80 studies conducted in the 1990s on the effects of strategies for teaching diversity in teacher education confirms this reality. Her review focused on general programmatic features (such as courses taught and field experiences), what was taught, and the effects of multicultural education learning experiences for prospective teachers rather than the specific instructional techniques (the "how" of teaching) of individual teacher educators. More recent scholarship, such as that of Adams, Bell, and Griffin (2007); Milner (2009); and Ball and Tyson (2011) indicate that these trends continue.

However, some emerging scholarship targets teacher educators (and college instructors in other disciplines) and their needed competencies and accountability for being ethnically, culturally, and racially responsive in their teacher education policies, programs, and pedagogies. Illustrative of this emergence is Mayo and Larke's (2013) summary of initiatives by professors in different disciplines to incorporate multiculturalism into their curricula after participating in a training institute. The present volume, *Talking Diversity with Teachers and Teacher Educators,* is another noteworthy contribution to these new developments for moving ideological and theoretical beliefs about cultural diversity into the actual instructional practices of college professors teaching others to do so.

Specialization and content mastery are preeminent in the professional training, socialization, and practice of college professors. It is, therefore, often difficult for them to personally embrace teaching needs and domains that cut across disciplinary boundaries as teaching cultural diversity and multicultural education do. These professors may endorse the general idea of diversity without doing anything pragmatically about it in the subject-specific courses they teach. The editors and contributing authors of *Talking Diversity with Teachers and Teacher Educators* were conscious of these tendencies as they put this volume together and deliberately set about counteracting them by showing how diversity is an integral feature of many disciplines that are common elements of most teacher education programs. Rather than continuing prior efforts that describe what the teacher education students should learn about diversity from these courses (thereby focusing on outcomes), they shift the focus to processes teacher educators can use in teaching for diversity.

These processes have another feature that is captivating, validating, and authenticating: they are introduced and illustrated with narratives describing the personal experiences and practices of teacher educators using strategies for engaging in diversity studies that are highly recommended in theoretical scholarship about multicultural education, teaching diversity, and culturally responsive teaching. Therefore, they model their messages, or demonstrate how theory about cultural diversity pedagogy can be translated into the actual practices of teacher educators. Creating images of ideas is good pedagogy in general and imperative in areas of study that are potentially contentious, as diversity in its various manifestations often is.

There are several other attributes of this volume that illuminate salient features of education for and about diversity, whether intended for teacher educators or for students in classrooms at all levels and within all domains

educators cannot anticipate and design everything prior to actually interacting with their students.

Talking Diversity with Teachers and Teacher Educators validates these ideas. A multitude of instructional techniques is presented across the chapters and sometimes even within chapters. For this reason, teacher educators reading this volume should resist the temptation to seek affinity and allegiance with only their areas of disciplinary specialization and read only those chapters that are directly related. If they do so, they will miss the richness of this volume and one of its most salient qualities, which stems from the many different ways of teaching presented that are applicable across disciplines. The compilation of strategies and recommendations from the various chapters gives functional meaning to the idea of routinely using multiple perspectives and multiple methodologies in teaching about and for diversity.

There is indeed truth to the claim that teachers teach through who they are, or that there is a strong personal presence in teachers' professional actions. Undoubtedly, this is as true for teacher educators as it is for teachers in any and all other aspects of the educational enterprise. A profound implication of this fact for preparing to teach diversity is that teacher educators and teachers need to deeply understand themselves and how who they are affects how they teach. Advancements in reflective self-study, auto-ethnographic, and narrative research are providing useful guidance and techniques for developing these interactions. The authors of *Talking Diversity with Teachers and Teacher Educators* exemplify some of them in presenting their "personal stories" of how they are talking and teaching diversity in their respective classrooms. These stories are both instructive and inviting, affirming and empowering. They encourage and entice other teacher educators to join in promoting diversity in action as well as ideology, and they provide some reasonable and viable windows of opportunity for how these participations can occur successfully. In this sense, the style of this volume is as enriching, enlightening, and insightful as diversity is itself. It is a conversation of necessity and significance, and certainly one worth joining!

—Geneva Gay

REFERENCES

Adams, M., Bell, L. A., & Griffin, P. (2007). *Teaching for diversity and social diversity* (2nd ed.). New York, NY: Routledge.

Ball, R. F., & Tyson, C. A. (2011). *Studying diversity in teacher education.* Lanham, MD: Rowman & Littlefield.

Gay, G. (Ed). (2003). *Becoming multicultural educators: Personal journey toward professional agency.* San Francisco, CA: Jossey-Bass.

Gay, G. (2010). *Culturally responsive teaching: Theory, research, and practice* (2nd ed.). New York, NY: Teachers College Press.

Mayo, S. M., & Larke, P. J. (Eds.). (2013). *Integrating multiculturalism into the curriculum: From the liberal arts to the sciences.* New York, NY: Peter Lang.

Milner, H. R. (Ed.). (2009). *Diversity and education: Teachers, teaching, and teacher education.* Springfield, IL: Charles C. Thomas.

Nieto, S., & Bode, P. (2012). *Affirming diversity: The sociopolitical context of multicultural education* (6th ed.). Boston, MA: Pearson Education.

Sleeter, C. E. (2001). Preparing teachers for culturally diverse schools: Research and the overwhelming presence of whiteness. *Journal of Teacher Education, 52*(2), 94–106.

Talking Diversit
with **Teacher**
and **Teacher Educator**

of learning; these are consensual points among scholars in the field of multicultural education. *Talking Diversity with Teachers and Teacher Educators* is unequivocal about the need for diversity to be explicitly, intentionally, and centrally present in all aspects of the preparation and practice of educators. This comprehensiveness and integration are signified by the wide range of disciplinary narratives provided as examples of the practice of diversity teaching and learning by teacher educators. These approaches move the discourse about diversity in teacher preparation and practice beyond the prevailing tendencies of presenting it as primarily a domain separate from other aspects of teacher education such as reading, math, science, and social studies methods. Furthermore, the authors are members of the professional (and sometimes demographic) communities from which (and to whom) they speak. They are teacher educators with expertise in diversity speaking to teacher educators. This shared professional membership increases the credibility of their explanations and recommendations.

Credibility and "place" gaps are continuing problems in teacher preparation for and classroom practice of diversity in PreK–12 education because frequently the "trainers" are not currently in these classrooms and have been away from precollegiate teaching for many years. While their suggestions may be sound ideologically, PreK–12 practitioners and teacher candidates often perceive them as too theoretical and impractical for the day-to-day realities of actual classrooms. The presentations in *Talking Diversity with Teachers and Teacher Educators* avoid these tensions by focusing on the "place" where much initial teacher education occurs. Consequently, there is no need for the contributing authors to spend time and energy defending their credibility since they are speaking to others of their own professional communities from within.

Evidence of the influential presence of ethnic, racial, cultural, social, and linguistic diversity in the distribution of educational resources, opportunities, and outcomes is too compelling to be ignored or dismissed. Yet many educators find it extremely difficult to talk about or do anything substantial and transformative about ethnic, racial, and cultural diversity. In fact, the mere mention of "diversity" is often silencing and incapacitating. Too often the response to these perceived challenges is, let's not talk about diversity (especially that which is race-based) at all, or if we must, let's do so in vague, global, and nondescript ways such that the resulting illusions of discourse are virtually useless. Fortunately, the chapters in this volume do not perpetuate these habits. Although the authors readily admit that talking about diversity is difficult, they proceed to engage in some real (not merely ritualistic) conversations about it. Some obvious yet profound lessons are taught about engaging in authentic conversations about any topic of any significance—you have to have something to talk about. The more important the topic is, the more it demands of discussants intellectually, ethically, emotively, and communicatively. When a topic, issue, event, or experience is personally significant to us, we work more diligently (and most often, effectively) at talking about it. Hence, if teachers and teacher educators are not willing to invest and engage in some kind of worthy actions, it is not surprising that they find it difficult to talk about diversity, because they have nothing to talk about. Conversely, action (whether imagined or actualized) is the sustenance of genuine conversation.

The authors in *Talking Diversity with Teachers and Teacher Educators* help the reader overcome the difficulty of engaging diversity by sharing some of what they are doing in their own classes and then proceed to have conversations about these actions. In so doing they demonstrate another powerful lesson for others to learn and emulate—that is, that talking about and teaching diversity are easier and more substantial when filtered through personal commitments and engagements. So, some of the difficulty typically attributed to talking about diversity may be more a proxy for inaction than a reason for noncommunication. *Acting before talking* also can move diversity out of the restrictive realms of only being perceived as pathological and problematic to focusing on its normative, generative, and transformative capabilities.

Unquestionably, teaching to, through, and for cultural diversity is challenging, but it also is invigorating and stimulating. But then, so is any creative and qualitative teaching. Some of the most challenging aspects involve defying conventions such as "business as usual" teaching techniques common among college professors and looking for a set of "best practices" that are applicable to all students, circumstances, and times. For college and university teachers, these often are actualized as some form of lecturing, with all students doing the same assignments in the same way *all the time* (usually some kind of academic writing and uniform test taking) and professors telling students what to do without doing the tasks themselves. Preparing teachers for diversity requires some fundamental challenges in these pedagogical conventions. Paramount among these challenges is the need for teacher educators to model what they recommend by doing as they expect their teacher candidates to eventually do in their classrooms. An important pedagogical idea for dealing effectively with diversity in classrooms is using multiple and varied instructional techniques to achieve high-level learning outcomes for diverse students. If teacher educators are to model this message, some variation of lecturing as the only teaching style will no longer suffice. Instead, a wide variety of approaches to teaching and learning, types and sources of knowledge, and performance assessments should be used routinely. These diverse instructional techniques need to be continually modified such that there is always an element of novelty in college classrooms since teacher

Introduction
and How to Use This Book

No one should be allowed to graduate from a teacher certification
program or be licensed to teach without being well grounded in how the
dynamic of cultural conditioning operates in teaching and learning.

—Geneva Gay, "Building Cultural Bridges:
A Bold Proposal for Teacher Education"

Increasingly, as our nation and our classrooms have become more diverse, colleges of education have been answering the call to prepare the next generation of teachers to be sensitive and responsive to issues of diversity. As Gay (1995) exhorts in the opening epigraph, it is imperative that colleges of education and other agencies that certify teachers prioritize issues of diversity.

The standards for teacher preparation by the Council for the Accreditation of Educator Preparation (CAEP) have diversity running as a theme throughout, with Standard 1.9 (Equity) specifically addressing culture, ethnicity, gender, sexual orientation, language, and learning differences (CAEP, 2013). Before that, the National Council for Accreditation of Teacher Education (NCATE) expected colleges of education to have conceptual frameworks that reflected a commitment to preparing teacher candidates to support the learning of all students (NCATE, 2010). For this reason and a host of others, diversity courses have been created and, in many colleges and universities, even required for graduation. Further, university presidents and college deans have pledged their commitment to faculty and staff hiring and student admissions that diversify their faculty, staff, and student bodies.

Despite these affirmative practices and improvements in higher education, in our teacher education experience, we have been less than satisfied with the information related to teaching about diversity in our respective fields. The problem is not a lack of print materials; textbooks on multicultural education abound (NCATE, 2008). What is lacking is a knowledge base of content-specific strategies grounded in the literature and research for examining diversity in education. For example, how can issues of diversity be effectively discussed in a science education classroom? How should language arts educators infuse multicultural perspectives? How can education majors develop sensitivity to diversity among special education students?

Each of us, authors of this book, has been alternately frustrated and encouraged by our experiences preparing culturally responsive and competent educators. What began as a hallway conversation between the editors of this book blossomed into a concerted effort to galvanize our work and share our experiences with others. We realized, as Gallavan (2000) points out, that talking with other multicultural educators is vitally important for professional support and personal revitalization. Soon we found ourselves leading a faculty-development workshop on "difficult conversations" dealing with diversity. Later, we (Cruz, Ellerbrock, Howes, & Vásquez, 2010) presented at the annual conference of the American Association of Colleges of Teacher Education (AACTE), leading a discussion on how best to foster and develop sensitivity for diversity in prospective teachers.

It was while we were at the AACTE conference, during the question-and-answer session at the end of our panel presentation, that the idea for this book came about. Having presented content-specific approaches and techniques that we used in our own teacher education courses, we were inundated with requests to publish our classroom-tested activities and strategies. When we returned to our home university, we invited other colleagues whose work was well-known in this regard to collaborate on a publication. As we came together to write, share drafts, and revise our respective chapters, we learned anew and became heartened at the encouraging work being done across the nation. This book is a culmination of that research and collaboration.

WHO SHOULD USE THIS BOOK?

We intend this book to be of primary interest to teacher educators, to enrich their instruction concerning diversity in subject-matter and general education courses. This book is not intended to replace the content-area methods book in teacher education programs but rather to be used as a support resource for instructors. Facilitators in professional development venues will also find ideas, strategies, and activities that can be useful in their work. We also envision this collection as a central reading in doctoral-level courses in teacher education programs. Especially in those advanced graduate courses where a mix of subject-area specialists is present (e.g., "Research in Teacher Education," "Policy and Contexts of Teacher Education," "Teaching and Learning," "Seminar in Teacher Education"), this book can serve as a catalyst in important and necessary conversations on diversity.

FORMAT AND COMPONENTS OF THE BOOK

First and foremost, this is a how-to book. That is, the book provides specific instructional exercises, case studies, and strategies that have been implemented in college-of-education classrooms and professional-development workshops. We are cognizant of the recent finding that new teachers say their training placed too much emphasis on theoretical learning relative to practical classroom issues (National Comprehensive Center for Teacher Quality, 2007). The exercises, case studies, and strategies included in this text represent exemplars used by the authors to foster substantive dialogue and self-reflection leading to personal transformation and, hopefully, transformation in preservice teachers' future classrooms. The authors present multiple topic areas and multiple possibilities for use. For instance, some activities are time sensitive (e.g., best done at the start of a semester), some have specific goals (e.g., developing a sense of community), and still others have multiple goals (e.g., self-reflection and examination of privilege). All have been found to be effective in engaging participants in courageous conversations and difficult dialogues in teacher education.

The book is divided into two sections. Part I, "Laying the Foundation: Diversity Education in Colleges of Education" (Chapters 1–3), offers an overview of diversity education and discusses cultural competence as it relates to teacher education and professional development, along with ways to foster a classroom learning environment conducive to holding quality conversations about diversity issues. Part II, "Content-Specific Diversity Education" (Chapters 4–10), presents action-oriented exercises, assignments, and strategies for inspiring and managing difficult dialogues in the college classroom at both elementary and secondary teacher education levels as well as in teacher professional-development workshops. Each of these chapters begins with a classroom-centered vignette that illuminates an issue discussed in the chapter and can be used as a discussion-starter in class. In addition, the Resources appendix provides an annotated list of resources for teaching about diversity in the college classroom and other venues.

In "A Vision of Diversity in Teacher Education" (Chapter 1), Cheryl Ellerbrock and Bárbara Cruz provide an overview of research in the field in teacher education. Additionally, a conceptual model of the Stages of Learner Awareness and Identity is offered and discussed. Of particular note is the dissonance with which instructors often struggle as they work through the stages of awareness and identity development in their own education. The chapter also provides general strategies for how faculty may approach the emotional as well as the cognitive content of their course material. Other important considerations examined include the general challenges faced by teacher educators who discuss diversity in their courses; the special challenges and advantages faced by minority professors when they address issues of diversity in the classroom; the special challenges and advantages faced by mainstream professors when they address issues of diversity in the classroom; considerations for tenure-track versus tenured faculty and implications for tenure and promotion; and what accommodations can be made when there's not much diversity represented in the student body in one's college classroom or community.

In "Cultivating Positive Learning Environments in College Classrooms" (Chapter 2), Cheryl Ellerbrock focuses on the importance of fostering a learning environment that is responsive to students' needs, where a community of learners is invested in supporting one another, and on how such learning environments help set the foundation for quality conversations to take place. This chapter specifically addresses the major elements of such an environment at the college level, the challenge of fostering a positive classroom learning environment, and specific activities that are appropriate for courses within teacher preparation programs that instructors can use to help nurture such an environment. This chapter concludes with specific activities that can help foster positive learning environments where difficult conversations can take place, including activities that help establish rules and communication guidelines, build relationships, promote cooperation, and encourage continuous self-reflection.

The author team of Vonzell Agosto, Zorka Karanxha, Deirdre Cobb-Roberts, and Eric Williams explores recent technological advancements in "Critical Media Literacy: Edutaining Popular Culture" (Chapter 3). From the Web 2.0 to social networking sites, students are accessing, sharing, producing, and consuming media, with both positive and negative outcomes. The authors describe how teacher educators can help both preservice and inservice teachers develop critical media literacy and facilitate transformative learning around diversity and equity issues.

Part II begins with English language arts (ELA) teacher educator Anete Vásquez's overview of how teachers of English language arts can support linguistically and culturally diverse learners in their classrooms in Chapter 4, "English Language Arts Education: Valuing All Voices." Subsequently, vignettes describing difficult dialogues surrounding sexual orientation, gender, race or ethnicity, language, social class, and abilities that have occurred in the author's ELA education classrooms are conveyed. The vignettes themselves can be used as a means to facilitate classroom discussion, so each vignette is followed by a brief list of discussion questions. After each vignette, teaching exercises and strategies are discussed that attempt to open the minds of teacher candidates to the richness that diversity can bring to the ELA classroom and to prevent the marginalization of any student voice.

Bárbara Cruz argues that diversity issues have long been at the core of social studies education in Chapter 5, "Social Studies Education: Promoting and Developing Inclusive Perspectives." However, many social studies educators are nonetheless reticent to broach such topics in class for fear that they don't know enough, that conflict may arise, or that they will not use appropriate strategies. This chapter offers a variety of strategies and in-class activities that will assist prospective and current social studies educators in exploring critical issues in preparation for service in our nation's diverse schools.

In "Mathematics Education: Challenging Beliefs and Developing Teacher Knowledge Related to English Language Learners" (Chapter 6), Eugenia Vomvoridi-Ivanović and Kathryn Chval address issues related to teaching mathematics to English language learners (ELLs). Specifically, the authors discuss how, through various activities, preservice teachers can grapple with the pedagogic and cognitive role of language and its interplay with the teaching and learning of mathematics. The authors first describe the preconceived notions that most of their preservice teachers have initially, which poses a challenge in their mathematics methods course. They then share classroom activities along with focus questions and discussion guidelines the authors have successfully used with preservice teachers.

In "Science Education: Exploring Diverse Visions of Science and Scientists" (Chapter 7), Elaine Howes and Miyoun Lim posit that science as currently constructed, practiced, and taught is not always welcoming to women, people of color, people of certain socioeconomic classes, and people who are learning English. Science is too powerful and too important a part of the human enterprise, past and present and around the world, to be left to those who are easily successful with traditional ways of teaching and learning science. Students preparing to teach science often come into their preparation programs with stereotypical visions of who can do science. Nonetheless, they are eager to help all of their students learn and enjoy science. Beyond engaging their students in interesting activities (and sometimes discussion), however, they are uncertain as to how to teach all students well. They learn about various cultures, ways of speaking, and attitudes toward schooling in "diversity" courses, but they do not necessarily know how these apply to teaching and learning science. Therefore, experiences that help them make connections between teaching the content of science in ways that are accessible and engaging for all students are the focus of this chapter.

In "ESOL Education: Empowering Preservice Teachers to Advocate for English Language Learners" (Chapter 8), Deoksoon Kim and Sylvia Celedón-Pattichis, specialists in world language education and English language learners, present teaching strategies and a case study assignment for preservice teachers that enables them to address the needs of culturally and linguistically diverse students; the authors ultimately embrace the role of advocate. The authors also showcase how preservice teachers can use Web 2.0 technologies, leading to ongoing discussion and co-constructed knowledge.

In "(Foreign) Language Education: Lessons from a Journey in Rethinking 'Diversity' and Thinking About Privilege" (Chapter 9), Adam Schwartz explores how ideas of culture are dependent on how students and teachers define and value race and ethnicity. This chapter introduces the notion that culture can be studied as an interpersonal process through which students use their emergent bilingualism to frame their own ideas of privilege, ethnicity, and ways of thinking about language and race. Through an analysis of Spanish classroom activities, accompanied by conversations with students and preservice methods teachers, this chapter suggests how to introduce identity, ideology, and imagination as conceptual tools used to reconsider "cultural education."

In Chapter 10, "Exceptional Student Education: Utilizing the Arts to Facilitate Inclusive Environments," Patricia Alvarez McHatton and Roseanne Vallice argue that while students with exceptionalities are increasingly served in general education settings, research indicates that many general education teachers lack an understanding of disabilities and question their ability to instruct students with diverse learning needs. This chapter explores the concept of disability from a sociocultural perspective, using readings, films, and experiential activities to engage students in reflection and dialogue about disability. The activities are varied and provide multiple mechanisms to engage teachers in a critical analysis of their own biases and beliefs regarding disabilities.

The Resources appendix provides an extensive and targeted annotated bibliography of websites, software, audiovisual matter, books, journals, newsletters, curriculum materials, organizations, and grant opportunities that may be useful for the subject-area specialist and anyone interested in educating for diversity. These resources are those found to be most useful by the authors of the book and are organized by both issue and content area.

HOW TO USE THIS BOOK

As we worked on this project, our belief in cross-disciplinary instruction was further confirmed. We found that we could easily modify many of the activities from a colleague's content-specific field and use them in our own classrooms. Readers are encouraged to read *all* the chapters, even those that are not within your area of subject specialization. Many of the strategies discussed in other chapters can be easily modified for a wide range of courses and your specific field. For example, creating learning circles (Chapter 2) can be done in any large college-classroom environment so that multiple, smaller groups can form their own bonds and identity within the larger classroom community. A Paideia seminar (Chapter 4) is a useful strategy for facilitating collaborative, intellectual dialogue about a given text, no matter the discipline. Diversity bingo (Chapter 5) can be modified and used in virtually every content field.

We have also found that many of the strategies can be used in several ways—as introductory activities as well exercises that delve deeper into a topic. The diversity bingo activity, for example, is often used as an icebreaker in a class, intended to help students get to know one another. However, because the activity also valorizes people with diverse backgrounds, a postactivity debriefing can easily be guided so that students consider asset and deficit models in instruction.

We have also discovered that just learning about what our colleagues do in their classrooms often inspires us to create a new activity for ours. It is our intent to help facilitate this cross-disciplinary approach by including icons throughout the book (see Table I.1).

EXPLANATION OF ICONS

In each of the chapters, in addition to content-specific activities, you will also find general strategies that are applicable to all content areas as well as strategies that can easily be altered to suit other content areas. The strategies result in learning outcomes important in all fields of study. These learning outcomes are denoted by icons throughout the book.

CONCLUSION

Finally, we encourage you to collaborate with colleagues to enhance and enrich the learning experiences of preservice and inservice teachers as they pertain to diversity issues. Educators who can address the needs of all learners are ultimately more effective in the classroom. In addition, we believe that teachers should facilitate students' acquisition of the knowledge and skills necessary to participate fully in the social world while also broadening their experience of the rich diversity of cultures that make up the United States and the world. Teachers who know, value, and are interested in this multiplicity of "ways of being" represented in their classrooms will be better able to attend to individual learners' needs, as well as portray the fundamental openness to diversity that is required to develop a strong democracy.

It has certainly been our experience that, as Renaissance philosopher Michel de Montaigne (1580/2006) famously observed, it is good to "whet and sharpen

Table I.1. Icons Used in This Book and Their Corresponding Intended Learning Outcomes

Icon	Learning Outcome
	Building Classroom Community
	Developing Perspective
	Examining Privilege
	Supporting Experiential Learning
	Promoting Discussion
	Facilitating Self-Reflection
	Appreciating Cultural Differences
	Making Cross-Disciplinary Connections

our wits by rubbing them against those of others." Working together as a cohesive group of teacher educators, we *can* provide students with the sensitivity and responsiveness to issues of diversity that are so desperately needed to teach and reach today's K–12 students and transform our society so that it is more equitable and responsive. It is our job, our mission, our opportunity to effect change.

ACKNOWLEDGMENTS

We thank Dr. Harold Keller and Dr. Michael Stewart, associate deans from the College of Education at the University of South Florida, for their gracious and steadfast support and commitment to this project.

We also want to thank the contributors to this book. Impromptu and passionate hallway conversations were the initial impetus for this book, as we comforted, advised, and cheered one another on in our classroom efforts to teach teachers to teach *for*, not in spite of, diversity. Thus we acknowledge one another's collegiality, wisdom, perseverance, and friendship (deepened through the development of this text) as the foundation of this volume.

REFERENCES

Council for the Accreditation of Educator Preparation (CAEP). (2013). *CAEP standards for accreditation of educator preparation.* Washington, DC: Author.

Cruz, B. C., Ellerbrock, C., Howes, E., & Vásquez, A. (2010, February). *Difficult dialogues: Struggles and strategies in the teacher education classroom.* Paper presented at the annual meeting of the American Association of Colleges for Teacher Education, Atlanta, GA.

De Montaigne, M. (2006). *The essays of Montaigne, complete.* Project Gutenberg. Retrieved from www.gutenberg.org/files/3600/3600-h/3600-h.htm (Original work published 1580)

Gallavan, N. P. (2000). Multicultural education at the academy: Teacher educators' challenges, conflicts, and coping skills. *Equity & Excellence in Education, 33*(3), 5–11.

Gay, G. (1995). Building cultural bridges: A bold proposal for teacher education. In J. Q. Adams & J. R. Welsch (Eds.), *Multicultural education: Strategies for implementation in colleges and universities, Vol. 4* (pp. 95–106). Springfield, IL: Illinois State Board of Higher Education.

National Comprehensive Center for Teacher Quality. (2007). *Lessons learned: New teachers talk about their jobs, challenges, and long-range plans.* New York, NY: Public Agenda.

National Council for Accreditation of Teacher Education. (2008). *Professional standards for the accreditation of teacher preparation institutions.* Washington, DC: Author.

National Council for Accreditation of Teacher Education (NCATE). (2010). *FAQ about standards.* Retrieved from www.ncate.org/Standards/NCATEUnitStandards/FAQAboutStandards/tabid/406/Default.aspx#faq9

Part I

LAYING THE FOUNDATION: DIVERSITY EDUCATION IN COLLEGES OF EDUCATION

CHAPTER 1

A Vision of Diversity in Teacher Education

Cheryl R. Ellerbrock and Bárbara C. Cruz

> Since culture and difference are essential to humanity, they should play a central role in teaching and learning. To ignore them is to assure that the human dignity and learning potential of ethnically, culturally, and racially diverse students are constrained or minimized.
>
> —Geneva Gay, "Teaching To and Through Cultural Diversity"

DIVERSITY IN TEACHER PREPARATION PROGRAMS

Understanding diversity[1] as it affects teaching and learning is of critical importance for those who are preparing to teach at the primary or secondary levels, as well as for teacher educators. Appreciating diversity and applying that understanding to our work as educators is vital to meeting the many learning styles, communication patterns, and cultural subtexts present in the student bodies we serve. In teacher education, diversity is regularly associated with race, ethnicity, and/or culture (Grant & Gibson, 2011). Contemporary visions of diversity also encompass age, gender, sexual orientation, (dis) ability, religion, language, and socioeconomic class. Precisely because the definition of diversity is multilayered, interconnected, and nuanced, our job as educators must take into account the multiplicity and mixture of human experience in schools.

As we learned while working on this book project, even though discussing diversity in teacher education should be a priority, many college instructors purposefully (and sometimes unconsciously) avoid discussing these issues. Reasons for this avoidance may include the following:

- a limited research base in the field, most of which is focused on K–12 education
- lack of familiarity with the breadth and depth of diversity issues
- difficulty providing a real-world context within a relatively homogenous college/university system or classroom
- resistance to infusing diversity in all programs throughout teacher preparation curricula
- lack of knowledge in the pedagogies for teaching controversial issues
- lack of confidence in handling potentially inflammatory comments
- concern over potential problems associated with tenure and promotion

Whatever the reason, such avoidance may result in education students' lack of opportunity to be well grounded on matters of diversity. Given the demographic changes of K–12 and postsecondary student populations, no other type of issue or topic may be as important to include in teacher education curricula as those related to diversity. It is critical for students to engage in deep reflection and enlightening conversations on diversity in order to best prepare to reach and teach today's K–12 student population. The myriad of learning styles, communication patterns, and cultural subtexts present in student bodies are just a few of the reasons why it is vital for future educators to appreciate diversity and apply that understanding in their work.

As teacher-preparation accrediting bodies, such as the Council for the Accreditation of Educator Preparation (CAEP), increasingly prioritize field experiences and professional disposition as criteria for institutional and programmatic accreditation, colleges of education are left to consider ways of assessing teacher candidates as "fit" for the profession in terms of their valuation of diversity (Cruz & Duplass, 2010). The CAEP Standards (2013) assert that "diversity must be a pervasive characteristic of any quality preparation program" (p. 29). Further, as the notion of cultural competence becomes more and more an ideal in teacher education, those of us who work in teacher preparation and professional development must develop our own knowledge base in this emerging field.

LIMITED RESEARCH BASE IN THE FIELD

Although the scholarship in K–12 multicultural education is fairly robust, there is a dearth of empirical studies in higher education. Most of the scholarship dealing with diversity issues in postsecondary education examines the many problems inherent in the proposition (see, e.g., Gallavan, 2000; Young &

Tran, 2001), calls for more infusion of diversity topics (see, e.g., Barceló, 1995; Gay, 1995; Mayhew & Grunwald, 2006), presents best practice approaches (see, e.g., Anderson, 1999; Betances, 1995; Meacham, 1995), or describes exemplary programs (see, e.g., Gaudelli, 2001, Maude et al., 2010). However, few research studies have been empirical in nature or been conducted in any systematic, longitudinal way.

Existing scholarly work reveals the difficulties faced by postsecondary institutions with respect to diversity. The twin challenges of recruitment and retention of diverse students and faculty come up time and again in the literature. Some institutions—especially those in rural or relatively isolated communities—lament that it is difficult to provide real-world context when there is not much diversity represented in the student body or the local community (Hickey & Lanahan, 2012). In such situations, there may be times when minority students feel like tokens in the classroom, which has the potential to lead to unwanted and unwelcomed attention (Marchesani & Adams, 1992) or increased alienation (Cabrera, 1994; Harris, 1996). Extant research suggests that variability within groups often increases when a few minority group members are used to represent the larger group (Mullen & Hu, 1989). The opposite may occur as well—students who are members of groups outside of the mainstream culture may be simply ignored and made invisible.

DIFFICULTY INFUSING DIVERSITY IN ALL PROGRAMS

It can also be a challenge to get all programs across a college or university campus to accept the need to embrace diversity as a goal and infuse diversity into the curricula. While it may be true that some disciplines have more "natural" connections to issues of diversity, every field has subject matter, leading thinkers, and controversial issues that can serve as an opportunity to discuss diverse thinking and practice. Yet some instructors may actively resist incorporating diversity into their courses, believing such topics have no place in their fields' curricula. In our experience, we have had faculty tell us that they simply have too much "core" content to cover and that, as a result, there simply is not enough time in the semester to address matters of diversity. We have also heard from school district development personnel who believe that in the era of accountability and high-stakes testing, devoting teacher development workshops to diversity topics might have a harmful impact on student test scores which, in turn, might cast a negative shadow back onto their teachers. Of course, in each case we point out the way in which helping teachers think about diversity, how it is manifested in their classrooms, and what they can do to provide equitable educational access for all students can ultimately improve student achievement.

FEELINGS OF INADEQUACY AMONG INSTRUCTORS

Faculty in both the privileged groups and the historically disadvantaged groups report that addressing diversity in class is not always easy and that they often find themselves wrestling with their own beliefs and experiences. Faculty from disadvantaged groups may worry they will become tokens, perceived as having a "chip on their shoulder," or as advocating a purely personal cause. Faculty from privileged groups sometimes fear that because of their background, they will not be seen as having enough credible expertise or life experiences to facilitate conversations on diversity.

College faculty often feel inadequately prepared in their own formal training to teach a diverse student population (Marchesani & Adams, 1992). It may be that neither their undergraduate nor specialized graduate programs addressed diversity in any systematic way. Even with formalized training in teacher education, many instructors find themselves ill-equipped to facilitate such difficult and potentially controversial conversations in their courses with their students. For example, what do you do as a teacher educator when a comment is made in class that offends or marginalizes a particular group? What do you do when the conversation devolves from an educational exchange to a passionate rant grounded in someone's personal belief system? Often, the fear of such situations results in the avoidance of the deep conversations that preservice teachers so desperately need to consider and engage in.

TENURE AND PROMOTION

Faculty working toward tenure and promotion also worry about implications for their application dossiers. They wonder if including potentially uncomfortable topics will have a negative impact on their classroom learning environment, course evaluations, reputation as a teacher educator, and chances for achieving tenure and/or promotion. The need for classroom control, positive course evaluations, and securing their professional career may be perceived as more important and outweigh the need to include diversity topics as part of their courses (Greenman & Kimmel, 1995; Kelly-Woessner & Woessner, 2006). To be sure, we personally have witnessed strong student reactions to some diversity-related discussions in our classes and wondered how this might impact our own end-of-course evaluations. However, we have also used the semester-long course format to "unpack" some of the students' misperceptions, lessen some prejudicial attitudes, and help pre- and inservice teachers feel empowered regarding both diversity content and pedagogical strategies.

Ultimately, our student course evaluations are among the highest in our college, and our students overwhelmingly express their gratitude for the skills they learned and now have in their teaching repertoire.

THE NEED FOR QUALITY EDUCATIONAL EXPERIENCES CONCERNING DIVERSITY IN TEACHER PREPARATION PROGRAMS

Even if students are exposed to diversity in their postsecondary education, one cannot assume that mere exposure to those of diverse backgrounds in their college classes will produce positive and meaningful interchanges between groups and across differences (Gurin, Dey, Hurtado, & Gurin, 2002). As a matter of fact, interviews conducted with 641 first-year teachers revealed that while more than three-quarters of these teachers reported that their preparation programs contained coursework that included working with diverse learners, only 39% felt that their training in this area helped them "a lot" when it came to working with ethnically and racially diverse learners, and only 47% felt that their training had prepared them adequately to work with students with special needs (Rochkind, Ott, Immerwahr, Doble, & Johnson, 2008). It may be important to consider not only the amount of exposure that students have to diversity but also the type and quality of interactions in which students engage. As college instructors, we are positioned to provide classroom-based experiences wherein students learn about diversity and are given opportunities to interact and engage with peers in meaningful and authentic ways. As Gurin et al. (2002) state, "Genuine interaction goes far beyond mere contact and includes learning about difference in background, experience, and perspectives, as well as getting to know one another individually in an intimate enough way to discern common goals and personal qualities" (p. 336).

DIVERSITY AWARENESS AND IDENTITY DEVELOPMENT

In our experience, when students are confronted with diversity issues, they typically engage in some measure of reflection, adjusting and tweaking their conception of self and their understanding of their own identity. Further, it seems most students go through a fairly predictable developmental process as they try to make meaning and sense of the issues vis-à-vis their own identities and experience. Anthropologists, sociologists, and psychologists have all posited models for the process by which people experience a new culture and make personal accommodations (see, e.g., Helms, 1990; Oberg, 1954; Schnell, 1994; and Ward, Bochner, & Furnham, 2001). We have adapted these ideas, applying them to our lived experiences of being teacher educators, arriving at a model of Diversity Awareness and Identity Development (See Figure 1.1).

In general, we have observed that our students go through a usually consistent trajectory of awareness, reflection, dissonance, and accommodation—although to varying degrees and with varying amounts of pushback and acceptance, as will be explained shortly. These observations lead us to share the following stages that teacher educators may find in their college classrooms.

Naiveté/Pre-Awareness

While some students may enter our college classrooms at a stage beyond the naiveté/pre-awareness stage, we have found that many of our preservice teachers often have little or no awareness of others' ethnic, cultural, or social identities and social justice issues in general. For those in privileged groups, there may be a lack of awareness that problems even exist. We can think of this as the "ignorance is bliss" stage. Sometimes there may be an awareness of difference, but not much meaning or understanding is attributed to these observations. Other times, students exhibit a fair amount of awareness, but some of their beliefs may be prejudiced or blatantly discriminatory. Those in disadvantaged groups may feel purposefully or unintentionally ignored, their concerns and issues minimized or dismissed completely.

Figure 1.1. Diversity Awareness and Identity Development

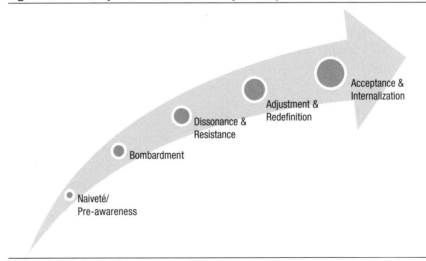

Source: Cruz, 2010

Bombardment

Students who are in the naiveté/pre-awareness stage are often shocked when diversity-minded instructors present them with experiences and information that contradict and challenge their existing worldviews and beliefs. The bombardment stage is characterized by intense and often dramatic exposure to new knowledge and perspectives. Members of privileged groups often deny that there are problems, differences, inequities, or injustices—or their own collusion; further, they may feel angry at having to confront these issues and resent somehow being implicated in the injustices. Those in disadvantaged groups may feel anger and/or shame at learning about or revisiting inequities and injustices; they may also resent being turned into representatives for their group.

Dissonance and Resistance

Of the five stages, this is the one of greatest discomfort and that harbors the most possibility of conflict. While some students begin to internally wrestle with and make sense of the information presented by the instructor in the bombardment stage, many others experience great cognitive dissonance and actively resist the lessons to be learned. Those in privileged groups often see assimilation as the way for people from nonprivileged groups to behave and be successful; they may rationalize or deny inequalities or "blame the victim." Those in disadvantaged groups may resent having to serve as spokespersons for their group, may want to distance themselves from other people like themselves, may be seen as the "special" or "different" one, or may not acknowledge that all members of their social group have not had the same opportunities they have had. It is important for instructors and students to work through dissonance and resistance despite potential conflict—both internally within the individual and externally among members of the class. Because, although this stage has the most potential for conflict, it also has the most potential for growth.

Adjustment and Redefinition

Fortunately, we have found the majority of students will make accommodations to their existing belief structures by incorporating new knowledge and perspectives. In this stage, learners seek to understand ways in which inequity is and has been manifested. Those in privileged groups acknowledge institutional forms of discrimination and even begin to "own" their own discriminatory behaviors. Those in disadvantaged groups may try to redefine themselves and find ways to challenge inequities in the system. It is important to provide concrete, real-world (both historical and contemporary) examples of hope and resolution so that students can see the potential and possibility of people working for justice and equity.

Acceptance and Internalization

If both students and instructors persevere through the stages of awareness and identity development, they will arrive at a place where they can have a better understanding of diversity while simultaneously acknowledging the dynamic and insidious interplay of discriminatory practice. For those in both the privileged and disadvantaged groups, this can result in a more complex sense of self and a deeper and more inclusive acceptance of others.

LESSONS LEARNED

All the authors of this book's chapters have experienced these stages—as both instructors and learners—to one degree or another. We offer the following observations and lessons learned as you reflect on your level of diversity awareness and identity development and consider ways to help your students do the same:

- Students may not progress through all stages or go through the stages in the same way or at the same rate.
- Ongoing nurturance and support is critical if students are to think deeply about diversity and take risks.
- It is vital to create a safe space for students to explore their perspectives on diversity, even for those who voice discriminatory or prejudicial beliefs.
- Students may not be aware of their own points of view.
- Many students may not know what to do when they themselves are confronted with diversity issues.
- Conflict is likely to arise when students are at different stages in the process, especially if they are two students from the same group (privileged/disadvantaged).
- The instructor will likely be the point of attack (both passive and overt) during the bombardment and dissonance and resistance stages.
- Student progress through these stages may be enhanced when there is consistency of approach across courses and throughout a program of study.

- Staying abreast of what students are thinking (but not necessarily saying aloud in class) is important to avoid misunderstandings and hurt feelings (see strategies below for ideas about how to monitor this).

BEST PRACTICE FOR DIVERSITY AWARENESS AND IDENTITY DEVELOPMENT

We have found and created a number of useful practices for teacher education faculty in an effort to help guide students through these stages. These practices include increasing awareness of self, engaging in ongoing self-education, planning with the purpose of fostering diversity awareness and identity development, fostering a learning environment that is caring and civil, crafting assignments that focus on the affective as well as intellectual domains, utilizing examples and experiences grounded in real-world contexts, providing opportunities for purposeful reflection, and self-disclosing one's own individual lived experiences.

Increasing Awareness of Self

As an instructor, you must first and foremost understand yourself and your own level of comfort with any issue that is to be discussed or studied in class. As you embark on your self-education in preparation for the course, you should reflect on your own life experiences, feelings, background, and upbringing with respect to the potential topics of the course. We agree with Martell's (2013) advice to examine one's own teaching practice. This is the time to honestly reflect on your own attitudes and beliefs, taking note of any that may be problematic or useful in authentically examining and studying an issue or phenomenon. Ongoing personal reflection with the intent of achieving personal growth and transformation is critical in being able to facilitate dialogues about diversity with college students.

Ongoing Self-Education

As any teacher will attest, feeling knowledgeable and confident about the subject matter results in more effective teaching. Likewise, as an instructor in today's diverse society, you must also develop your own knowledge about diverse and often sensitive issues by researching such topics, attending faculty development workshops, making the most of professional conferences and, wherever possible, experiencing firsthand some of the topics and issues under study. Students, too, should be encouraged to embark on a course of self-study in which they come across an issue or topic about which they know very little. It is our job as teacher educators to provide these experiences grounded in real-world contexts for students through which they can not only reflect on their feelings, perceptions, and lived experiences, but also learn more about necessary topics and dispel their misunderstandings.

Purposeful Planning for Fostering Diversity Awareness and Identity Development

Thoughtful and purposeful planning is paramount in diversity education. In constructing the course syllabus, instructors should choose readings that not only inform, but also challenge students to self-reflect and respond in thoughtful ways. In-class activities and field experiences should be selected in such a way that there is built-in time for students to talk, ask questions, and seek clarification as needed. Gatewood and Hall's (2012) usage of "disruptive movement" theory can be helpful in engaging education majors in critical conversations and interactions. In-class activities should move from low-risk to high-risk, gradually building students' trust and confidence while also helping them to feel safe and secure in opening up to their classmates and instructor.

Fostering a Classroom Environment That Is Caring and Civil

Before discussion of sensitive issues can begin, it is imperative that a positive, caring, and civil classroom environment be established (see Chapter 2). Instructors must establish ground rules and discussion guidelines, engendering care, respect, and trust for one another. Community building throughout the semester wherein opportunities to interact with one another are purposefully planned and implemented is critical. During discussions, careful moderation is vital. We agree with Johnson and Johnson (2009) that using "constructive controversy" can be an effective instructional tool that results in student learning.

Crafting Assignments That Focus on the Affective Domain

While facts and figures are authoritative, effective intercultural-communication pedagogy includes teaching strategies that promote cognitive, affective, and behavioral growth (Kim & Gudykunst, 1999). Chapters 4 through 10 of this book offer a plethora of approaches and exercises that tap into this important learning domain by bringing a human face to an issue through including case studies, personal stories, and experiential learning.

Instructors should use class time to guide students through discussions and exercises that illuminate their thinking on issues. They should also facilitate community- and school-based experiences that provide real-world context for discussions in the college classroom. We encourage students to write cultural autobiographies (Phillips, 2012) and cultural memoirs (Johnson, Kang, & Katz, 2012) to consider how past experience may impact current beliefs and practices.

Utilizing Examples and Experiences Grounded in Real-World Contexts

As much as possible, we have found that examples grounded in true scenarios (past and present), readings based on genuine experiences, and authentic assessments are powerful in developing diversity awareness and understanding. As Gay (2010) observes, examples can serve as "*meaningfulness bridges* for students between academic abstractions and their experiential realities" (p. 147).

Time and time again this has been the case for our students. As teacher educators we have developed a collection of examples and scenarios from multiple perspectives, above and beyond our own individual experiences, to provide students with opportunities to engage in their own authentic experiences and thus unpack diversity in real time. Many students do not truly understand such issues until they are placed in field experiences where they witness diversity firsthand. Early field experiences in diverse school settings embedded within teacher education coursework is one avenue for obtaining increased real-world contextualized examples. But even in communities that are relatively homogeneous, case studies and scenarios that put students in vicarious decision-making roles can be instrumental in developing awareness and understanding.

Providing Opportunities for Purposeful Reflection

In addition to providing students with opportunities to explore and unpack examples and experiences that focus on diversity, students also need to learn who they are as individuals and as contributing members of society. Instructors can support students' personal transformation and identity development by providing opportunities to reflect on their own thoughts, perceptions, and feelings regarding self and others. Assigning reflective tasks throughout the course is one way instructors can aid this journey. Reflective assignments are valuable when students are asked to critically evaluate their stances, viewpoints, and responses to a situation involving diversity and consider how they would respond to that same situation if they were to encounter it in their own lives or classrooms. For example, on a daily basis, students can be asked to write a short "exit slip" at the conclusion of class. A reflection or learning log, assessed periodically, can also be a useful strategy to gauge understandings and feelings. Requiring reflective assignments can also help instructors monitor students' thought processes and growth over time and provide individual students with an opportunity to witness and review their personal growth as well.

Self-Disclosing Individual Lived Experiences

Finally, we have found that using examples from our own lives in class can be a powerful vehicle for teaching and learning. Research on instructor self-disclosure suggests that instructors who share about themselves promote trust and student participation (Goldstein & Benassi, 1994). While you should not disclose anything that will make you extremely uncomfortable, it is important to model that all of us are in a continuous process of learning and growing. Sharing experiences of discrimination, intolerance, or acceptance may help students understand that diversity education is a lifelong learning process. Further, discussing your lived experiences with students may help to promote a learning environment in which all members, instructor included, are viewed as contributors to the conversation who stand to benefit from the discussion. However, it is important to note that while it is a powerful practice, using examples from your own personal experience alone may at times be counterproductive as students from differing backgrounds may not have similar personal experiences or reference points (Gay, 2010). Still, we have found that this approach gives voice to lived experience and models for students how culturally sensitive and responsive teachers wrestle with the issues themselves.

CONCLUSION

This book seeks to provide those involved in teacher education with a framework for understanding diversity and identity development and to empower them to make use of action-oriented strategies and interventions to manage difficult but critical conversations in the college classroom and other professional development venues. The framework of student learner identity and awareness referenced in this chapter is woven throughout the content chapters (Chapters 4–10). It is our hope that by understanding the stages through which learners progress and by considering classroom-tested strategies and interventions for promoting constructive dialogue on diversity issues, instructors can begin to help pre- and inservice teachers become more culturally competent educators.

NOTE

1. In this chapter and throughout this book, the term "diversity" will be used in the most inclusive fashion (e.g., race, age, ethnicity, culture, gender, socioeconomic class, religion, (dis)ability, language, and sexual orientation). Every effort has been made to use people-first language. When referring to students with disabilities, this volume uses three terms interchangeably that occur repeatedly in literature on disabilities studies: students with disabilities, students who are differently abled, and students who are (dis)abled. Because there is no consensus on terminology, the editors determined that the use of any of the three is acceptable.

REFERENCES

Anderson, J. A. (1999). Faculty responsibility for promoting conflict-free college classrooms. *New Directions for Teaching and Learning, 77*, 69–76.

Barceló, S. (1995). The multicultural campus: Facing the challenges. In J. Q. Adams & J. R. Welsch (Eds.), *Multicultural education: Strategies for implementation in colleges and universities, Vol. 4* (pp. 15–22). Springfield, IL: Illinois State Board of Higher Education.

Betances, S. (1995). Diversity reading clubs. In J. Q. Adams & J. R. Welsch (Eds.), *Multicultural education: Strategies for implementation in colleges and universities, Vol. 4* (pp. 51–53). Springfield, IL: Illinois State Board of Higher Education.

Cabrera, N. A. (1994). College students' perceptions of prejudice and discrimination and their feelings of alienation: A construct validation approach. *Review of Education/Pedagogy/Cultural Studies, 16*, 387–409. Retrieved from www.cirtl.net/index.php?q=node/5435

CAEP Commission on Standards and Performance Reporting. (2013). *CAEP accreditation standards and evidence: Aspirations for educator preparation.* Retrieved from caepnet.files.wordpress.com/2013/02/commrpt.pdf

Cruz, B. C. (2010, February). *Difficult dialogues in the social studies education classroom: A model for diversity awareness and identity development.* Paper presented at the annual meeting of the American Association of Colleges for Teacher Education, Atlanta, GA.

Cruz, B. C., & Duplass, J. A. (2010). Professional dispositions: What's a social studies education professor to do? *The Social Studies, 101*, 140–151.

Gallavan, N. P. (2000). Multicultural education at the academy: Teacher educators' challenges, conflicts, and coping skills. *Equity & Excellence in Education, 33*(3), 5–11.

Gatewood, C., & Hall, K. (2012). Making the uncomfortable comfortable: How deliberate conversation and interaction among education majors can bring about more profound awareness of self with respect to diversity. In G. Hickey & B. K. Lanahan (Eds.), *Even the janitor is white: Educating for cultural diversity in small colleges and universities* (pp. 61–76). New York, NY: Peter Lang.

Gaudelli, W. (2001). Reflections on multicultural education. *Multicultural Education, 8*(4), 35–37.

Gay, G. (1995). Building cultural bridges: A bold proposal for teacher education. In J. Q. Adams & J. R. Welsch (Eds.), *Multicultural education: Strategies for implementation in colleges and universities, Vol. 4* (pp. 95–106). Springfield, IL: Illinois State Board of Higher Education.

Gay, G. (2010). Acting on beliefs in teacher education for cultural diversity. *Journal of Teacher Education, 61*(1–2), 143–152.

Gay, G. (2013). Teaching to and through cultural diversity. *Curriculum Inquiry, 43*(1), 48–70.

Grant, C., & Gibson, M. (2011). Diversity in teacher education: A historical perspective on research and policy. In A. F. Ball & C. A. Tyson (Eds.), *Studying diversity in teacher education* (pp. 19–62). New York, NY: Rowman & Littlefield.

Greenman, N. P., & Kimmel, E. B. (1995). The road to multicultural education: Potholes of resistance. *Journal of Teacher Education, 46*(5), 360–368.

Goldstein, G. S., & Benassi, V. A. (1994). The relation between teacher self-disclosure and student classroom participation. *Teaching of Psychology, 21*(4), 212–217.

Gurin, P., Dey, E. L., Hurtado, S., & Gurin, G. (2002). Diversity in higher education: Theory and impact on educational outcomes. *Harvard Educational Review, 72*(3), 330–366.

Harris, L. (1996). Diversity in the classroom: Bridging difference and distance through computer-mediated communication. *Chronicle of Higher Education: Almanac, 43*(1). Retrieved from www.diversityweb.org/diversity_innovations/faculty_staff_development/teaching_strategies_practices/computer_mediated.cfm

Helms, J. E. (1990). *Black and white racial identity: Theory, research, and practice.* New York, NY: Greenwood Press.

Hickey, G., & Lanahan, B. K. (2012). *Even the janitor is white: Educating for cultural diversity in small colleges and universities.* New York, NY: Peter Lang Publishing.

Johnson, D. W., & Johnson, R. T. (2009). Energizing learning: The instructional power of conflict. *Educational Researcher, 38*(1), 37–51.

Johnson, E. C., Kang, H. Y., & Katz, L. (2012). "What's a cultural memoir?" An action research study of future teachers' understandings of themselves as cultural persons. In G. Hickey & B. K. Lanahan (Eds.), *Even the janitor is white: Educating for cultural diversity in small colleges and universities* (pp. 49–60). New York, NY: Peter Lang.

Kelly-Woessner, K., & Woessner, M. C. (2006). My professor is a partisan hack: How perceptions of a professor's political views affect student course evaluations. *Political Science and Politics, 39*(3), 495–501.

Kim, Y. Y., & Gudykunst, W. B. (1999). Teaching intercultural communication. In A. L. Vangelisti, J. A. Daly, & G. W. Friedrich (Eds.), *Teaching communication: Theory, research, and methods* (pp. 171–180). New York, NY: Routledge.

Marchesani, L. S., & Adams, M. (1992). Dynamics of diversity in the teaching–learning process: A faculty development model for analysis and action. In M. Adams (Ed.), *Promoting diversity in college classrooms: Innovative responses for the curriculum, faculty, and institutions* (pp. 9–20). San Francisco, CA: Jossey-Bass.

Martell, C. C. (2013). Race and histories: Examining culturally relevant teaching in the U.S. history classroom. *Theory & Research in Social Education, 41*(1), 65–88.

Maude, S. P., Catlett, C., Moore, S., Sánchez, S. Y., Thorp, E. K., & Corso, R. (2010). Infusing diversity constructs in preservice teacher preparation: The impact of a systematic faculty development strategy. *Infants & Young Children, 23*(2), 103–121.

Mayhew, M. J., & Grunwald, H. E. (2006). Factors contributing to faculty incorporation of diversity-related course content. *Journal of Higher Education, 77*(1), 148–168.

Meacham, J. (1995). Conflict in multicultural education classes: Too much heat or too little? *Liberal Education, 81*(4), 24–29.

Mullen, B., & Hu, L. (1989). Perceptions of ingroup and outgroup variability: A meta-analytic integration. *Basic Applied Social Psychology, 25*, 525–559.

Oberg, K. (1954). *The social economy of the Tlingit Indians of Alaska* (Unpublished doctoral dissertation). University of Chicago, Chicago, IL.

Phillips, M. (2012). Shagging in the South: Using cultural autobiographies to deconstruct preservice teachers' perceptions of culture. In G. Hickey & B. K. Lanahan (Eds.), *Even the janitor is white: Educating for cultural diversity in small colleges and universities* (pp. 27–36). New York, NY: Peter Lang.

Rochkind, J., Ott, A., Immerwahr, J., Doble, J., & Johnson, J. (2008). *Lesson learned: New teachers talk about their jobs, challenges and long-range plans.* New York, NY: National Comprehensive Center for Teacher Quality; Public Agenda Foundation.

Schnell, J. (1994). *Understanding the shock in "culture shock."* ERIC Document Reproduction Service, ED 398 616.

Ward, C., Bochner, S., & Furnham, A. (2001). *The psychology of culture shock* (2nd ed.). Philadelphia, PA: Routledge.

Young, R. L., & Tran, M. T. (2001). What do you do when your students say, "I don't believe in multicultural education?" *Multicultural Perspectives, 3*(3), 9–14.

CHAPTER 2

Cultivating Positive Learning Environments in College Classrooms

Cheryl R. Ellerbrock

> The college classroom, with norms and values often in odds with
> student developmental needs, can be both a facilitator and hindrance
> to classroom community. When students perceive barriers to learning
> and acceptance, they disengage which subsequently affects their
> academic effort.
>
> —Keonya C. Booker, "The Role of Instructors and Peers in Establishing
> Classroom Community"

Facilitating conversations about diversity with college students who all
have unique personal histories and values can be so daunting that Schmitz,
Stakeman, and Sisneros (2001) refer to engaging students in such dialogue
as "walking through a minefield" (p. 613). This chapter focuses on how to
foster a classroom learning environment that is responsive to students' needs
and how such environments help set the foundation for high quality, often
difficult conversations to take place. Specifically, in this chapter I elaborate
on the major elements and challenges associated with fostering a positive
classroom learning environment at the college level and describe activities
that promote opportunities for successful difficult dialogues that are appropriate for courses within teacher preparation programs. By creating a learning environment that is responsive to students' needs prior to engaging in
difficult conversations, the instructor proactively minimizes the number of
"mines" in the "field."

MAJOR ELEMENTS OF A POSITIVE
CLASSROOM LEARNING ENVIRONMENT

The work of various scholars such as Glasser (1998), Maslow (1943, 1954), Noddings (2003), and Deci and Ryan (1985, 2000) posits that humans have a set of needs that are central to life and motivation. Needs that are important to our conversation on cultivating a positive classroom learning environment include the need for physical, emotional, and psychological safety; care; and relatedness/belonging (Deci & Ryan, 1985, 2000; Glasser, 1998; Maslow, 1943, 1954; Noddings, 2003, 2005; Ryan & Deci, 2000). In addition to these needs, cultivating a sense of civility helps nurture a positive classroom learning environment (Forni, 2002). When all are attended to, students and teacher alike have the potential to experience a true sense of community within the classroom (McMillan & Chavis, 1986; Osterman, 2000; Solomon, Battistich, Kim, & Watson, 1997).

Physical, Emotional, and Psychological Safety

Physical, emotional, and *psychological safety* are attended to in classroom environments where students feel physically safe; where they are free from worry of being bullied, harassed, ridiculed, or embarrassed; where they can express themselves freely; and where they can openly take academic risks. In a study of 11 college campuses, Garcia, Hoelscher, and Farmer (2005) found that volatile interpersonal exchanges within the college classroom tended to occur in unsafe and ineffective learning environments. Feeling safe within the college classroom is essential in order to create a learning environment where conversations about diversity and other related issues can take place in a caring and civil manner (Brown, 2004; Middleton, 2002; Torok & Aguilar, 2000).

Care

Care is identified as one of the most noted characteristics of exemplary college instructors, yet caring within the context of college classrooms is neither seen as a priority for many instructors (Lowman, 1996; Meyers, 2009) nor has it been the focus of much research (Straits, 2007). As Straits states:

> Unfortunately, the vast majority of studies regarding teacher caring have focused on elementary and, to a much lesser extent, secondary settings. Caring as a component of college teaching has been relatively ignored. (p. 171)

Care itself is rather hard to define. Rogers and Webb (1991) note that "our knowledge of caring is tacit: it is implicit in action. In other words, although we have difficulty in defining it, we know it when we see it" (p. 177). Noddings (2005) suggests that care is a fundamental human need:

> The desire to be cared for is almost certainly a universal human characteristic. Not everyone wants to be cuddled or fussed over. But everyone wants to be received, to elicit a response that is congruent with an underlying need or desire. (p. 17)

Caring may include a sense of mutuality, connection, the desire to understand and help one another reach his or her fullest potential and become self-actualized, and/or the wish to be understood (Chaskin & Rauner, 1995; Hayes, Ryan, & Zseller, 1994; Mayeroff, 1971). Many believe caring is not accomplished without action. According to Noddings (2003, 2005), a caring relationship involves an interpersonal connection between two people in which one is the deliverer of care and the other is the receiver of care. Applying this concept to the classroom, if the teacher is the deliverer of care and the student is the receiver, it is imperative that the student recognizes and receives the care in order for the caring act to be completed. As Noddings (2005) writes, "No matter how hard teachers try to care, if the caring is not received by students, the claim 'they don't care' has some validity" (p. 15). Simply stated, all students, even those in college, desire to have instructors who care about them and from whom they receive acts of care. Straits (2007) suggests that caring college instruction includes the following indicators: being available to assist students, showing students respect as individuals, giving extra effort, encouraging discussion in and beyond the class, getting to know students, wanting students to learn, providing multiple opportunities for student learning, employing multiple teaching strategies, making available a multitude of resources, and encouraging higher-level thinking.

Belonging and Relatedness

Intimately associated with care, *belonging* is described as "a pervasive drive to form and maintain at least a minimum quantity of lasting, positive, and significant interpersonal relationships" (Baumeister & Leary, 1995, p. 497). Viewed by Glasser (1998) as *the* most important basic need of all humans and by Maslow (1943, 1954) as the next important need after fulfilling one's basic needs, belonging involves feelings of value, connection, capability, and contribution to the group. *Relatedness* includes a sense of connection to others within a social group environment (Osterman, 2000) and is seen as a basic psychological need for intrinsic motivation (Deci & Ryan, 1985, 2000). Relatedness is intimately connected to the need to belong (Osterman, 2000). In a study about the sense of classroom and university belonging, Freeman, Anderman, and Jensen

(2007) found that college freshmen who experience a sense of belonging to a specific class report positive motivational beliefs about the class, feel increasingly confident about achieving their academic goals for the course, perceive the course content as meaningful, and are more prone than other students to participate in class based on their personal interest in truly learning and mastering the material.

Civility

Civility involves the compassionate awareness of those around you and the readiness to adjust your behavior for the benefit of others (Forni, 2002). At the core, civility consists of respect, responsibility, and restraint. In the book *Choosing Civility: The Twenty-five Rules of Considerate Conduct*, Forni outlines a series of rules that are essential to the development of civility (e.g., acknowledge others, be inclusive, respect others' opinions; see Forni for descriptions of each rule). By following these rules, Forni believes people are able to successfully connect with others, an essential element in creating a civil society. At the classroom level, civil learning environments are led by instructors who are respectful, relate to their students, use hands-on approaches, communicate and listen exceptionally well, and actively encourage student participation in class. Instructors promote an environment where students truly trust and listen to one another. Booker (2008) found that college students' perceptions of their favorite courses are greatly influenced by how well the instructor fosters a sense of civility and upholds students' sense of dignity. In a study conducted by Boice (1996), faculty members with the deepest understanding of classroom civilities and its effects were the least likely to have acts of incivility take place within their classroom learning environments. Classrooms that take on an uncivil nature tend to have students who are apathetic, uninvolved, oppositional, and argumentative (e.g., coming in late, leaving early, cynical talk, negative body language; Boice, 1996). Because civility is a learned skill, it is important that instructors consciously exemplify the ideal of civility in the classroom and explicitly teach students how to be civil (Boice, 1996).

A true sense of classroom community can be a by-product of a classroom learning environment that cultivates a sense of safety, care, belongingness, relatedness, and civility. The term *community* describes "a social organization whose members know, care about and support one another, have common goals and a sense of shared purpose, and to which they actively contribute and feel personally committed" (Solomon et al., 1997, p. 236). Communities are made up of four elements: membership, influence, a shared emotional bond, and integration and satisfaction of needs (McMillan & Chavis, 1986).

McMillan and Chavis suggest that a community is present when every member experiences a sense of importance, support, value, satisfaction, care, and belonging to the group. As Osterman (2000) affirms, community is intimately associated with belonging and care:

> A community exists when its members experience a sense of belonging or personal relatedness. In a community, the members feel that the group is important to them and that they are important to the group. Members of the community feel that the group will satisfy their needs; they will be cared for or supported. Finally, the community has a shared and emotional sense of connection. (p. 324)

The cultivation of a positive classroom learning environment requires instructors to place a keen focus on students' needs for physical, emotional, and psychological safety; care; relatedness; and belonging as well as the importance of civility. When present, students may begin to perceive themselves as part of a positive classroom environment and function as members of a community, setting the foundation for quality discussions and learning to take place.

CHALLENGES TO CULTIVATING A POSITIVE LEARNING ENVIRONMENT

There are many challenges associated with cultivating a positive learning environment in college classrooms. Educational institutions today, including postsecondary institutions, are becoming increasingly more diverse. With a diverse student population holding an array of values, perceptions, and skills gained through lived experiences, diversity within the classroom has the potential to enrich the learning environment and educational experience. However, if the classroom environment is not nurtured in a way that values diversity while simultaneously fostering alliances among all learners and the instructor, the classroom environment can quickly become a source of discontinuity and conflict (Anderson, 1999). In a study on social boundaries within the university learning environment, Ituarte and Davies (2007) report that group formation based on common features such as language, ethnicity, race, and personal appearance occur in all aspects of the university experience, including classrooms. Such divisions within the classroom have the potential to separate and alienate students, which results in an unwelcoming environment. Further, while college instructors are experts in their content area, they may not be as skilled in fostering positive relationships and a responsive classroom learning environment (Anderson, 1999). Many lack formal training or have not been given opportunities to learn *how* to promote such a learning environment.

Another challenge is that many college instructors incorrectly assume that their students have respect for one another, including their differences in learning styles and worldviews. As Anderson (1999) states, "Many instructors tacitly assume that when college students enter a classroom, they are aware of their responsibility for learning and of the standard of civility that should be operative" (p. 70). On the contrary, most students do not enter the classroom with a deep understanding of others and how they are to interact with colleagues and need to be taught how to build respectful relationships (Middleton, 2002; Torok & Aguilar, 2000). Whether consciously or unconsciously, students look to the instructor to provide this information, foster an environment necessary for their success, and model the type of respectful relationships expected. Brown (2004) found that multicultural education instructors who model how to create such a classroom atmosphere may have more of an impact on students' ideas of diversity and personal beliefs than the actual course content. However, not knowing how to create a positive classroom learning environment coupled with a lack of understanding and resources to communicate behavioral expectations to students often makes developing such an environment challenging for instructors (Johnson & Johnson, 2009). As a result, instructors often mimic the types of teaching and learning environments they experienced as a learner rather than seeking new ways to be more effective with their student population (Anderson, 1999; Boice, 1996).

A MULTIFACETED APPROACH TO CULTIVATING A POSITIVE LEARNING ENVIRONMENT

Cultivating a positive learning environment requires a multifaceted approach that takes into consideration the importance of supporting student needs, cultivating civility, and promoting community at the classroom level. This approach should, at minimum, include a focus on establishing rules and communication guidelines, building relationships, promoting cooperation, and encouraging continuous self-reflection. In this section, I will provide multiple activities that can be used in teacher preparation programs to cultivate a positive classroom learning environment. I, along with many of the authors of this text, have used these activities in both small and large classes; undergraduate-only, graduate-only, and mixed-level classes; and in auditorium-style as well as smaller, more intimate classroom settings. It is important to consider your specific context, the student population, and the physical layout of the classroom when determining how to best implement the ideas described below. Most of the activities should take place early in the semester, preferably within the first few class sessions unless otherwise indicated.

ESTABLISH RULES AND COMMUNICATION GUIDELINES

Research by Van Soest (1994) suggests that in safe environments, students are able to empathize with others, especially members of underprivileged groups. Instructors can model how to promote a positive classroom environment by instituting structured guidelines for behavior and dialogue within the classroom so students have a clear understanding of the expected code of conduct. For example, guidelines for classroom communication may include rules such as confidentiality, using "I" statements, active listening, working toward equal participation, acknowledging the emotions of others, showing respect, suspending one's personal beliefs, and not interrupting others or putting down their ideas (Garcia & Van Soest, 1997; Johnson & Johnson, 2009; Nagda et al., 1999; Schmitz et al., 2001; Van Soest, 1994).

It is important for instructors to teach and enforce classroom rules and guidelines in order to promote a safe and respectful environment where everyone can share their points of view without feeling fear of being attacked or mocked (Goodman, 1995). Nilson (2010) suggests that instructors should proactively attempt to reduce classroom incivilities by engaging students in a process of developing an agreed-upon set of guidelines. Ideally, guidelines for behavior and dialogue should be co-created, introduced early in the semester, agreed to by all members of the class, and be an integral part of the daily classroom routine. Further, the instructor should be willing to follow the same set of guidelines that were established for students. Collaborative rule-making, a classroom code of conduct, classroom communication guidelines, and constructive versus nonconstructive dialogue are tools I use to help establish classroom rules and communication guidelines in my college classrooms.

Collaborative Rule-making

The purpose of this activity is for students to wrestle with the idea of rules and ultimately create a well-defined list of three to five rules to serve as guiding expectations for all members of the class. I first ask students to engage in a think-write-stand-and-share based on the following questions; for 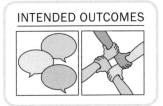 each question, they are asked to think about it, spend a few minutes individually writing a response, and then stand up and share their response with the class:

- What rules are you currently implementing or thinking about implementing in the classroom?
- Why are these rules important to you?

After engaging the class in a discussion centered on their responses to these questions, I explain that even college classrooms should function on a set of agreed-upon rules. Students then engage in a classroom meeting at which they collaboratively discuss the necessity of rules, what kinds of rules may be important in college classrooms, and what rules they would like for this particular class. Then, as a group, they discuss their perceptions of what each rule means, come to an agreement about the definition of each rule, and then vote on each rule. I always encourage the class to consider a few rules (e.g., respect self and others), but let the class know that even these rules are up for negotiation and must be thoroughly defined and voted on. It is my job as the instructor to ensure that the rules selected cover all essential components that are necessary to produce a positive learning environment. I post the rules in the classroom and ask all students to keep a copy of the rules with their course materials. I refer back to the rules throughout the semester as needed.

Classroom Code of Conduct

As an alternative to collaborative rule-making, this activity asks students to create a classroom code of conduct that functions as the rules and expectations for all members of the class. Albert's (1996) work on cooperative discipline in the classroom suggests that a classroom code of conduct is an essential element in the creation of a safe and orderly classroom. Albert refers to such codes as "encouragement in action," where students are given the necessary information to "feel *capable* of choosing responsible behavior in *our* classroom" (p. 129).

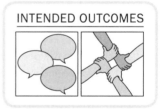

INTENDED OUTCOMES

To create a classroom code of conduct, first ask students to envision the ideal college classroom. After gathering this information, determine what operating principles are necessary to achieve this vision. The following is an example of a classroom code of conduct from one of my college-level courses:

- I will help foster a safe learning environment.
- I will be responsible for contributing to my learning and the learning of others.
- I will be respectful of all members of the classroom community.

- I will be prepared for class.
- I will learn something new every day.

Creating the code of conduct is not sufficient in and of itself. Students must also clearly understand exactly what each principle means. This can be accomplished by holding a discussion on appropriate and inappropriate behaviors as they relate to each principle. Additionally, there must be a plan for holding students accountable for each principle within the code of conduct. This plan must be clearly articulated to students and enforced by the instructor.

Classroom Communication Guidelines

The purpose of this activity is to teach students the interpersonal communication skills that are necessary to engage in difficult conversations in a respectful and constructive manner. Often college instructors assume students know how to properly talk to one another. However, my experience has proven that this 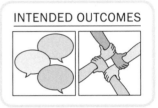 is not always the case. The following 11 principles that students must adhere to when engaging in conversations that might evoke controversy are taken directly from Johnson and Johnson (2009):

1. Be critical of ideas, not people.
2. Separate my personal worth from criticism of my ideas.
3. Remember that we are all in this together, sink or swim. Focus on coming to the best decision possible, not on winning.
4. Encourage everyone to participate and to master all the relevant information.
5. Listen to everyone's ideas, even if I do not agree.
6. Restate what someone has said if it is not clear.
7. Differentiate before I try to integrate.
8. Try to understand both sides of the issue.
9. Change my mind when the evidence clearly indicates that I should do so.
10. Emphasize rationality in seeking the best possible answer, given the available data.
11. Follow the *golden rule of conflict*. (pp. 42–43, italics in original)

I share these principles with students on the first day of class. Over the course of the next few class sessions, students are given the opportunity to create their own classroom communication guidelines. Samples of previous communication guideline statements from colleagues and my classrooms include:

- I will suspend my thoughts/beliefs so I can concentrate on what others are saying.
- I will find strengths in others' viewpoints.
- I will search for a balance between my thoughts/beliefs and others' thoughts/beliefs.
- I believe all people hold a key to the solution.
- I will try my best to communicate my thoughts/beliefs in the most constructive way possible.
- I will practice self-reflection.

For each constructive dialogue guideline statement, students are also asked to come up with a nonconstructive statement. For example, for the constructive dialogue statement "I find strength in others' viewpoints," a nonconstructive statement would be, "I search for weakness in others' viewpoints." Each statement is discussed in detail to help students understand the importance of talking with one another in a constructive manner. All guidelines are voted on and students receive a copy to place with their course materials. I urge all students to help fellow class members follow these guidelines. It is important to note that the instructor must also adhere to the guidelines. In fact, students regularly remind *me* of a guideline I fail to follow.

Constructive Versus Nonconstructive Dialogue

The purpose of this activity is to help students analyze conversations for the various elements that make up constructive and nonconstructive dialogue. This activity requires the use of the classroom communication guidelines from the activity above, along with a video, article, or other example of a dialogue between two 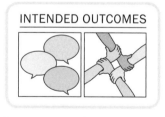 or more people. I tend to choose examples that show aspects of nonconstructive dialogue. Examples of such dialogues are plentiful (e.g., online, on television). One example I like to use is a video clip highlighting a 2005 interview between Matt Lauer and Tom Cruise that can be located on YouTube. In this video, Tom Cruise dialogues with Matt Lauer about psychiatry and antidepressants. While watching and/or reading a transcript of the dialogue, students are asked to use their classroom communication guidelines to think about aspects of constructive and nonconstructive dialogue present in the video. Students

INTENDED OUTCOMES

are also asked to think about how they felt when watching the dialogue. After previewing the dialogue example, students engage in a whole-class conversation centering on their responses and the importance of adhering to our classroom communication guidelines.

BUILD RELATIONSHIPS

Beginning on the first day of class, instructors should provide multiple opportunities for students to interact with one another and build respectful relationships grounded in care. In *McKeachie's Teaching Tips: Strategies, Research, and Theory for College and University Teachers,* Svinicki and McKeachie (2011) suggest the first class session of the semester be devoted to "breaking the ice," including activities in which classmates introduce themselves to one another and get to know the instructor (p. 22). It is important that the instructor actively participate in all activities so students see her or him as part of the community. Through implementing classroom activities and other structures aimed at building a sense of relatedness, students are provided with examples of ways they can promote positive and respectful relationships within their future classrooms. The semester-long structure I call *learning circles* and an activity called Past, Present, and Future are intended to help "break the ice" and build positive instructor–student and student–student relationships.

Learning Circles

Learning circles (LCs) are designed to break down large numbers of students into multiple small groups that form their own community and identity within the larger classroom. In such communities, genuine relationships and a sense of belonging and relatedness can develop and be nurtured. I have used LCs with classes as small as 12 and as large as 100. Students in an LC work together as a team to facilitate the professional growth and academic achievement of LC members and the whole

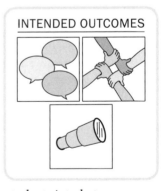

INTENDED OUTCOMES

class. At the beginning of the semester, I arrange students into heterogeneous LCs where they will remain for the duration of the semester (see Figure 2.1 for a visual representation of how to break down a class of 28 students into LCs). Each LC is made up of no more than five students. Students create an LC name

Figure 2.1. Learning Circles

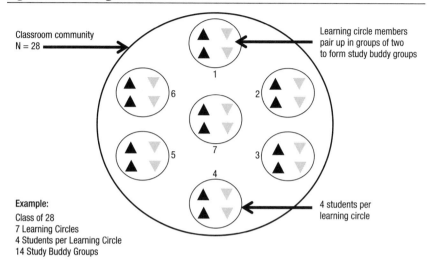

that is used when referring to the group. Each LC member also selects a study buddy for the semester. Throughout the semester, LC members work collaboratively to better understand class readings, analyze and synthesize course topics, engage in class activities, and make presentations.

Past, Present, and Future Collage

The purpose of this icebreaker activity is to have all class members, instructor included, get to know one another and build a sense of relatedness, respect, and care. All class members are asked to create a visual display that represents their past, present, and future and to create a key that describes each item. Although the purpose of this activity can be accomplished in many different ways, I require that a poster board be cut into a 25.5" x 11" rectangle and folded into three equal 8½" x 11" sections. Students are then asked

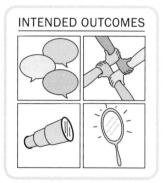

to display items that represent their past on the left section, present on the center section, and hopes and wishes for their future on the right section. I encourage students to be creative. My students have used pictures, parts of magazines, computer graphics, two-dimensional items, words, phrases, and quotations. For each item on the collage, students create a key that explains its significance.

During class, students choose one item from each section to share with their LC members. I also create a visual and a key that I share with the class. The collages and keys are collected, and I carefully examine each in an effort to get to know my students. After I've returned them, I have students staple them onto the cover of their notebook or binder. A colleague of mine initially thought college students would consider this activity juvenile and was surprised to find how much her students actually enjoyed it and the extent to which it helped build community. Further, it is an example of an activity that preservice teachers can one day do with their K–12 students.

PROMOTE COOPERATION

In order to cultivate a positive college-classroom learning environment, it is important that all members of the classroom community share responsibility and be invested in one another's learning in a cooperative, rather than competitive, nature (Johnson, Johnson, & Smith, 2007). The instructor needs to set a tone of mutual responsibility for student learning early in the academic semester and provide frequent opportunities for students to learn from one another throughout the duration of the course. Cooperative learning is a noteworthy teaching method to promote this type of learning environment from all members of the classroom. Grounded in social interdependence theory, cognitive developmental theory, and behavioral learning theory, cooperative learning is "an accepted, and often the preferred, instructional procedure at all levels of education [that] is being used in postsecondary education in every part of the world" (Johnson et al., 2007, p. 16).

Cooperative learning is *not identical* to group work. It is a structured teaching method that consists of a series of elements essential to its success, including these defined below (Johnson, Johnson, & Smith, 1998, 2007):

- *Positive interdependence* includes making sure each student perceives that he or she cannot succeed at the learning task unless others are also successful.
- Making sure that each student can be assessed based on his or her performance is known as *individual accountability*.
- *Promotive interaction* involves encouraging the success of others by helping, praising, and supporting others.
- Supporting students' leadership, communication, and conflict-management skills is an essential part of *social skill* development that is necessary for effective cooperative learning.
- *Group processing* includes focusing on how to improve the cooperative experience in the future.

Advocated by Kagan (2010), PIES (positive interaction, individual accountability, equal participation, and simultaneous interaction) is another way of thinking about cooperative learning that shares some similar elements with Johnson and colleagues' conceptualization listed above (for more information on Kagan's PIES, visit www.kaganonline.com). Such elements are necessary for cooperative learning to be most effective.

Positive outcomes of cooperative learning include, but are not limited to, higher achievement, increased long-term retention, improved critical thinking and problem-solving skills, greater intrinsic motivation, transferability of learned skills, greater social support, and improved interpersonal relationships (Johnson, et al., 2007). Williams (2004) found that by using the jigsaw method at the college level, a type of cooperative learning activity discussed in detail below, intergroup relations improved. Johnson, Johnson, and Smith (2007) state, "The positive interpersonal relationships promoted by cooperative learning are the heart of the learning community" (p. 20). Such relationships help to set the foundation for a learning environment where difficult, often confrontational, conversations can take place without the typical conflict, resistance, and hostility often associated with such dialogues. Learning Circle Reading Roles and Jigsaw are two examples of activities I use in my classes to promote cooperation.

Learning Circle Reading Roles

The purpose of learning circle reading roles, adapted from the literature circle concept, is for students to work together cooperatively so they can deepen their understanding of assigned readings. Reading roles provide the individual accountability and group interdependence necessary to make this activity truly cooperative. Required materials include course reading(s), any technology necessary to fulfill the reading roles task, and access to the course online discussion board. Each member will select a reading role to complete based on the assigned readings for a given class (see Table 2.1).

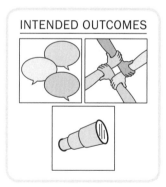

INTENDED OUTCOMES

Each student within an LC is responsible for reading the assigned reading(s), responding to the reading(s) based on his or her assigned role, responding to the work of fellow LC members, and holding in-class discussions on the reading(s) (see Figure 2.2 for a graphic representation of how reading roles work within LCs). It is expected that personal thoughts will be shared. For example, for the discussion director, it is not enough to simply list questions;

Table 2.1. Learning Circle Reading Roles

Reading Role	Description	Guiding Questions
Discussion Director	Your role is to identify the important aspects of your assigned reading(s) and develop questions for your group to discuss. Focus on the major themes or "big ideas" in the reading(s) and your reaction(s) to those ideas. Make sure to answer your own question. You are also responsible for facilitating the group discussion during class.	• What did the reading(s) make you think about? • What do you think the reading(s) was/were about? • What are the most important ideas/moments in the reading(s)? Why?
Summarizer	Your role is to prepare a summary of the major elements of the reading(s). You will need to decide what you perceive to be the most important elements of the reading(s) and explain each in a way that is easy to understand.	• What are the most important pieces of information from the reading(s)? • Why are these pieces of information important?
Connector	Your role is to connect the reading(s) to other coursework, lived experiences, news events, political events, and/or popular trends. Make sure to provide clear and meaningful connections.	• What is the most interesting or important connection that comes to mind? • What connections can you make to your own life? News events, political events, and/or popular trends? • What connections can you make to previously learned information?
Word Watcher	Your role is to watch out for words and/or phrases from your reading(s) that are worth knowing. These words might be interesting, new, and/or important. Make sure to define each word or phrase and indicate the specific location in the reading(s) (author, title, page, or paragraph number) so the group can discuss these words in context.	• Which words and/or phrases are especially important to understand? • What new words are introduced in the reading(s)? • What words/phrases do you perceive to be the most interesting?
Illuminator	Your role is to find passages in the reading(s) that you would like to discuss with the group in depth. These passages should be memorable, interesting, puzzling, and/or important. Your notes should include the exact passage along with a short description stating why you selected the passage.	• Why does this quote stand out? • What does this quote mean to you? • How might other people (of different backgrounds) think about this text/passage?
Illustrator	Your role is to illustrate an aspect or multiple aspects of the reading(s) you believe to be most memorable, interesting, puzzling, and/or important. Make sure to provide a short description that explains your illustration and how it pertains to the reading(s).	• How does your illustration relate to the reading(s)? • Why did you illustrate the reading(s) the way you did? • What, if anything, did illustrating the reading(s) help you realize about the content of the reading(s)?

Figure 2.2. Learning Circle Reading Roles

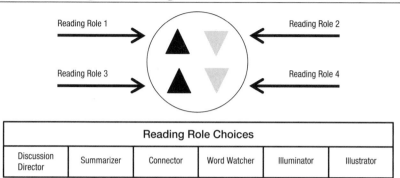

Reading Role Choices					
Discussion Director	Summarizer	Connector	Word Watcher	Illuminator	Illustrator

students must also answer their own questions. Each LC member selects a different role for each set of readings. Students do not repeat a role until they fulfill every role. Prior to class, I have LC members post their roles to an online LC group-discussion board where members of their LC write a response before the beginning of class. This activity is used to place accountability on each student to read and comprehend assigned readings, elicit thought-provoking conversations about the readings before the beginning of class, and improve the quality of classroom discussions. This activity can be a regular and integral part of class sessions at which readings will be discussed.

Jigsaw

The purpose of this more complex, yet popular cooperative learning activity is to allow students the opportunity to take on the role of teacher and learn from one another. Jigsaw promotes, among other things, positive interdependence, individual accountability, and social skills. It can take place at any time during the semester but will be most effective once a classroom community is established. Either the students or the instructor decides upon a topic of study with numerous subtopics. Students are placed in heterogeneous groups, referred to for the sake of this activity as *home teams*. Students analyze the topic of study and decide the subtopics about which they will become experts. *Expert teams* convene and are given an assignment created by the instructor to help guide their time together and master the topic. All experts will be expected to report back to their home team and teach this team what they learned. At the conclusion of this process, all students have had the opportunity to learn all topics through teaching their own

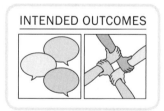

INTENDED OUTCOMES

topic to their home-team peers and learning about other base-team peers' topics. To extend this activity, home teams can then integrate the information they have learned and create a final project that exemplifies their combined understanding.

ENCOURAGE CONTINUOUS SELF-REFLECTION
(FOR INSTRUCTOR AND STUDENTS)

Instructional leaders have a unique opportunity to create a positive, caring, and civil community of learners within the college classroom. In order for this to truly occur, it is important that both the instructor and students practice self-reflection in an effort to personally transform their beliefs, thoughts, and behaviors. Such opportunities help to increase what Villegas and Lucas (2002) call sociocultural consciousness, the "awareness that one's worldview is not universal but is profoundly shaped by one's life experience, as mediated by a variety of factors, chief among them race/ethnicity, social class, and gender" (p. 27). Instructors who frequently pontificate on their own beliefs run the risk of being insensitive to students' needs, reprimanding students, creating an un-welcoming atmosphere, and creating an atmosphere that can lead to student resistance (Garcia & Van Soest, 1997; Van Soest, 1994). Instructors can begin to ponder their own personal belief systems regarding students, diversity, their teaching, and student learning by asking themselves questions such as,

- Do I hold an attitude that is asset-oriented, unconditional, and positive toward all of my students?
- Do I believe that all members of the classroom community, including myself, have room for personal growth?
- Do I make equitable classroom decisions?
- Do I believe all my students can learn at a high level?
- Do I suspend my own beliefs to hear the opinions of others?
- Do I do everything I can to demand excellence from all of my students?
- Do I foster opportunities for students to learn from and with one another?

Acknowledging and being willing to change one's thoughts, beliefs, and behaviors are crucial elements to fostering a positive classroom learning environment.

In addition to instructors, students must also be given opportunities to practice self-reflection based on prior life experiences. Smith (2000) and Garmon (2004) found that preservice teachers build their awareness and consciousness when given opportunities to reflect on their past experiences with culturally diverse people. It is important to scaffold students' understanding of self and others based upon where students are, encouraging growth from that point (Schmitz, Stakeman, & Sisneros, 2001; Van Soest, 1994). By strategically designing activities that promote self-reflection, awareness, and knowledge building, instructors can help students think critically about their understandings and provide opportunities for increased personal and multicultural awareness. Activities I use to encourage self-reflection include The Paseo, Circles of Comfort, "Who Am I?," Iceberg, and "I Am Different." Each of these activities can take place at any point in the semester after a sense of community has been established.

The Paseo

The purpose of the Paseo[1] is to have students reflect on who they are, make connections between who they are and their own thoughts and behaviors, share aspects of their personal life story with fellow classmates, and learn about the life stories of classmates. Required materials include a circle web example, preferably one filled out by the instructor, paper and writing utensils, and enough classroom space for students to arrange themselves into inside-outside circles. Inform students that they will create a circle web about themselves (see Figure 2.3 for an example; I show my completed circle web as a way to break the ice and to provide a visual model). After introducing the example, instruct students to start making their own circle webs.

INTENDED OUTCOMES

Make sure your students write their names in the center circle. For each of the outside circles, tell students to write a word or phrase that describes who they are (as they perceive themselves and/or how others perceive them). Once everyone has created a "web," have students stand and arrange themselves into inside-outside circles of an equal number of students (two circles, with one circle inside the other, where students in each circle are shoulder to shoulder). Students should pair off, with one member in the inside circle facing his or her partner in the outside circle. Explain to students that you will ask them a series of questions, one at a time. They can use their diagrams to help answer each question. They are to take 1 minute to think about their responses to the question. Then, when instructed, the inside circle partner shares his or her response to the question in 2 minutes. The outside partner practices active listening skills and does not interrupt. Once time expires, roles switch so the outside partner can share. After both partners share their responses, allocate

Figure 2.3. The Paseo Circle Web

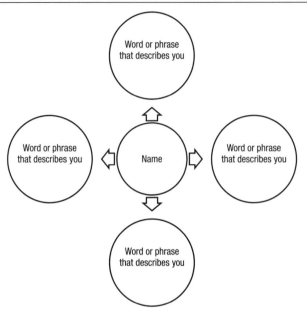

1 minute for open dialogue between partners. At the end of the open dialogue time, have each group thank their current partner and shift the inner or outer circles so that everyone has a new partner. Repeat the entire process with a new question. Sample questions/prompts include:

- What word/phrase in your circle web do you believe best represents who you are?
- What word/phrase would others perceive to best represent you?
- Describe a time when one of the aspects of who you are listed on your web served to your advantage.
- Describe a time when one of the aspects of who you are listed on your web served to your disadvantage.
- Discuss a time when one of the aspects of who you are listed on your web prevented you from standing up against an inequity.
- Discuss a time when one of the aspects of who you are listed on your web prompted you to stand up to an inequity.

Once students discuss all questions/prompts, ask them to take a few minutes to do a quick think-write-share about what they saw, heard, and felt during the process. Afterward, debrief the activity. Possible debriefing questions include:

- How do you feel after engaging in this activity?
- What did you learn from this activity?
- Why did we engage in this activity?
- How might you adapt this activity and use it in your current/future classroom?

Circles of Comfort

The purpose of the Circles of Comfort[2] activity is for students to reflect on their levels of comfort regarding personal and educational situations. Students draw a diagram of three circles and label the smallest circle "Comfort," the next circle "Risk," and the outside circle "Danger" (see Figure 2.4 for an example). Suggest situations

that students may encounter during their practicum, internship, or professional teaching experiences. Some examples of situations include teaching a student in the preproduction stage of language acquisition, teaching a student with special needs, and working in a high-poverty school. Have students think about the aspects of the situation that make them comfortable, those that are more risky, and those they perceive as dangerous and thus may cause them to be defensive or avoid the situation. Students should then fill in their circles based on this topic and their possible issues with the topic. Follow up by asking students, "What will it take to move some of your issues from the danger and risk circle to the comfort circle?" Help students brainstorm a step-by-step plan for moving one of their issues to a less threatening zone. I find it powerful to have students journal about this experience afterward.

Figure 2.4. Circles of Comfort

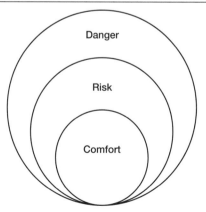

"Who Am I?" Iceberg

The purpose of this activity is to have students analyze and self-reflect about visual aspects of their persona as well as those aspects that may not be visible to others. Using the "Who Am I?" Iceberg (see Figure 2.5), students are asked to record their own thoughts regarding things people see or know about them and

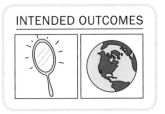

things people do not see or know. Volunteers share their iceberg with the class. This activity lends itself well to talking about what we really show people, what we keep hidden, the various "masks" one person may wear, the differences between people, the value of differences, and the importance of truly getting to know someone. This activity is followed up with a discussion on cultural diversity and cultural competence, this time using a cultural iceberg metaphor; that is, some aspects of our culture (e.g., behaviors and beliefs) are visible to others while a large part of our culture is hidden below the surface. Numerous cultural iceberg graphics can be found online.

I Am Different

The purpose of this activity is to have students make connections between their past experiences and their current thoughts and behaviors. First, students identify and then reflect on their earliest memory of being different—and this can be any difference: skin color, age, body size, clothing, dialect, ability

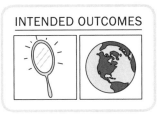

level, et cetera. Students then either draw a picture or jot down words that

Figure 2.5. "Who Am I?" Iceberg

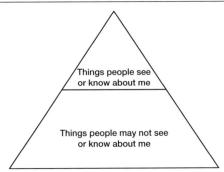

depict this memory. Ask students to ponder and record (1) how they determined they were different (e.g., did someone communicate that explicitly or implicitly?); (2) what institutions (e.g., schools, church, or home) were involved; and (3) what feelings they had about this difference. Have students share their discoveries with a small group, typically their LC group. Then have the entire class compile a list of the responses generated for the three items. This is followed by a class discussion using the following questions:

- Do your early memories influence your behavior and interactions? Why or why not?
- Do you see any influence of your early memories in your current professional/personal life (e.g., impact on your interaction with friends, employees, or students)?
- How do you believe your past experiences impact the larger organization to which you belong (school)?

Through this activity, students tend to gain a deeper sense of appreciation of difference and an increased sense of empathy toward and understanding of others.

CONCLUSION

In this chapter I urge educators to place a keen focus on fostering a safe, caring, and civil college-classroom learning environment that meets students' needs and where students experience a sense of belongingness. This type of learning environment sets the foundation for a true sense of community and enables the types of subject-specific activities and diversity-related conversations outlined in Part II of this book. In such communities, instructors can engage students in critical yet difficult conversations on issues of diversity that students in teacher education programs need so desperately to explore.

NOTES

1. The Paseo protocol was adapted from the National School Reform Faculty Harmony Education Center. Website: www.nsrfharmony.org/protocol/doc/paseo.pdf

2. The Circles of Comfort protocol was adapted from the Zones of Comfort protocol from the National School Reform Faculty Harmony Education Center. Website: www.nsrfharmony.org/protocol/doc/zones_of_comfort.pdf

REFERENCES

Albert, L. (1996). *Cooperative discipline*. Circle Pines, MN: American Guidance Services.

Anderson, J. A. (1999). Faculty responsibility for promoting conflict-free college class-rooms. *New Directions for Teaching and Learning, 77*, 69–76.

Baumeister, R. F., & Leary, M. R. (1995). The need to belong: Desire for interpersonal at-tachments as fundamental human motivation. *Psychological Bulletin, 117*(3), 497–529.

Boice, R. (1996). Classroom incivilities. *Research in Higher Education, 37*(4), 453–486.

Booker, K. C. (2008). The role of instructors and peers in establishing classroom communi-ty. *Journal of Instructional Psychology, 35*(1), 12–16.

Brown, E. L. (2004). What precipitates change in cultural diversity awareness during a multicultural course: The message or the method? *Journal of Teacher Education, 55*(4), 325–340.

Chaskin, R. J., & Rauner, D. M. (1995). Special section on youth and caring. *Phi Delta Kap-pan, 76*(9), 665–719.

Deci, E. L., & Ryan, R. M. (1985). *Intrinsic motivation and self-determination in human behavior*. New York, NY: Plenum Press.

Deci, E. L., & Ryan, R. M. (2000). The "what" and "why" of goal pursuits: Human needs and the self-determination of behavior. *Psychological Inquiry, 11*(4), 227–268. doi:10.1207/S153-27965PLI1104_01

Forni, P. M. (2002). *Choosing civility: The twenty-five rules of considerate conduct*. New York, NY: St. Martin's Press.

Freeman, T. M., Anderman, L. H., & Jensen, J. M. (2007). Sense of school belonging in col-lege freshmen at the classroom and campus levels. *Journal of Experimental Education, 75*(3), 203–220.

Garcia, B., & Van Soest, D. (1997). Changing perceptions of diversity and oppression: MSW students discuss the effects of a required course. *Journal of Social Work Education, 36*(2), 261–278.

Garcia, J. E., Hoelscher, K. J., & Farmer, V, L. (2005). Diversity flashpoints: Understanding difficult interpersonal situation grounded in identity difference. *Innovative Higher Ed-ucation, 29*(4), 275–289. doi:10.1007/s10755-005-2862-9

Garmon, M. A. (2004). Changing preservice teachers' attitudes and beliefs about diversity: What are the critical factors. *Journal of Teacher Education, 55*(3), 201–213.

Glasser, W. (1998). *Choice theory: A new psychology of personal freedom*. New York, NY: HarperCollins.

Goodman, D. (1995). Difficult dialogues: Enhancing discussions about diversity. *College Teaching, 43*(2), 47–52.

Hayes, C. B., Ryan, A., & Zseller, E. B. (1994). The middle school child's perceptions of caring teachers. *American Journal of Education, 103*, 1–19.

Ituarte, S., & Davies, G. (2007). Perception of "self" and "other": Social boundaries that in-fluence teaching and learning in increasingly diverse US classrooms. In D. Palfreyman & D. McBride (Eds.), *Learning and teaching across cultures in higher education* (pp. 74–92). New York, NY: Palgrave Macmillan.

Johnson, D. W., & Johnson, R. T. (2009). Energizing learning: The instructional power of conflict. *Educational Researcher, 38*(1), 37–51. doi:10.3102/0013189X08330540

Johnson, D. W., Johnson, R. T., Smith, K. A. (1998). Cooperative learning returns to college. *Change, 30*(4), 26–35.

Johnson, D. W., Johnson, R. T., & Smith, K. (2007). The state of cooperative learning in postsecondary and professional settings. *Educational Psychology Review, 19*, 15–29. doi:10.1007/s10648-006-9038-8

Kagan, S. (2010). Structures optimize engagement. Retrieved from www.kaganonline.com/free_articles/dr_spencer_kagan/ASK28.php

Lowman, J. (1996). Characteristics of exemplary teachers. *New Directions for Teaching and Learning, 65*, 33–40.

Maslow, A. H. (1943). A theory of human motivation. *Psychological Review, 50*(4), 370–396.

Maslow, A. H. (1954). *Motivation and personality*. New York, NY: Harper and Row.

Mayeroff, M. (1971). *On caring*. New York, NY: Harper and Row.

McMillan, D. W., & Chavis, D. M. (1986). Sense of community: A definition and theory. *Journal of Community Psychology, 14*, 6–23.

Meyers, S. A. (2009). Do your students care whether you care about them? *College Teaching, 57*(4), 205–210.

Middleton, V. A. (2002). Increasing preservice teachers' diversity beliefs and commitments. *Urban Review, 34*(4), 343–361.

Nagda, B. A., Spearmon, M. L., Holley, L. C., Harding, S., Balassone, M. L., Moise-Swanson, D., & de Mello, S. (1999). Intergroup dialogues: An innovative approach to teaching about diversity and justice in social work programs. *Journal of Social Work Education, 35*(3), 433–449.

Nilson, L. (2010). *Teaching at its best: A research-based resource for college instructors* (3rd ed.). San Francisco, CA: Jossey-Bass.

Noddings, N. (2003). *Caring: A feminine approach to ethics and moral education* (2nd ed.). Berkeley: University of California Press.

Noddings, N. (2005). *The challenge to care in schools: An alternative approach to education. Advances in contemporary educational thought* (2nd ed.). New York, NY: Teachers College Press.

Osterman, K. F. (2000). Students' need for belonging in the school community. *Review of Educational Research, 70*(3), 323–367.

Rogers, D., & Webb, J. (1991). The ethic of caring in teacher education. *Journal of Teacher Education, 42*(3), 173–181. doi:10.1177/002248719104200303

Ryan, R. M., & Deci, E. L. (2000). Self-determination theory and the facilitation of intrinsic motivation, social development, and well-being. *American Psychologist, 55*(1), 68–78. doi:10.1037/0003-066X.55.1.68

Schmitz, C. L., Stakeman, C., & Sisneros, J. (2001). Educating professionals for practice in a multicultural society: Understanding oppression, and valuing diversity. *Families in Society: The Journal of Contemporary Human Service, 82*(6), 612–622.

Smith, R. W. (2000). The influence of teacher background on the inclusion of multicultural education: A case study of two contrasts. *Urban Review, 32*(2), 155–176.

Solomon, D., Battistich, V., Kim, D., & Watson, M. (1997). Teacher practices associated with students' sense of the classroom as community. *Social Psychology of Education, 1*, 235–267.

Straits, W. (2007). "She's teaching me": Teaching with care in a large lecture course. *College Teaching, 55*(4), 170–175.

Svinicki, M., & McKeachie, W. J. (2011). *McKeachie's teaching tips: Strategies, research, and theory for college and university teachers* (13th ed.). Belmont, CA: Wadsworth Cengage Learning.

Torok, C. E., & Aguilar, T. E. (2000). Changes in preservice teachers' knowledge and beliefs about language issues. *Equity and Excellence in Education, 33*(2), 24–31.

Van Soest, D. (1994). Social work education for multicultural practice and social justice advocacy: A field study of how students experience the learning process. *Journal of Multicultural Social Work, 3*(1), 17–28.

Villegas, A. M., & Lucas, T. (2002). *Educating culturally responsive teachers: A coherent approach.* Albany: State University of New York Press.

Williams, D. (2004). Improving race relations in higher education: The jigsaw classroom as a missing piece to the puzzle. *Urban Education, 39*(3), 316–344. doi:10.1177/0042085904-263063

Critical Media Literacy
Edutaining Popular Culture

Vonzell Agosto, Zorka Karanxha,
Deirdre Cobb-Roberts, and Eric Williams

Recent technological advancements—from the Web 2.0 to social networking sites—have resulted in increased opportunities that allow people to communicate and share media. In turn, the consumption and production of media has become more accessible to educators and students. Kellner (2004) argues that education needs to be re-envisioned, and in the process educators need to consider whether education should primarily be restructured to promote democracy and human needs or the global economy and needs of business. In deliberation about the purpose and direction of education, Kellner situates new technologies as powerful tools that can liberate or dominate, manipulate or enlighten—and, therefore, he urges educators to teach students how to use and critically analyze these media.

More than 90% of today's students are using personal devices and school computers to access and disseminate media before, during, and after school (Williamson & Johnston, 2012). They are regularly disciplined for bypassing district content filters to access potentially harmful materials using school computers or their own devices. Such filters have the effect of censoring information and blocking access. Censorship and blocking access to websites limits students' abilities to find and critically examine the validity of informational sources gathered from global information networks, an essential skill for students preparing for college and careers. More broadly, media serve as prime vehicles for cultural expression. Therefore, the exploration of how cultures and cultural groups are treated and how culture is performed, appropriated, or represented is a relevant area of inquiry for those concerned with educating students from diverse cultural backgrounds and educating students who will likely interact with people reflecting broad diversity.

We have become aware of the need for attention to cultural diversity, popular culture, and the role of critical media literacy in preparing educators and teacher educators, largely due to the reporting of current local events involving educators' and students' use and/or abuse of social media in particular.

Current local events involving educators' and students' use and/or abuse of social media have come to our attention as several of these incidents have involved students in our courses who are either teachers or administrators at the schools where these incidents have occurred. In order to understand the needs of leadership in a district where several incidents involving the use or abuse of social media had recently occurred, we conducted an informal survey of principals and select teacher leaders in all the schools of this local district during 2012. They were asked to list their primary concerns regarding the use of social media in schools. Among the seven principals (29%) who responded, most identified cyber-bullying, invasions of privacy, student and staff training needs, and inability to use social networks to disseminate information about school events as their primary concerns. Among the 12 teacher leaders (50%) who responded to the survey, most also identified cyber-bullying and student and staff training needs as their primary concerns. Teacher respondents also indicated concerns with loss of instructional time, protecting test security, and the inability to access quality online resources to support instruction as a result of filtering. While all had legitimate concerns, none was an advocate of completely shutting down access to social networks. Instead, most wanted to advance responsible use through information sharing and, therefore, focused on training and access opportunities rather than enacting stricter policies and tighter controls.

This chapter aims to support educators in critically examining media at the nexus of popular culture, ethnic culture, and diversity. For instance, educators are encouraged to examine deficit perspectives and stereotypes about subjugated ethnic groups that prevail through mass media and social media as a form of public entertainment. More specifically, we point to media representations and narratives that are constructed by educators, administrators, or students or that target them. Our examples demonstrate how the nexus of popular culture or ethnic culture and media is being realized in school events, classroom projects, and Internet-based postings among educators. We take the perspective that popular culture is a form of "edutainment," meaning that as it entertains it educates (Agosto, 2014; Giroux, 2001).

We provide a rationale and strategies for the inclusion of critical media literacy to support the development of educators who will be able to acknowledge and confront media production and consumption that serves as a mechanism of oppression. We describe how we advanced a critical media literacy framework to support preparation that values diversity and engenders cultural competence. Some of the strategies we engaged with include targeting various levels of professional experience, inviting guests, and facilitating dialogue about emotions. We also provided historical and contemporary perspectives; examples of oppressive and anti-oppressive media products; theoretical frameworks; and examples of local, national, and international media. We imagine that these or similar strategies can be used in various contexts and guided by the theoretical underpinnings we describe below.

CRITICAL MEDIA LITERACY

In the literature on educator and administrator preparation, popular culture has been understood and explored as a resource that helps to develop teacher identity, promote critical reflection among teachers (Ryan & Townsend, 2012), cultivate student leadership (McMahon & Bramhall, 2004), and promote representations of teachers in the movies (Dalton, 2004). Furthermore, popular culture has been identified as being useful in developing critical media literacy with the intent to facilitate transformative learning regarding diversity and equity issues (Tisdell, 2008). Tisdell positions critical media literacy as a classroom tool to critique the way hegemony is reinforced by the media. Thus critical media literacy is an educational response that views literacy as inclusive of different forms of mass communication, popular culture, and new technologies (Kellner & Share, 2007).

Social Oppression

Critical media literacy is based on critical social theory and is advanced here as an anti-oppressive approach that can be used to challenge social oppression. Social oppression refers to "the vast and deep injustices some groups suffer as a consequence of often unconscious assumptions and reactions of well-meaning people in ordinary interactions, media and cultural stereotypes, and structural features of bureaucratic hierarchies and market mechanisms" (Young, 2011, p. 41). More simply put, social oppression is a structural outcome embedded in the processes of everyday life (i.e., norms, values, habits, symbols, ideologies). In consideration of media as an art form and aesthetic experience, Duncum (2002) describes *everyday aesthetic experience* [emphasis in original] (p. 315) as sites where ideological struggles occur:

> Ideology works not because it calls particular attention to itself, but because it grounds itself in taken-for-granted, common-sense assumptions. Ideology works through ordinary cultural artifacts, and it can be hard to resist because it so often appears to belong to the realm of the natural. (pp. 5–6)

Young (2011) argues that there are five "faces" that can help us to understand and name social oppression along with its associated practices: violence, exploitation, marginalization, powerlessness, and cultural imperialism. While each is relevant to the conversation, for our purposes, cultural imperialism is the most prominent face of social oppression: "Cultural imperialism involves the universalization of a dominant group's experience and culture and its establishment as the norm" (p. 59). From a theory of social oppression, group experience and group liberation from cultural imperialism are the focus of inquiry rather than individual experience with faces and practices of oppression. In the classroom, the expectation is for students to consider how what appears as a single event in the media can signal larger patterns of representation for people who have similar social identities, experiences, and positions in the social structure. This expectation and opportunity to consider patterns in group experience can also deter students from reducing social oppression to an isolated or single event. Educators helping students to develop critical media literacy based in a critical social theory of oppression can require that students weigh historical evidence or consider whether the negative political implications for the individual and those with whom that individual shares a sense of connectedness (as group membership) can be overcome with little time or effort. For groups whose experiences historically and presently reflect the faces of oppression, the media representation must be read in conversation with a trajectory of representations circulating within the larger sociocultural narratives about people of similar social and political position.

Educators are in a unique position to encourage media literacy that is critical by empowering students to acknowledge and challenge positions of power and privilege related to the multiple and intersecting identities of actors and the intertextuality of narratives that are written or performed. For instance, educators might encourage students to consider whether local perspectives on an event gained by a reporter might belong to a particular group, reflecting a limited yet shared perspective. Students might also be asked to consider the possibility that some perspectives are invited to give credibility to the story or discredit opposing perspectives. In such cases, the power of the media can also be interrogated for how it constructs an apparently seamless narrative rather than one in which multiple and competing narratives are presented or left absent. Teacher educators can ensure that cultural critique and media analysis are central to teacher education by helping their students see that daily life and the policies affecting classrooms are both strongly influenced by media (McRobbie, 2000; Meiners, 2007). More specifically, critical media literacy requires that we examine media through an analytical lens grounded in critical social theory.

Critical Social Theory

Critical social theory (CST) weds critical theory and elements of sociological theory, cultural theory, and race/ethnic theory (Williams, 2008) and has as its goal to advance the emancipatory function of knowledge (Leonardo, 2004). The development of critical media literacy also includes self-examination of one's biases and acts that involve the differential privileging of members of different groups. In part, differential privileging of members of different racial groups is perpetuated through schooling by those working in schools. For example, Young (2011) claims that many teachers engage in unconscious aversion, in which they unconsciously behave differently toward Black or Latino students than they behave toward White students. We bridge the concept of cultural imperialism to culturally competent education (and other synonymous or convergent terms— i.e., culturally relevant, culturally consonant) through our discussion of media. Media are powerful tools that can be used to advance liberatory or oppressive education, and critical media literacy is an analytical tool with which to examine and critique media with the understanding that despite the multiple meanings we may glean from them, they are not neutral. Additionally, this approach is cognizant of the potential of media to support, mobilize, and immobilize populations. In other words, critical media literacy is not only about engaging students in media analysis but also about developing the critical lenses through which the analysis is conducted. Our approach to critical media literacy is tied to the enhancement of democracy and civic participation (Kellner & Share, 2007).

The discussion strategies we describe are meant to promote students', educators', and administrators' abilities to develop critical literacy with regard to media. More specifically, we expect that readers will be able to engage their knowledge of media and diversity and their critical dispositions to

- ask questions about language, power, social groups, and social practices;
- raise questions about the author's intent, the images used in texts, how those images represent various groups and relationships, and the effects of those elements on the reader and those around them;
- look for issues of (un)fairness;
- challenge textual constructions of reality that marginalize individuals or groups or that privilege or suppress views for specific purposes (Centre for Addiction and Mental Health [CAMH] Centre for Prevention Science, 2013).

One of the major goals we had in using critical media literacy with students and faculty was to support the development of educators and promote an institutional culture that reflects cultural competence. Our working defini-tion of cultural competence is having an awareness of one's own cultural iden-tity and views about difference, the ability to learn and build on the varying cultural and community norms of students and their families, and the ability to understand the within-group differences that make each student unique while celebrating the between-group variations (National Education Asso-ciation, 2013). Cultural competence is reflected by practices that recognize, affirm, and value the worth of individuals, families, and communities as they protect, preserve, and promote the dignity of each (adapted from Barrera & Kramer, 1997, and NASW Standards for Cultural Competence in Social Work Practice). We also relied on definitions of schoolwide cultural competence focused on school and community contexts whereby cultural competence is indicated by how well a school's policies, programs, practices, artifacts, and rituals reflect the needs and experiences of diverse groups in the school and surrounding school community (Bustamante, Nelson, & Onwuegbuzie, 2009; National Center for Cultural Competence, 2005; Nelson, Bustamante, Wilson, & Onwuegbuzie, 2008). These definitions of cultural competence span in their focus from K–12 school to college and coincide with our focus on increasing cultural competence college-wide.

In our planning for events we aimed to have faculty, and others who teach or counsel, think about building college-wide cultural competency with an emphasis on teaching and learning through the production and consumption of media and its analyses. To increase critical media literacy among faculty and teaching assistants, we utilized some of the methods Kellner and Share (2007) suggest for teaching critical media literacy to students: namely, critical discussion, debate, and analysis. Kellner and Share (2007) assert that teachers ought to be guiding students in an inquiry process that deepens their criti-cal exploration of issues that affect them and society. We intended to guide teacher educators and teaching assistants in subjecting their practice to in-quiry focused on the production and consumption of media and culture in teaching/learning contexts.

CRITICAL MEDIA LITERACY STRATEGIES

In the following section we discuss strategies we use to introduce and infuse critical media literacy into the discourse of faculty who prepare aspiring edu-cators and other school personnel. With some modifications, these strategies and activities can also be used in both preservice and inservice teacher edu-cation courses and, indeed, we have done so in our own classroom practice.

Pedagogical and Curriculum Interventions:
Connecting Culture, Media, and Diversity

Through our service to a College of Education Diversity Committee, we were able to offer critical media literacy as a way for students and faculty to consider how media can support structural oppression. To introduce the framework to faculty during a faculty meeting, we used popular culture in the form of a media clip from the movie *They Live* (1988).

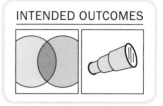

INTENDED OUTCOMES

In the movie *They Live* (1988), the main character finds a pair of sunglasses through which he is able to see messages on magazine covers and billboards. The messages, such as "consume" and "procreate," are broadcast unknowingly to humans by aliens who are attempting to establish a new world order in which they become the elite class to displace humans, who are being socialized and economically marginalized to become underclass. Like the main character, who donned sunglasses to see what was not readily apparent, critical media literacy supports the acquisition of knowledge, skills, and dispositions toward the development of heightened consciousness and criticality about the use and abuse of media, its varying influence, and related outcomes. Our intention in showing the clip was to "edutain" (entertain, educate) and entice. By entertaining faculty with an art form that is not generally presented in faculty meetings, we hoped to create dissonance that would provoke interest in attending future events. By connecting the idea of consciousness or awareness of mass media, we intended to educate faculty about the broader significance and pervasiveness of media and concerns about how mass communications circulate through popular culture unaccompanied by critical thinking or critical perspectives. By introducing this clip, we wanted to entice the faculty to attend forthcoming forums, meetings, and a retreat that would focus on teaching, learning, and implications for preparing educators and administrators. The movie clip of the sunglasses provided a metaphor for the development of critical media literacy. This previewing approach can be used in a teacher education course at the beginning of the semester to prepare students for the kind of critical thinking and analysis that will occur as the course unfolds.

Teacher's Use of Social Media

To foreshadow the critical discussions of media we wanted to incite in upcoming events, we showed a news clip involving a teacher posting racially

derogatory comments about one of her students
on her personal social media page. The news
headline read: "Parents infuriated over Manatee
teacher's Facebook comment" (tbo.com/news/
education/parents-infuriated-over-manatee
-teachers-facebook-comment-428806). At the
time we were able to view a clip that featured

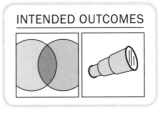

INTENDED OUTCOMES

the mother of an 8-year-old boy (who is Black), whose music teacher (a White
woman) commented about him on her social media website, referring to him
as the evolutionary link between humans and orangutans. When others in-
quired about the identity of the student, the teacher posted his initials on her
Facebook page. The news clip began with the anchorperson situating the story
as one about being careful about what you post on social media. In the clip,
the boy's mother suggested that more attention be given to teachers who bully
students. Also featured in the clip was the district superintendent who commented on the principal's decision to verbally reprimand the teacher.

After showing the clip, we asked faculty to discuss its salient themes in
small groups and then share the focus of their discussions with the large group.
Providing time for brief discussion in small groups first allows participants to
defuse (that is, express) the more emotional responses that may be difficult to
share in a larger group. The brief discussion in small groups also allows the participants to gain insight into others' interpretations, make connections between
their roles as educators, and assess their capacity to critically engage media.
While planning for the workshop, we wondered what faculty would view as
the most salient themes, which would be absent or marginalized in their discussions, and what skills of critical media literacy would be exhibited. In other
words, we wanted an activity that would allow us to assess the audience and
encourage self-assessment about their preparedness to engage in and facilitate
critical media literacy using culturally relevant pedagogy with their students.
We turned the metaphorical sunglasses on the faculty in order to capture the
messages they perceived as salient and the skills of media analysis they engaged
through the use of a web-based polling platform (polleverywhere.com). The
poll (taken by mobile phone) allows anonymous responses and immediately
captures and presents the highlights of the discussion resulting from the small
groups' deliberation about which themes they considered to be salient and provides an archive of the responses. Construction of the poll and identification
of the salient themes requires co-facilitators to view the media, discuss the issues, predict what other issues might be of interest to the audience or ignored,
and reach consensus about the few themes that will be polled. The themes we
identified as salient were privacy, teacher consequences, student well-being,
racism, and media representations of groups. Poll results can be used to inform

planning for future professional development events, provide topics for meetings, spur resource acquisition, guide syllabus revision of media guidelines, or prompt reflective journaling on areas of desired growth in knowledge, skills, and dispositions associated with cultural competence.

The results of our poll were that faculty paid primary attention to the consequences for the teacher and only little attention to race. Our observation during the large-group sharing about small-group discussion was that some of the skills associated with critical media literacy were being employed by a few members of the faculty. For instance, some questioned the framing of the story by the White female anchorperson (to be careful about what is posted) and the decision to end the story with the White male superintendent's perspective. We used this information as well as information from a string of email exchanges that were later sent via the faculty listserv to plan the diversity retreat for the following semester. From an instructor's perspective, the tabulation of this data can be a useful tool in organizing and planning a curriculum.

After the faculty meeting, email messages were sent to us applauding the introduction of critical media literacy. Highlighting the need for conversations on cultural competence soon developed into a discussion of bullying, with an emphasis on bullying among students. The issue of teachers bullying students was pervasively absent in the emails, although it was clearly presented by the mother in the news clip. We celebrated when the introduction of the theme and activities sparked an email conversation among faculty but lamented when concerns of the mother (who was Black) and the treatment of her child by the teacher (bullying) were not a point raised in the emails. These email exchanges also informed our preparation for the Diversity Forum—namely, the need to confront issues of race and racism more directly and at the intersection of multiple identities and cultural performances.

Those planning such events need to discern whether their intentions are to assess, to educate, or both. Our intention was to use the 30 minutes allotted to introduce critical media literacy, educate faculty about its relevance for teachers and students in schools, and entertain in order to incite interest in participating in more educative events (e.g., forums, retreats, and colloquia). Others, who have the time and conditions, may also choose to address the marginalized themes and provoke dialogue that delves into how the story is framed by an anchorperson or by captions; whose perspective is given prominence through placement and juxtaposition of narratives; or how the social hierarchy of society is reflected and reproduced in the production of the media product and construction of the narrative. In other words, the extent to which educators model and elicit critical media literacy utilizing the discussion strategies outlined earlier in this chapter (see CAMH Centre for Prevention Science, 2013) will be dependent on the intent of the educator, the conditions, and the context.

Oppressive and Anti-Oppressive Edutainment

At a diversity forum directed to an audience primarily composed of aspiring teacher educators, we presented faculty and students with an opportunity to engage in dialogue on media with presenters who were invited to discuss the intersection of race, gender, and dis/ability in Hollywood movies portraying Black, dis/abled males and the intersection of dis/ability, gender, and sexual orientation through a presenter's life history. Our strategy in designing the forum was threefold: to promote macro- and micro-level perspectives from those participating in the culture of the institution (student, professor), to present perspectives of those concerned about media constructions of others' identity, and to present media that challenges dominant narratives (namely those that minimize the robustness of identity and experience lived by people with dis/abilities). Overall we wanted to provide a bridge that would allow the audience to walk across the structural, societal, and individual dimensions of social oppression that are perpetuated through the media and coalesce in the experience of students as producers and consumers of media.

Presenting and engaging students in a critical analysis of major motion pictures (i.e., *The Bone Collector, Unbreakable, Source Code, Hancock, Battleship, The Avengers*) allowed them to consider how their perceptions of race, class, dis/ability, gender, and/or sexual orientation have been shaped through their exposure to mass media. After a presentation on dis/ability narratives that included illustrative clips from major motion pictures, the students were presented with a promotional interview with an actor from the film *Battleship* (2012), who is a Black, dis/abled male (Gregory D. Gadson). The students were then asked to identify the dis/ability tropes that were operating in the 30-second media clip. They were able to identify most of the dis/ability narratives (i.e., life not worth living, patriotism as an indication of worth, paternalism/maternalism from a White female, emphasis on action over thought; Agosto, 2014). One student even noted that the actor's physical condition (amputated legs and titanium prosthetics) was seemingly insufficiently robotic for the movie, so his abilities were enhanced by machinery to overexaggerate his masculinity and aggressiveness. The associations of Black men with dis/abilities with violence, White women as friends and not lovers, dehumanization (i.e., cyborg narrative) and overcoming dis/ability (i.e., a sense of despair) through being a productive citizen (in the armed forces) were not lost on the students.

To conclude the forum, a film produced as a capstone project by a master's student who has cerebral palsy helped to challenge other dis/ability narratives. The film focused on the slogan "It Gets Better" from the It Gets Better Project (www.itgetsbetter.org), which supports the idea that young adults should persist through times when society challenges who they are/are becoming, as lesbian, gay, bisexual, transgender, queer, questioning, or explorers of multiple points within the spectrum of sexual and/or gender identity. His film and presentation, focused on his own sexual identity development as a gay youth, challenged the trope that dis/abled people are asexual or straight and that those with disabilities are victims rather than survivors who persist. His presence as a filmmaker, whose speech is labored and perhaps difficult to understand by those who are unfamiliar with speech made with a different level of muscle tone, challenged the students to think about who can make a film, what film communicates, and the barriers that some groups face in having their perspectives shared via media. The presentation allowed students to consider how anti-oppressive media can be constructed by students in the context of courses. An anti-oppressive approach, for those working with youth in particular, is to use critical media literacy (CAMH Centre for Prevention Science, 2013; Choudhury & Share, 2012). Educators who welcome media that students create or use into the classroom should subject these media to the same process of critique, for students are not impervious to the infiltration of mass-produced stereotypes, tropes, or paradigms that influence decisionmaking about what media to disseminate or create.

Examining Stereotypes: The Usage of Blackface

Popular culture can be a source of stereotypical views and images about people from different social groups. It may be the primary source of information about a group for individuals who have had little to no opportunity for personal interaction with people of that group. For instance, one of the characters in the television sitcom *Martin* was Shenene (pronounced "Sha-nay-nay"), a stereotypical portrayal of a Black woman by the show's star, Martin Lawrence. This show originally aired during the 1990s, and its reruns air in most major cities today. This is just one example of how negative characterizations of Black women (i.e., annoying, violent, source of comic relief) are promoted through popular culture. We encouraged faculty to consider this by showing a video clip of students presenting their film *Teaching Diversity in Higher Education,* in which a White female impersonated (in blackface) a Black

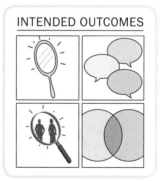

INTENDED OUTCOMES

student whom they named Shenene. After showing the video to the class, the students were questioned about why they chose this name. The girl who played the role in blackface shrugged and responded, "for comic relief."

The student-produced video was not an anomaly, unfortunately; there are many industry movies and amateur videos of White students and actors donning blackface for the purpose of performing the prevailing stereotypes of the time (e.g., *Gangs of New York, Soul Man, Trading Places, Tropic Thunder, Here Comes the Navy, Birth of a Nation, Amos and Andy*). Given the polysemic nature (i.e., having multiple meanings) of media artifacts, we aimed to model and encourage sensitivity to different readings, interpretations, and perceptions of the complex images, scenes, narratives, meanings, and messages of media culture (Luke, 1997).

Emotional load generally intensifies when dialogues on culture include race, racism, or antiracism. In turn, as emotional response intensifies, deflection to redirect dialogue (in order to avoid the stress it is generating) generally accompanies discussions addressing privilege and oppression (Johnson et al., 2012). Thus, we asked participants to write words on index cards representing the emotions the video generated in them; if no emotions were prompted by the video, they were instructed to write "none" on an index card. After airing the first clip from the video, we witnessed what we have identified as attempts to deflect the dialogue from race to the practice of the professor (who was not in the clip) and the quality of the video. Some of the emotions expressed on the notecards were anger, frustration, confusion, and disgust among some who perceived that the White student presenters were perpetuating stereotypes of Black students. Given the discomfort that some people have with allowing emotions to be expressed in the classroom, we did not want to give the impression that engaging emotions was easy, nor did we want to avoid them as if they are irrelevant or only function to diminish academic purposes (hooks, 1994). To the contrary, affective reflection and critical analysis are required for social change (Simpson, 2003).

However, some participants chose to verbalize their reactions immediately instead of recording their thoughts on the index card. We wanted each person to have the opportunity to respond to the prompt without being influenced by others' comments or interpretations of the media clip. In our planning, we considered the tendency for some voices to dominate in spaces where others remain silent. Still, we were unable to stave off the verbal interruptions from faculty. In our debriefing, we read and named them as interruptions to equitable participation.

Facilitators can benefit from anticipating subtle forms of resistance and understanding that emotional intensity and deflection are common responses when engaging in dialogue that one finds difficult due to the subject matter and their position with regard to it, whether that position is ideological or identity based (e.g., professional, group affiliation). For instance, one could provide direct instructions for participants to (1) focus on the content of the video rather than the quality of the video, (2) refrain from sharing impressions of the video aloud and instead write them on the index card for discussion in 5 minutes, and (3) allow for equitable participation in discussion to ensure that everyone is heard.

When the video ended, we provided the following prompts:

1. Discuss the emotions of groups in connection to the video (i.e., what prompted responses).
2. Analyze the video using a critical media literacy lens.
3. Discuss the findings.
4. Discuss whether some images should be censored in the classroom.

Blackface, through the lens of social oppression, is an example of cultural imperialism. To experience cultural imperialism "means to experience how the dominant meanings of a society render the particular perspective of one's own group invisible at the same time as they stereotype one's group and mark it out as other" (Young, 2011, p. 58). A critical media literacy approach can provoke educators to consider how blackface might be experienced by those who ascribe or are ascribed to the racial category Black. None of the media examined— neither the student-generated video on "teaching diversity" nor the interviews conducted by the anchorperson in the news coverage of students performing blackface—included a perspective from someone who is Black.

A YouTube search using "blackface" as a search term yields videos ranging from the racist rants of White college students to White students portraying President Barack Obama in a classroom drama. Also, there are books that focus on the perception of Black life through the eyes of a White male (i.e., *Black Like Me*) that can be used to support dialogue on how others have attempted to represent or gain knowledge of cultural groups' experiences to increase their level of cultural competence. Regardless of the source, critical media literacy urges us to problematize media and subject them to analysis.

This discussion was followed by a presentation on minstrelsy by a university librarian and historian who had curated an exhibition on sheet music (blackface and minstrelsy) in order to provide cultural and historical contextualization of blackface. This presentation provided history and information about available resources at the university (exhibits.lib.usf.edu/exhibits/show/minstrelsy). Other examples were also provided (e.g., www.pbs.org/wgbh/amex/foster/sfeature/sf_minstrelsy.html, digital.denverlibrary.org/cdm/search/searchterm/blackface, digital.library.louisville.edu/cdm/search/field/descri/searchterm/blackface).

Unpacking Microaggressions and Institutional Culture

Over the semester we focused on using and consuming media in the K–12 context, thus enabling faculty and students to focus on the education of children in schools and the ways in which media can be oppressive as well as liberatory and emancipatory. In another attempt to remind faculty and students of the connection

INTENDED OUTCOMES

between the national and local context and between the individual and the institutional culture, we asked participants to reflect and dialogue on our campus environment through the construct of racial microaggressions (Sue et al., 2007). Sue and colleagues describe racial microaggressions as "brief and commonplace daily verbal, behavioral, and environmental indignities, whether intentional or unintentional, that communicate hostile, derogatory, or negative racial slights and insults to the target person or group" (p. 273). Racial microaggressions framework is a way for faculty and students to develop cultural competence in their practice and facilitate that development among students.

We posted these prompts:

1. List and discuss the kinds of racial microaggressions you have witnessed or experienced at the university and how you responded.
2. If you were to intervene, do you feel that the leadership of your program, department, or college would support you?
3. What would/does that support look like?

Our intention in providing these prompts for discussion was to redirect the focus from the consideration of racial microaggressions at the individual level to include consideration of how racial microaggressions are perpetuated at the institutional level. For instance, in our planning we considered a case in which a colleague was searching the university's bank of stock photos for a photo of students using technology in a learning context. When asked why the photos selected for a presentation were only of students who appeared White (by color of eyes, skin, hair, and phenotype), the colleague responded that there were no photos available of students of color. Upon checking, we found the same and concluded that such an absence was more reflective of the choices of those making decisions about what photos are taken and who is included and excluded than it was a reflection of the practices of students of color. We believe that this environmental indignity helps to promote a cultural climate in which people of color are insulted by hidden or indirect messages that suggest they do not belong.

We wanted our participants to note other such instances and consider the challenges and opportunities for changing the climate of the institution beyond just the classroom toward one that reflects cultural competence in how the institution operates. Faculty can use this framework to analyze their practice and the class environment they create. Additionally, educators can engage in a similar activity by using these prompts or adding a few more depending on the context. The activity can be utilized with colleagues as well as students to examine their institutions and to gauge the level of support or resistance present in their specific context.

Students and Faculty Producing Video

Providing media that is empowering for students at the margins is important when attempting to challenge stereotypes and center the voices of students who are "othered" (Kumashiro, 2000). So to close, we featured another student-produced video that we viewed as anti-oppressive and emancipatory. For a class project, a class member who taught K–12 students who were speakers of languages other than English informed the students that she wanted to feature them in a video to provide personal stories from their perspectives that would be partnered with survey data. The goal of the project was to conduct action-based research on her role as a curriculum leader. Upon hearing about the project, her students became actively engaged in all aspects, from videotaping to editing and mixing the soundtrack. Each created a poster responding to a question asking them to make a statement about what they wanted from their teachers. The class member compared her students' statements to the best practices being circulated in the district that informed curriculum development and pedagogy; she then communicated her findings locally in the district as well as nationally at a professional conference. The students were empowered to say what they wanted from their teachers and communicate that through media and other arts-based approaches (i.e., music selection, audio mixing, drawing). Not only did the video bring awareness to the issues facing students who are native speakers of myriad languages (and generally marginalized for this in U.S. schools), but it also helped to give a human face and story to an issue and paved the way for the class member to facilitate change in practices and policies beyond her classroom.

Similarly, faculty can produce media or design an assignment requiring students to produce videos that are empowering for students at the margins. For example, teachers can ask students or preservice teachers to produce video to express their views on how institutions treat them and how they would like to be treated. Inservice teachers can have such an assignment designed for their students as well. For example, they can ask English language learners or students with dis/abilities or any "othered" group of students to tell their teachers how they want to be treated at school.

CONCLUSION

Overall, we provided multiple constructs such as critical media literacy, collegewide cultural competence, and racial microaggressions to analyze media in the form of news clips and images from popular culture and considered both historical and contemporary examples of how media can be oppressive and anti-oppressive. We worked collaboratively to plan the events in order to increase the college's cultural competence and facilitate the development of the critical media literacy skills of students, faculty, staff, and administrators. Faculty, students, and inservice teachers can work together to design assignments and staff development activities that are collaborative and increase the critical media literacy skills in their colleges, schools, and classrooms.

In our work as co-chairs of the College of Education Diversity Committee, we attempted to create "a safe haven" (quote from a participant in the retreat) for faculty, students, staff, and administrators to discuss issues of diversity in relation to social oppression and more specifically cultural imperialism as generated through media appropriated by students. The space we attempted to create was a haven *for* difficult dialogues, not safety *from* them. The foundation for this space was carved the prior year through surveys of students and faculty, task-force meetings, and networks of like-minded people who were finding little opportunity in their own departments to express critical perspectives or focus on cultural competence as an institutional issue with implications for their performance and performance ratings. Furthermore, others are approaching us with opportunities that include publishing, hosting events, serving as sounding boards, and operating in an advisory capacity. We recommend the foundation for critical media literacy be paved in advance through an inquiry process in which collaborators consider their guiding philosophy, networks of supports, resources in and outside of the immediate context, and sources of institutional support.

In order to move toward institutional cultural competence, we recommend fostering an inclusive culture (inclusivity of diverse ideas, perspectives, and participants). We included students, faculty, staff, and administrators throughout the process. We sought different perspectives and contributions throughout the process (from planning to implementation). Prior discussions on the direction of the Diversity Committee had revolved around excluding students from the retreat. However, we pushed for student participation and centered their experiences and perspectives in the forums and retreat (but we narrowed it to graduate assistants at the retreat). This push for student partici-pation has resulted in a new study being conducted that includes students and faculty as co-researchers.

Further, we recommend that instructors vet rather than censor the mate-rials students will be presenting in class. Instructors can ask students to send the topic or an outline of a presentation and any media material well in ad-vance so the professor can prepare to receive material and engage students in the skills of critical media literacy. Critically literate educators will have spent the time preparing students to interrogate and analyze materials, thus cen-soring would be a practice counter to the purpose and importance of critical media literacy. We could bury our heads in the proverbial sand and sweep our problems under the proverbial rug, simply hoping that upon graduation our students will have inherited the social skills they need to traverse the interper-sonal digital divide (Bugeja, 2005). Or we can encourage students to question the world and their place in that world and to consider the varied perspectives in preparation to work collaboratively toward critiquing and challenging op-pressive and hegemonic systems.

Popular culture specifically gave us an opportunity to entertain and edu-cate (edutain). Although our audience was composed of those in a college of education, we work in different subfields, so finding common ground around which to begin our difficult dialogues can be challenging at times. Popular culture provides common points of reference, whether through song, music, dance, theater, visual culture, or film. According to Share and Thoman (2007), "If teachers respect their students' popular culture while engaging it in mean-ingful inquiry, they open up possibilities for their students to critically use, analyze, and create media in the school setting" (p. 15).

REFERENCES

Agosto, V. (2014). Scripted curriculum: What movies teach about dis/ability and Black males. *Teachers College Record, 116*(4). Retreived from www.tcrecord.org/Content. asp?ContentId=17403

Barrera, I., & Kramer, L. (1997). From monologues to skilled dialogues: Teaching the process of crafting culturally competent early childhood environments. In P. J. Winton, J. A. Mc-Collum, & C. Catlett (Eds.), *Reforming personnel preparation in early intervention: Issues, models and practical strategies* (pp. 217–251). Baltimore, MD: Paul H. Brookes.

Bugeja, M. (2005). *Interpersonal divide: The search for community in a technological age.* New York, NY: Oxford University Press.

Bustamante, R., Nelson, J. A., & Onwuegbuzie, A. J., (2009). Assessing school-wide cultural competence: Implications for school leadership preparation. *Educational Administra-tion Quarterly, 45*(5), 793–827.

Centre for Addiction and Mental Health (CAMH) Centre for Prevention Science. (2014). *Free lesson plans: Critical media literacy.* Retrieved from www.youthrelationships. org/free-lesson-plans#critical

Choudhury, M., & Share, J. (2012). Critical media literacy: A pedagogy for new literacies and urban youth. *Voices from the Middle, 19*(4), 39–44.

Dalton, M. (2004). *The Hollywood curriculum: Teachers in the movies.* New York, NY: Peter Lang.

Duncum, P. (2002). Theorizing everyday aesthetic experience with contemporary visual culture. *Visual Arts Research, 28*(2), 4–15.

Giroux, H. A. (2001). Breaking into the movies: Pedagogy and the politics of film. *JAC-AMES, 21*(3), 583–598.

hooks, b. (1994). *Teaching to transgress: Education as the practice of freedom.* New York, NY: Routledge.

Johnson, J. R., Gonzalez, M., Ray, C., Hager, L. D., Spalding, S., & Brigham, T. (2012). Daring pedagogy: Dialoguing about intersectionality and social justice. In S. M. Pliner & C. A. Banks (Eds.), *Teaching, learning and intersecting identities in higher education,* (pp. 179–200). New York, NY: Peter Lang.

Kellner, D. (2004). Technological transformation, multiple literacies, and the re-visioning of education. *E-Learning, 1*(1), 9–37.

Kellner, D., & Share, J. (2007). Critical media literacy is not an option. *Learning Inquiry, 1,* 59–69.

Kumashiro, K. (2000). Toward a theory of anti-oppressive education. *Review of Educational Research, 70*(1), 25–53.

Leonardo, Z. (2004). Critical social theory and transformative knowledge: The function of criticism in quality education. *Educational Researcher, 33*(6), 11–18.

Luke, C. (1997). Media literacy and cultural studies. In S. Muspratt, A. Luke, & P. Freebody (Eds.), *Constructing critical literacies: Teaching and learning textual practice* (pp. 19–49). Cresskill, NJ: Hampton Press.

McMahon, T. R., & Bramhall, R. (2004). Student affairs teaching and practice related to leadership. *New Directions for Student Services, 108,* 61–70.

McRobbie, A. (2000). *Feminism and youth culture* (2nd ed.). London, England: Routledge.

Meiners, E. (2007). Life after Oz: Ignorance, mass media, and making public enemies. *Review of Education, Pedagogy, and Cultural Studies, 29*(1), 23–63.

National Education Association. (2013). *Why cultural competence?* Retrieved from www. nea.org/home/39783.htm

Nelson, J., Bustamante, R. M., Wilson, E., & Onwuegbuzie, A. J. (2008). The school-wide cultural competence observation checklist (SCCOC): An exploratory factor analysis. *Professional School Counseling, 20*(4), 20–32.

Ryan, P. A., & Townsend, J. S. (2012). Promoting critical reflection in teacher education through popular media. *Action in Teacher Education, 34*(3), 239–248.

Share, J., & Thoman, E. (2007). *Teaching democracy: A media literacy approach.* Los Angeles, CA: National Center for the Preservation of Democracy.

Simpson, J. S. (2003). *I have been waiting: Race and U.S. higher education.* Toronto, Canada: University of Toronto Press.

Sue, D. W., Capodilupo, C. M., Torino, G. C., Bucceri, J. M., Holder, A. M. B., & Esquilin, M. (2007). Racial microaggressions in everyday life: Implications for clinical practice. *American Psychologist, 62*(4), 271–286.

Tisdell, E. J. (2008). Critical media literacy and transformative learning: Drawing on pop culture and entertainment media in teaching for diversity in adult higher education. *Journal of Transformative Education, 6*(1), 48–67.

Williams, A. D. (2008). The critical cultural cypher: Remaking Paulo Freire's cultural circles using hip hop culture. *International Journal of Critical Pedagogy, 2*(1), 1–29.

Williamson, R., & Johnston, J. H. (2012). *The school leader's guide to social media.* New York, NY: Routledge.

Young, I. M. (2011). *Justice and the politics of difference* (2nd ed.). Princeton, NJ: Princeton University Press.

Part II

CONTENT-SPECIFIC DIVERSITY EDUCATION

CHAPTER 4

English Language Arts Education
Valuing All Voices

Anete Vásquez

Reading multiple texts is a requirement in my Teaching Adolescent Literature course. Preservice teachers (PSTs) participate in literature circles that have rotating memberships based upon text selections in each of ten categories. In one of the categories of books, each book has a protagonist who is questioning his or her sexual orientation: *Keeping You a Secret* (Peters, 2007); *Empress of the World* (Ryan, 2003); *Boy Meets Boy* (Levithan, 2009); *Deliver Us from Evie* (Kerr, 2009); and *Annie on My Mind* (Garden, 2007). During class one semester, after describing this category, I noticed two of my PSTs looked uneasy.

> "Some of you have worried looks on your faces," I stated. "Does anyone have a question or a comment?"
>
> "Can we really teach books like this in school, Dr. Vásquez? I mean, won't parents complain?" asked Carol.
>
> "Forget parents, I don't want to introduce my students to books about gay people," retorted Marc. "Homosexuality is wrong. Besides, you'd be inviting all kinds of uncomfortable conversations into the classroom."

I was amazed he had just blurted out that "homosexuality is wrong" as if it were fact. For all he knew, classmates of his or I might be members of the lesbian, gay, bisexual, transgendered, queer/questioning, or intersex (LGBTQ$_2$I) community. And, I was certain, all of these PSTs would one day have students who may question their own sexual identities. I also knew that all of the books on the list dealt with other potentially controversial issues, such as immigration, race, politics, and religion. After all, the very definition of adolescent literature is "a story that tackles the difficult, and oftentimes adult, issues that arise during an adolescent's journey toward identity" (Stephens, 2007, pp. 40–41). It was clear that this group of students, like many, could benefit from guidance and guidelines for creating a caring and civil community of learners. As a result, I began by building a positive learning community using many of the activities outlined in Chapter 2 of this text and by introducing the PSTs to the tenets of our professional organizations concerning diversity and culturally responsive teaching.

CULTURALLY RESPONSIVE TEACHING IN THE ENGLISH CLASSROOM

Culturally responsive teaching has been defined as "using the cultural knowledge, prior experiences, frames of reference, and performance styles of ethnically diverse students to make learning encounters more relevant to and effective for them" (Gay, 2000, p. 29). *Supporting Linguistically and Culturally Diverse Learners in English Education*, a position statement by the National Council of Teachers of English (NCTE), outlines eight principles for culturally responsive teaching in the English language arts (ELA) classroom (2005). It encourages teachers to acknowledge that we all, teachers and students, have diverse identities. Unlike Mr. Gradgrind, the schoolmaster in Charles Dickens's *Hard Times,* who believes his students are "little vessels . . . ready to have imperial gallons of facts poured into them" (Dickens, 1854, p. 4), culturally responsive teachers do not believe that students are blank slates; students arrive in school with funds of knowledge. As teachers we need to develop complex understandings of our students to create learning environments and activities that facilitate academic achievement for all. English teachers can use a variety of approaches to do this, including (1) incorporating multicultural literature; (2) engaging students in active learning; (3) allowing student choice; (4) teaching critical literacy skills; (5) applying content to real life; (6) creating physical and cultural adaptations; (7) using cooperative learning structures; and (8) differentiating instruction to meet the individual needs of learners (McNeal, 2005).

Beyond these eight suggestions, the NCTE (2005) position statement urges teachers to realize that "teaching is a political act" that requires educators to "cross traditional, personal, and professional boundaries" in pursuit and advocacy of social justice and equity (para. 4). Teachers must acknowledge their limits of understanding students' backgrounds. Moreover, they must work to expand their understanding through activities such as attending community meetings, getting to know the adults in the community, studying the history of diverse cultures, and conducting community ethnographies.

The vast majority of teachers in the United States represents a middle-class, European American population (Gay, 2000). This is particularly true in the

English teaching profession, where 85% to 90% of teachers are White and female (Snyder & Hoffman, 2002). The demographic landscape of the United States, however, is rapidly changing, and the potentially different cultural backgrounds and experiences of teachers and their students underscore the need for teachers to understand the racial and social inequities that have existed and still exist in American schools (Gay, 2000). Furthermore, teachers must recognize the privileges that middle-class Whiteness has afforded them. Teachers must act as agents of change by examining what constitutes "official knowledge" and how some forms of knowledge privilege one set of students while restricting others. Boyd et al. (2006) write, "When educators support unquestioned ideas and ideals that reflect a single, dominant view of society, the result is a marginalization of the contributions, potential, and capabilities of learners who come from diverse linguistic, ethnic, and cultural backgrounds" (p. 330).

SELECTED INSTRUCTIONAL ACTIVITIES

Teacher educators are seeking ways to expand what PSTs accept as official knowledge by widening the scope of the curricula to include culturally relevant course material and employing alternative activities and real-world experiences to promote social justice and equity in their classrooms and beyond. Teacher educators can do this by creating assignments that help their PSTs cultivate critical perspectives through meaningful dialogue, self-interrogation, and action research—as outlined in Chapter 1 of this text—as ways to facilitate PSTs' journey through diversity awareness and identity development.

The remainder of this chapter provides vignettes that have occurred in my English education classrooms. Each vignette highlights a classroom situation in which gender orientation, race or ethnicity, language, social class, or abilities became a topic of sometimes unsettling discussions. The vignettes themselves can be used as a means to promote dialogue, so each is followed by a list of discussion questions. Subsequently, the teaching activities attempt to open the minds of PSTs to the richness that diversity can bring to the ELA classroom in an attempt to prevent the marginalization of any student voice.

SEXUAL ORIENTATION

The vignette provided in the introduction of the chapter introduces the opportunity to discuss two issues. One is the statement made by the student that "homosexuality is wrong." If ignored, PSTs might interpret silence as tacit consent. The second issue involves the other student's question, "Won't parents complain?"

Vignette discussion questions:

1. You will have students in your class with values, beliefs, or lifestyles very different from your own. You may even have moral and/or philosophical issues with some differences. How will you make these students feel welcome, an integral part of the classroom, and safe to take academic risks?
2. Your classes are very likely going to be made up of students from families with very diverse perspectives. How will you select course materials? Will you stick to material that avoids controversial issues? Do such materials even exist? How will you handle complaints about curriculum?

Thematic Analysis of Reader Reviews

Assign PSTs to read reviews of the books you have in this category at booksellers' websites such as Barnes and Noble, Amazon, and Powell's Books and do a thematic analysis of the reviews. Ask PSTs to categorize the reviews and consider the gathered information when trying to answer their own question, "Can we really teach books like this in school?" One bookstore website my students examined had 171 reader reviews posted about *Keeping You a Secret* (Peters, 2007). My PSTs' thematic analysis led them to

INTENDED OUTCOMES

realize that LGBTQ$_2$I readers identified with the characters in important ways, and non-LGBTQ$_2$I readers expressed a deeper understanding of the LGBTQ$_2$I community. One reviewer wrote that the "theme . . . taught me a lesson about the particular challenges gay people face with assorted prejudices from peers and family [and] to be more compassionate and understanding . . . more open-minded" (www.amazon.com). PSTs also found that all readers, regardless of sexual orientation, were highly engaged with the text and expressed a heightened appreciation of all types of diversity, not just gender identity.

Creation of a Position Statement on Safe Schools

Share with PSTs some of the findings of the *2011 National School Climate Survey* of 7,261 LGBTQ$_2$I students between the ages of 13 and 21 (Kosciw, Greytak, Bartkiewicz, Boesen, & Palmer, 2012):

- 81.9% reported being verbally harassed.
- 38.3% reported being physically harassed.
- 55.2% experienced electronic harassment or cyber-bullying.
- 18.3% reported being physically assaulted at school in the past year.
- 84.9% heard "gay" used in a negative way frequently at school.
- 71.3% heard other homophobic remarks such as "dyke" or "faggot."
- 63.5% reported feeling unsafe in school.
- 31.8% missed a day of school in the past month because of feeling unsafe.
- 16.8% reported being taught positive representations of LGBTQ$_2$I people, history, and events.

Discuss the fact that some of the most famous authors and poets are members of the LGBTQ$_2$I community—Lord Byron, Truman Capote, Gore Vidal, Oscar Wilde, Tennessee Williams, Thornton Wilder, Virginia Woolf, Walt Whitman—and how easy it is for ELA teachers to include this information when teaching. Ask PSTs to research other positive steps that individual teachers and schools can take to create safer schools for LGBTQ$_2$I teens and share their findings with the class. Then

INTENDED OUTCOMES

have PSTs write a position paper on their synthesized findings. Many excellent resources can be found on the Gay, Lesbian, and Straight Education Network (GLSEN) website (www.glsen.org).

Panel Presentation—LGBTQ$_2$I Students' Experiences in School

Contact a chapter of GLSEN, your university's LGBTQ$_2$I student organizations, regional chapter of Parents, Families, and Friends of Lesbian and Gays (PFLAG), or local high schools' Gay-Straight Alliance (GSA) groups to ask if they have members who are willing to serve on a panel discussion entitled "LGBTQ$_2$I Students' Experiences in School." I facilitated such a panel discussion with my PSTs and found it to be highly informative and poignant. Prior to the discussion, I made certain that PSTs knew acceptable terminology (gay rather than homosexual, sexual orientation rather than sexual preference, etc.), and we reviewed our mutually created and agreed-upon classroom discussion guidelines.

Panel members spoke about when and how they came out to their family and friends and what their school experiences were as an LGBTQ$_2$I student, including stories of inclusive teachers and of those who made disparaging comments or turned a deaf ear to the harassment of LGBTQ₂I students. Panel members' comments echoed facts PSTs had read and put a person behind the statistics they found when they researched initiatives that teachers and schools can enact to create safer schools for LGBTQ₂I teens.

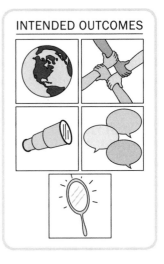

Of all of the issues we discuss in my methods courses, working with LGBTQ₂I adolescents is the one that makes PSTs the most uncomfortable. Many cite strong religious views that prevent them from supporting LGBTQ₂I rights. After our panel presentation, one such PST posted this comment on our online discussion board:

> Insightful discussion in class. I appreciate the fact that I was allowed to respectfully disagree with the LGBTQ experience . . . while still being shown respect from my classmates. I hope everyone knew that I also have great respect for all of them, even though they might not agree with me as well. We don't have to agree on all the particulars of all issues, as long as we show respect for one another. This makes disagreeing much less painful! I appreciate being given the opportunity to voice my opinion in a safe and respectful environment without fear of condemnation. I feel that we all have that in this class.

I include this student comment because I want to be honest. Not all of these activities will change the hearts and minds of all PSTs on all issues. If a caring and civil classroom environment is created, however, powerful discussions can take place that encourage PSTs to reconsider their own beliefs. Sometimes PSTs will choose resistance; sometimes they will choose transformation. In the end, they have experienced profound self-examination and gained knowledge that may not change their views but has broadened their perspective.

RACE AND ETHNICITY

I use cases from Johannessen and McCann's *In Case You Teach English: An Interactive Casebook for Prospective and Practicing Teachers* (2002) to promote discussions on race and ethnicity in my methods courses. One case study, entitled

"Do We Have to Read *Huck Finn*?" always sparks heated conversations about the place of race talk in the ELA classroom, as the following excerpt illustrates.

> "This case must be old. Students today wouldn't have such an issue with the use of the n-word. No one uses it anymore in a derogatory way," commented Laura, a White student. "Kids today know that the novel reflects the culture of the time, not the present day."
>
> "What present day are you living in where there's no racism?" asks D'Jenane, one of the two Black PSTs in the class.
>
> "Yea, wherever that is—I want to live there," adds Hector, who is Puerto Rican.
>
> Dwight, the other Black PST in class, comes to Laura's defense, "I know what Laura is trying to say. It's not like back when Twain was writing. There's not as much racism now as there used to be."
>
> "Besides, the n-word has been de-stigmatized in some ways by hip-hop culture," interjects Ryan. "It's in lyrics, Black people call each other the n-word. Of course, I'm White, so I would never use the n-word . . ." Ryan's voice trails off uncomfortably.
>
> "Whatever," interjects Michelle, who is of mixed race. "I just don't think you should be talking about race in the classroom. Just treat all students the same—with respect."

Michelle's comment exposes the fact that many undergraduates, in particular, still ascribe to a "color-blind" philosophy of race, where racial and ethnic group membership is considered irrelevant to the way one is treated. Proponents of Critical Race Theory (CRT) argue the "color-blind" approach is the antithesis of fairness and suggest that race and ethnicity cannot be ignored. Schofield (2009) traces the color-blind philosophy to sentiments expressed in Supreme Court Justice John Marshall Harlen's 1896 dissenting opinion in *Plessy v. Fergusson,* in which he asserts that the Constitution is "color-blind." The multicultural perspective is traced to Justice Harry Blackmun's comment in the 1978 case of the *Regents of the University of California v. Bakke,* "In order to get beyond racism, we must first take account of race . . . And in order to treat persons equally, we must treat them differently. We cannot—we dare not—let the equal protection clause perpetuate racial supremacy" (p. 407).

Vignette discussion questions:

1. Should teachers discuss issues of race in the classroom? If so, how?
2. Should we treat all students as if they were the same, or should we acknowledge differences in race? Why?

Paideia Seminar

Part of our role as teacher educators is to support PSTs in encouraging critical thinking and participation in their future classrooms. The Paideia Seminar, or Socratic Circle, is a teaching strategy that meets this goal while providing PSTs with a safe venue in which to discuss difficult topics, including but not limited to race and ethnicity. This student-centered strategy requires that the instructor give students a "text" to study, such as a picture, an original document, a film, a commercial, or song lyrics. Suggestions of powerful "texts" include Norman Rockwell's painting *The Problem We all Live With* (1964); a news article about the 2006 racial incident in Jena, Louisiana; an excerpt from the nonfiction book *The Other Wes Moore: One Name, Two Fates* (Moore, 2011); or any text that focuses on race and education.

INTENDED OUTCOMES

Give PSTs time to study the text and write brief statements about important features or questions. Arrange desks in a circle and sit with the students. Encourage a PST to read his or her statement or question and allow discussion to unfold. This often invites other PSTs to share what they have written. Once the first PST's comments have been discussed, the next person in the circle reveals his or her written comments or questions until each class member has had an opportunity to share. Optimally, the role of the teacher educator is simply to record comments. Initially the teacher educator may need to be more active, prompting PSTs to analyze the texts by asking open-ended questions. To conclude, ask PSTs to recap major points of the seminar and discuss the procedure itself. Did the PSTs think it went well or that it could be improved? If so, how? The Paideia Seminar can lead to extraordinary discussions of race, power, history, and education in America.

Using Counter-Stories

Counter-storytelling "aims to cast doubt on the validity of accepted premises or myths, especially ones held by the majority" (Delgado & Stefancic, 2001, p. 144) and serves "as a means for giving voice to marginalized groups" (DeCuir & Dixson, 2004, p. 27). Have PSTs listen to counter-narratives to explore the insidious nature of racism and how it is manifested in educational contexts. StoryCorps, an independent nonprofit oral history project, is an excellent source for such stories. I have used the following three stories from StoryCorps: (1) sisters Sylvia Mendez and Sandra Mendez Duran discuss *Mendez v. Westminster*, their family's lawsuit that won Mexican-American children the right to attend White schools in 1945 (Mendez & Mendez Duran, 2013); (2) Ricardo Pitts-Wiley tells his son Jonathan about getting bussed from an all-Black school to a school where African Americans made up only 2% of the school population (Pitts-Wiley, 2013); and (3) Mweupe Mfalme Nguni tells the story of his first day at an integrated elementary school in 1965, where a teacher chastised a classmate for calling him the n-word by proclaiming, "I don't ever want to hear you say that again. He can't help it that he was born a little nigger. And it's just by the grace of God that you wasn't born a little nigger." Mweupe concludes that the comment made him feel like "God had no grace upon me" (Nguni, 2013).

INTENDED OUTCOMES

Such counter-stories may provide opportunities for PSTs to think from another's perspective. As Delgado and Stefancic (2001) state, counter-stories "help us to understand what life is like for others, and invite the reader into a new and unfamiliar world" (p. 41). The StoryCorps website also provides a "Do-It-Yourself Guide" that instructs students in the basic skills of interviewing and storytelling. Assign students to collect counter-stories from friends and families about their own schooling experiences, both positive and negative, as part of a larger research project. Have PSTs share their stories and compare and contrast experiences.

Demographic Research and the Privilege of Whiteness

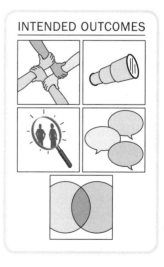

INTENDED OUTCOMES

Another way to investigate issues of culture, ideology, power, and history presents itself in an analysis of standardized test scores of Whites and non-White K–12 students. Rather than grounding the discussion in personal feelings or the findings of researchers, have PSTs examine the state's school indicator reports, which include information found in Table 4.1.

Require PSTs to work in cooperative groups to analyze data in various ways, including the relationship between highly diverse schools versus hegemonic schools in relationship to

Table 4.1. School Indicator Report Information

School Information	Test Scores	Student Information	Teacher Information
Absentee rate	ACT	Demographic makeup	Percentage teaching outside of field
Average class size	SAT	Percentage in special education	
	State exam scores	Percentage in gifted programs	Percentage at each degree level
Per-pupil expenditures	School grade	Percentage of English language learners	
Graduation rate			Years of teaching experience
Incidents of crime/violence		Percentage receiving free or reduced-price lunch	
Suspensions		Mobility rate	
Dropout rate		Stability rate	
		Percentage employed after graduation	
		Percentage continuing education	

standardized test scores, school climate (e.g., class size, suspension rates, absenteeism, expenditure per student, crime/violence, dropout rates, graduation rates, mobility, and stability), and teacher characteristics (e.g., percentage out-of-field, advanced degrees, years of experience). As findings are reported, discuss the underlying mechanisms at work that contribute to the disparity in test scores by directing conversation to topics such as the minimum wage, health care, child care, and other larger social issues. PSTs realize that the "achievement gap" is not a result of race and ethnicity but of power and the distribution of resources. They become cognizant, too, that the expression itself—"achievement gap"—is problematic in terms of working toward equity because it reflects a deficit view that blames the individual. Groups begin to understand the permanence of racism created by hierarchical structures that privilege Whiteness and marginalize people of color. This activity can also help develop what Murrell refers to as *community teacher knowledge*—that is, "contextualized knowledge of the culture, community, and identity of the children and families [a teacher] serves and [the ability to] draw on this knowledge to create the core teaching practices necessary for effectiveness in a diverse setting" (2001, p. 52).

LANGUAGE

Constance Weaver's *Grammar to Enhance and Enrich Writing* (2008) illuminates how labels send messages. The term Standard American English (SAE), which presupposes there is one right way to speak, has been replaced by the language of wider communication (LWC) (Conference on College

Composition and Communication, 1988). African American English (AAE) and "interlanguage" (Gass & Selinker, 2001) are stigmatized. Speakers of AAE are following grammatical rules—the rules of the "language of nurture" (Weaver, 2008, p. 240), and "interlanguage" is the natural process by which English language learners' (ELLs) native language and second language merge and separate in creative ways as they stretch to learn another language. Many PSTs are language purists and cannot accept that ELA teachers are charged with recognizing the linguistic validity of students' home languages and that "we must ensure that students have the opportunity to share their linguistic and cultural wealth in our classrooms" (Groenke, Scherff, & Rodriguez, 2008, p. 1). Teaching students to code-switch, the practice of moving back and forth between two languages or between two dialects or registers of the same language, is one way to honor students' home language. Encouraging students to change their dialect or register dependent upon the context of the situation is a powerful lesson. Sometimes it is appropriate to speak in the LWC; other times it is more effective to speak in another register or dialect. PSTs also have a narrow conception of the fact that "all learners need opportunities to explore every facet of what it means to be communicatively competent in multiple dialects, multiple linguistic registers, and for multiple audiences with varying communicative expectations" (Boyd et al., 2006, p. 345), as the following exchange from my classroom demonstrates:

"Why should we respect the fact that a kid has not bothered to learn Standard American English?" blurts out Peter. "If you were born and raised in the U.S., speak proper English. If not, learn English before you enroll in taxpayer-funded schools. Requiring teachers to get ESOL-endorsed is ridiculous!"

The class sat in silence for a few seconds, stunned.

Laura timidly raised her hand. "I don't feel as vehemently as Peter does, but earlier we talked about the NCTE's position statement on culturally and linguistically diverse students and how all students need to be taught mainstream power codes and discourses to become critical users of language. How do you honor a student's home language while still telling them they need to learn to speak a certain way?"

Discussion questions:

1. Why have many states enacted legislation requiring English Language Arts teachers to become endorsed in English for Speakers of Other Languages (ESOL)? Do you agree with this policy? How are English teachers in a primary position to help ELLs acquire language skills?

2. How can teachers simultaneously respect students' home language while also teaching them the language and discourse of power?

3. Is it possible that one day there will no longer exist something such as the language of wider communication? What would the ramifications be either way?

One-Syllable Conversations

Organize PSTs into discussion groups and assign each group a "hot topic" issue, one about which they will have strong and divergent opinions that they want to express and debate. "Hot topic" issues depend upon the context in which you teach. Currently, among my PSTs, "hot topics" include Common Core State Standards, disparity in learning opportunities, standardized assessments, charter schools, and items in the local and national news, just to name a few. Give groups 5 to 7 minutes to discuss the issue with one caveat: they may use only one-syllable words. Stop them when time is up and have each group prepare a statement, in one-syllable words, summarizing their group's feelings on the topic. Allow one-syllable discussion to follow. Conclude by asking PSTs how they felt when restricted to one-syllable words. My PSTs were frustrated because they had good ideas but could not express them adequately with the constraint. They felt new empathy for ELLs and realized that lack of participation often has little to do with cognitive ability and more to do with communicative ability.

INTENDED OUTCOMES

Children's Books and Translation Dictionaries

INTENDED OUTCOMES

PSTs are required to differentiate instruction for ELLs in their lesson plans. Typically they suggest inadequate assistance for ELLs, such as providing translation dictionaries and pairing them with other students for help. For this activity, have PSTs select a partner. Give each pair a selection of a children's story in a little-known language and a translation dictionary for that language. I generally give them *Stasts par Benjaminu* by Beatrise

Potere and a Latvian-English dictionary because of my family's Latvian heritage. I preview the text by stating that it is a story about a little rabbit that gets into all sorts of trouble. It is an easy read with pictures that assist understanding. They may use the dictionaries, and they have a partner to help them. After reading they should be able to answer the following questions:

1. How are Peter and Benjamin related?
2. What caused Peter's clothes to shrink?
3. What perplexed Mr. McGregor when he returned home?

When the PSTs cannot answer the three questions, they realize how inadequate their accommodations are because they have a difficult time comprehending the Latvian translation of Beatrix Potter's *The Tale of Benjamin Bunny*. They become more eager to learn strategies that will truly create language-rich classrooms for ELLs.

Code-Switching

Ask PSTs to record and transcribe a 5-to-10-minute segment of an informal conversation with friends and bring it to class to share in small groups. Have them rewrite the conversation using the register they would speak in if their grandmother were part of the conversation. Ask them to rewrite it again using an ap-  propriate register if a potential employer were a party to the conversation. This activity is successful because even if some students speak in the LWC in their initial conversation, they still find that it is very informal. For instance, they use "gonna" rather than "going to" and "hafta" rather than "have to." If your classes are not made up of diverse speakers, it is also fruitful to take a published speech such as Martin Luther King's "I Have a Dream" or a portion of a presidential State of the Union address and play with linguistic register based upon a variety of speaking situations. PSTs come to understand that style of content is dependent upon place and audience of context.

INTENDED OUTCOMES

SOCIAL CLASS

My English methods class discussed *The Genteel Unteaching of America's Poor* (2009), in which Kylene Beers asserts that some teachers have convinced themselves there is a population of students who cannot withstand the demands of an academically challenging curriculum. Beers writes, "In the end we are left with an education of America's poor that cannot be seen as anything more than a segregation by intellectual rigor, something every bit as shameful and harmful as segregation by color" (p. 3). As I was insisting upon holding all students to high expectations, my PSTs, who knew only that my last few years of public high school teaching were spent in a very affluent school, argued with me.

> Taylor quipped, "It's easy for you to believe that all kids can learn. C'mon, now, you taught in that rich, White school where the students drive nicer cars than the teachers."
>
> "Yea," piped in Stephanie. "You didn't teach in south county where drug dealers and prostitutes hang out, and kids are raised by grandmas and aunties. South county kids have too much on their minds to focus on school."
>
> "I agree. They've got to get jobs or take care of little brothers or sisters cause mama's working all the time. You can't expect the same of them academically as you do your rich, White kids," concurred Kiana.

Discussion questions:

1. Discuss the impact on education that may result from growing up in poverty.
2. Can you hold all students, regardless of economic situation, to the same standards? Why or why not?
3. What are some ways to promote equity in learning for all students regardless of economic status?

Writing Feedback

Provide PSTs with copies of Figure 4.1 and Figure 4.2, two authentic writing samples completed by 4th-grade boys in response to the prompt "Describe a day when you had a very good day."

INTENDED OUTCOMES

Ask PSTs to outline the feedback they would give each student and to be prepared to share it with the class. Inevitably, PSTs praise the writing sample in Figure 4.1 and comment positively on the length of the piece, the amount of detail, word choice, imagery, and sentence structure. Suggestions for improvement are to work on spelling, punctuation, and use of dialogue. Overall, they think the piece is wonderful.

Figure 4.1. Writing Sample 1

It was an, delighttul wensday when I was seven years old. I was walking my dog down the street. was looking at the great pretty houses in my neighboorhood. There wer Mantions, and tiny houses, some were rusty and, some were just there. I was feeling happy because it was friday and I had a thee -day weeke WOW! while I was walking, I come to a house were an elderly person lived. she had lived there alone for eight years I could see inside her liveing room window from the road and somthing didn't look right. it looked like she was on the ground and not able to get up. I sprited up to her door and went in. "Help?! Do you need some help?! I said. I was a little nervous that I had just walked in without knocking, so I walked very slow Over here I heard a little voice yelled I have fallen and I can't get up?? I saw her layingon the floor and went right to work I put my arm under hers and lifted her up AA! I pulled withe all of my strenth but she didn't more. I took a deep breath, bent down, tried again. "One, Two, Three ... lift I hollared, trying to pretend that I was on a team, and not alone. slowly, she started to lift of the ground. in a few minutes, she was completely on her feet. "Oh, my, thank you sweetie" she whisperd, she looked really happy that I was there to help. from that day forword, I always stopped by her house on my walk, Just to make sure she was alnght and she was always ther to welome me with fresh-bucked cookies!

Figure 4.2. Writing Sample 2

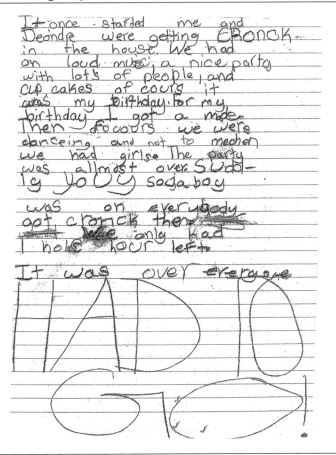

The writing sample in Figure 4.2 stuns PSTs. Most go immediately to out-rage: "This is inappropriate, particularly for a fourth-grader." They cannot be-lieve the student has written about getting "cronk," a term that can mean anything from partying to getting high. The initial conversation is about what disciplinary actions they would take. I agree with them that the content is inappropriate but, pedagogically, what feedback would they give about the piece? PSTs admit that the student has a great imagination; that he interweaves popular culture nicely into the story; that his transitions are good; and that he understands sentence structure somewhat. They suggest that areas of improvement should focus on classroom appropriateness, punctuation, and the proper use of pronouns.

Then ask the PSTs to explain what they surmise about these two boys based on their writing. They paint an asset-oriented picture of the first boy: he lives in a middle-class neighborhood with a family that is supportive of his education.

PSTs' views of the second boy reflect deficit thinking: He lives in low-income housing with a single mother who has little interest in or time for her son's education. PSTs are surprised to learn that these two boys were good friends at the time of this assignment and live on the same block in the same neighborhood, both being raised by their grandmothers. Discuss the academic impact their initial responses to the boys' writing would have on each boy in the long run.

Debunking Deficit Thinking

The American Association of Colleges of Teacher Education (AACTE) and the Southern Poverty Law Center have partnered to develop the Teaching Diverse Students Initiative (TDSI), which offers online tools to help teachers improve the instruction of racially and ethnically diverse students. To introduce this activity, use a video clip from the website of Sonia Nieto (2010), who discusses how educators often express a deficit view of the experiences students bring with them to school to introduce this activity. Instead of focusing on what students do not have, educators should seek out and build upon students' strengths. Give PST the list of characters found in Table 4.2.

INTENDED OUTCOMES

Assign PSTs to small groups to identify the strengths of their assigned character and to identify how each strength could be built upon to help that character succeed in a middle or high school ELA class. This activity facilitates PSTs' understanding of what is meant by the term "funds of knowledge" (Moll, Amanti, Neff, & Gonzalez, 1992) as they uncover the strengths each character would bring to their classroom.

Public Transportation and Library Computers

Hearing a teacher candidate adamantly assert that "all of my students will turn in typed papers. If they can't afford computers at home, they can go to the public or school library to do research and type their papers" prompted me to create this activity. Collaborate with local libraries and require your PSTs to use public transportation and to type their response to this assignment on a computer at the public library. Leave mini-research questions with the

INTENDED OUTCOMES

Table 4.2. Asset-Oriented Approach Activity

Character	Novel	Author and Year
Carla Garcia	*How the Garcia Girls Lost Their Accents*	Julia Alvarez (1992)
Marguerite Johnson	*I Know Why the Caged Bird Sings*	Maya Angelou (1969)
Esperanza	*The House on Mango Street*	Sandra Cisneros (1984)
Ishmael Beah	*A Long Way Gone: Memoirs of a Boy Soldier*	Ishmael Beah (1998)
Little Bee	*Little Bee*	Chris Cleave (2009)
Tayo	*Ceremony*	Leslie M. Silko (1977)

librarians to give to your candidates when they sign up to use the computers. Here is a sample assignment:

> Identify three initiatives that one of the following could take to improve the education of children living in poverty: (a) the federal government, (b) local schools, or (c) classroom teachers. Your response should be no longer than two pages in length and cite three resources. Your assignment must be completed, typed, and printed at the library. Upon completion, submit your paper along with your bus ticket and verification of authenticity signed by the librarian.

This activity provides the opportunity to discuss not only the research they gathered but also the physical experience of taking public transportation and completing the assignment at the library. PSTs develop an understanding of what they are asking of their students. They are often irritated with public transportation and surprised by the distractions in the library. They are frustrated when the computer "times them out" after 30 minutes, and they are annoyed that they need coins to print their papers.

ABILITIES

After introducing an assignment that required PSTs to differentiate instruction for students with learning disabilities, I heard one candidate whisper to a friend, "God, I don't plan on teaching retards. I'm going to teach literature. Those kids won't be in my class. What a waste of time." The friend snickered in response.

Discussion questions:

1. When you were in school, were kids with special needs included or segregated?

2. What message did you receive in school about kids with special needs?
3. What does the term "inclusive education" mean to you?
4. What are some of the challenges of inclusive education?
5. What are some of the benefits of inclusive education?

With a greater percentage of students with disabilities receiving services in general education classrooms, PSTs must feel prepared to work with special populations by knowing teaching strategies and accommodations that will help all students succeed. PSTs should also have opportunities to work in a co-teaching setting. And, as illustrated in the vignette, there is a need to modify attitudes regarding people who are differently abled. Unfortunately, many teacher education programs attempt to achieve this last goal through "disability performances." To many, such performances, even when educative, are offensive because

> they show more about nondisabled differently-abled bodies than about the "real" situation of an experienced wheelchair user, or a visually impaired person navigating her world. Instead of bringing a wheelchair user's or a blind person's life nearer and showing it as a dignified life full of potential and specialized skills, many simulation exercises merely reinforce negative stereotypes of disabled people as victims. (Kuppers, 2007, pp. 80–81)

Flower, Burns, and Bottsford-Miller (2007) examined 41 studies dealing with disabilities simulations and found their use did little to modify attitudes regarding people who are differently abled. Similar to the findings of Sandler and Robinson (1981), they found that opportunities for people without disabilities to interact in equal-status relationships with people who have disabilities is more effective. Films presenting positive images of differently abled people (Eichinger, Rizzo, & Sirotnik, 1992) and accurate information about people who are differently abled (Pfeiffer, 1989) are also effective ways to foster positive attitudes.

Focus Films

To provide accurate information about people who are differently abled and to facilitate equal-status interaction between people with and without disabilities, work with your campus's differently abled student support services and ask willing students who are differently

INTENDED OUTCOMES

abled to be guest lecturers in your class. This has been a powerful activity in my class, particularly when the lecturer first showed a video he brought about his learning disability. It was titled *A Mind of Your Own* (Sweeney, 1999) and presents Henry, Matthew, Max, and Stephanie, four middle-school students who speak candidly and knowledgeably about what it is like to grow up with a learning disability and what it takes to succeed in school by capitalizing on strengths and abilities.

Our guest lecturer described his perception of the film and explained how his learning disability impacted his life in both positive and negative ways. He spoke specifically about his school experiences and provided helpful suggestions for PSTs' future work with students with learning disabilities. Fanlight Productions is a company that produces documentaries about children and young adults with various disabilities that can be used to educate PSTs. A list of documentaries can be found at their website: fanlight.com.

Simulation of a Response to Intervention Meeting

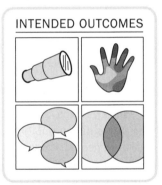

In Response to Intervention (RTI), schools identify students at risk for poor learning outcomes, monitor student progress, provide evidence-based interventions, adjust the intensity and nature of those interventions based upon students' responsiveness, and identify students with learning disabilities. RTI also provides a mechanism for general and special education staff to work together to increase the number of students who are successful in the general education curriculum (Witt, 2006).

Many PSTs, however, graduate from general education preparation programs without ever having worked with a special educator. Invite practicing special education teachers, faculty, and/or undergraduate and advanced degree PSTs to attend a session or two of your English education methods classes. Put your students in small groups with a special educator, and provide the group with a case study of a student with a disability. Have groups follow the steps involved in the collaborative process of intervention planning: discuss and clarify issues, prioritize concerns, target the behavior or skill that needs improvement, define the behavior or skill in a clear and measurable way, brainstorm intervention techniques, select the ones they will use, and write an intervention plan. Also, have groups discuss formative assessment, or progress monitoring, which will enable educators to monitor the child's success in mastering No Child Left Behind–specified standards-based learning and to respond with effective, personalized, instructional strategies.

PSTs appreciate the realism of the activity, learn the skills needed for this type of collaboration, develop collegial relationships with peers in the field of special education, and benefit from the opportunity to problem solve and identify strategies for learning and behavior issues they will most likely face in the classroom (Arthaud, Aram, Breck, Doelling, & Bushrow, 2007).

Co-teaching in Pre-internship Field Experiences

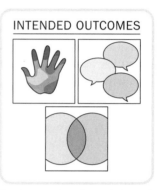

INTENDED OUTCOMES

True collaborative teaching has four essential components: (1) two or more professionals (2) jointly delivering instruction (3) to a diverse group of students (4) in a shared classroom space (Friend & Cook, 2009). Few teacher education programs adequately prepare graduates to teach collaboratively, however. One way to remedy this is to pair your English education majors with special education majors for placement in field experiences.

All participants in the co-teaching model should be well-versed in the conceptual framework of Friend and Cook (2009) as outlined in the four essential components listed above and learn the distinct variations of co-teaching: (1) one teaching and one assisting or observing; (2) station teaching, where each teacher is responsible for one station and students circulate; (3) parallel teaching, where both teachers deliver the same lesson but to smaller groups of students; (4) alternative teaching, where one teacher instructs a larger group while the other teacher facilitates review, practice, or enrichment for a smaller group of students; and (5) team teaching, where teachers share teaching responsibilities and interact throughout the entire lesson. Have pairs co-write lesson plans that reflect shared teaching with the roles and responsibilities of each teacher candidate clearly delineated.

Hoppey, Yendol-Silva, and Pullen (2004) conducted a similar pre-internship experience with elementary education majors. PSTs in this study experienced enhanced collegiality, satisfaction with teaching, and a sense of shared responsibility for *all* students' success by meeting the unique demands of the learners in their classrooms. PSTs also developed an escalated level of teacher talk as pairs planned instruction, received feedback on their plans from the collaborative teacher, worked to improve their lessons before and after delivery, and learned how to resolve disagreements about best practices.

CONCLUSION

The activities in this chapter give equal weight to the five strands of Language Arts instruction and model for PSTs the integration of reading, writing, listening, speaking, and viewing. They promote the goals of English educators while at the same time incorporating the dimensions of multicultural education (Banks, 2004) by providing examples of how PSTs can integrate content from a variety of cultures, assist students in the interrogation of how knowledge is constructed, reduce prejudice, promote equity, and create an empowering classroom culture. The vignettes and teaching activities can be woven seamlessly into the English education curriculum and lend themselves most easily to courses such as methods of teaching, teaching grammar, teaching adolescent literature, pure literature courses, and others. Most important, however, is the fact that these activities encourage our PSTs to question and cross traditional, personal, and professional boundaries in pursuit of social justice and equity for all learners.

REFERENCES

Arthaud, T. J., Aram, R. J., Breck, S. E., Doelling, J. E., & Bushrow, K. M. (2007). Developing collaboration skills in pre-service teachers: A partnership between general and special education. *Teacher Education and Special Education, 30*(1), 1–12.

Banks, J. A. (2004). Multicultural education: Historical development, dimensions, and practice. In J. A. Banks & C. A. M. Banks (Eds.), *Handbook of research of multicultural education* (2nd ed., pp. 3–29). San Francisco, CA: Jossey-Bass.

Beers, K. (2009). *The genteel unteaching of America's poor.* Urbana, IL: National Council of Teachers of English.

Boyd, F. B., Ariail, R. W., Jocson, K., Sachs, G. T., McNeal, K., Fecho, B., & Morrell, E. (2006). Real teaching for real diversity: Preparing English language arts teachers for 21st-century classrooms. *English Education, 38*(4), 329–350.

Conference on College Composition and Communication. (1988). *The national language policy* [Policy statement]. Urbana, IL: National Council of Teachers of English. Retrieved from ncte.org/cccc/resources/positions/123796.htm

DeCuir, J., & Dixson, A. (2004). "So when it comes out, they aren't that surprised that it is there": Using critical race theory as a tool of analysis of race and racism in education. *Educational Researcher, 33*(5), 26–31.

Delgado, R., & Stefancic, J. (2001). *Critical race theory: An introduction.* New York, NY: New York University Press.

Dickens, C. (1854). *Hard times.* London, England: Bradbury and Evans.

Eichinger, J., Rizzo, T. L., & Sirotnik, B. W. (1992). Attributes related to attitudes toward people with disabilities. *International Journal of Rehabilitation Research, 1*, 53–56.

Flower, A., Burns, M. K., & Bottsford-Miller, N. A. (2007). Meta-analysis of disability simulation research. *Remedial and Special Education, 28*(2), 72–79.

Friend, M., & Cook, L. (2009). Interactions: Collaboration skills for school professionals (6th ed.). New York, NY: Longman.

Garden, N. (2007). *Annie on my mind.* New York, NY: Farrar, Straus, & Giroux.

Gass, S. M., & Selinker, L. (2001). *Second language acquisition: An introductory course.* (2nd ed.). Mahwah, NJ: Erlbaum.

Gay, G. (2000). *Culturally responsive teaching: Theory, research, and practice.* New York, NY: Teachers College Press.

Groenke, S. L., Scherff, L., & Rodriguez, R. J. (2008). ELL and the English/language arts. *English Leadership Quarterly, 30*(3), 1.

Hoppey, D., Yendol-Silva, D., & Pullen, P. (2004). We became teachers together: Understanding collaborative teaching as innovation in unified teacher education. *Action in Teacher Education, 16*(1), 12–25.

Johannessen, L. R., & McCann, T. M. (2002). *In case you teach English: An interactive casebook for prospective and practicing teachers.* Boston, MA: Allyn & Bacon.

Kerr, M. E. (2009). *Deliver us from Evie.* New York, NY: HarperCollins.

Kosciw, J. G., Greytak, E. A., Bartkiewicz, M. J., Boesen, M. J., & Palmer, N. A. (2012). *The 2011 National School Climate Survey: The experiences of lesbian, gay, bisexual and transgender youth in our nation's schools.* New York, NY: GLSEN.

Kuppers, P. (2007). The performance of disability. *TDR: The Drama Review, 51*(4), 80–88.

Levithan, D. (2009). *Boy meets boy.* New York, NY: Random House.

McNeal, K. (2005). The influence of a multicultural teacher education program on teachers' multicultural practices. *Intercultural Education, 16,* 405–419.

Mendez, S., & Mendez Duran, S. (2013, August 23). *I remember being in court every day* . . . [Audio recording]. Retrieved from storycorps.org/?s=mendez&post_type=listen

Moll, L. C., Amanti, C., Neff, D., & Gonzalez, N. (1992). Funds of knowledge for teaching: Using a qualitative approach to connect homes and classrooms. *Theory into Practice, 31,* 132–141.

Moore, W. (2011). *The other Wes Moore: One name, two fates.* New York, NY: Random House.

Murrell, P. (2001). *Community teacher.* New York, NY: Teachers College Press.

National Council of Teachers of English (NCTE). (2005). *Supporting linguistically and culturally diverse learners in English education* [Policy statement]. Retrieved from www.ncte.org/cee/positions/diverselearnersinee

Nguni, M. M. (2013, August 23). *Recess came and the boys had a football* . . . [Audio recording]. Retrieved from storycorps.org/listen/mweupe-mfalme-nguni/

Nieto, S. (2010). *Debunking deficit views* [Video]. Teaching Diverse Students Initiative. Retrieved from curry.virginia.edu/fipselibrary/debunking-deficit-views

Peters, J. A. (2007). *Keeping you a secret.* New York, NY: Little, Brown.

Pfeiffer, D. (1989). Disability simulation using a wheelchair exercise. *Journal of Postsecondary Education and Disability, 7,* 53–60.

Pitts-Wiley, R. (2013, August 23). *I got bussed to a high school in my sophomore year* . . . [Audio recording]. Retrieved from storycorps.org/?s=pitts+wiley&post_type=listen

Plessy v. Ferguson, 163 U.S. 537 (1896).

Regents of the University of California v. Bakke, 438 U.S. 265 (1978).

Rockwell, N. (1964). *The problem we all live with* [Painting]. Stockbridge, MA: Norman Rockwell Museum.

Ryan, S. (2003). *Empress of the world.* New York, NY: Penguin Books.

Sandler, A., & Robinson, R. (1981). Public attitudes and community acceptance of mentally retarded persons: A review. *Education and Training of the Mentally Retarded, 16,* 97–103.

Schofield, J. (2009). The colorblind perspective in school: Causes and consequences. In J. A. Banks & C. A. M. Banks (Eds.), *Multicultural education: Issues and perspectives* (7th ed., pp. 257–284). Hoboken, NJ: John Wiley & Sons.

Snyder, T. D., & Hoffman, C. M. (2002). *Digest of education statistics 2001* (No. NCES 2000-130). Washington, DC: U.S. Department of Education, National Center for Educational Statistics.

Stephens, J. (2007). Young adult: A book by any other name . . . Defining the genre. *The ALAN Review, 35*(1), 34–42.

Sweeney, G. (director). (1999). *A mind of your own* [Documentary]. Canada: Fanlight Productions.

Weaver, C. (2008). *Grammar to enhance and enrich writing.* Portsmouth, NH: Heinemann.

Witt, J. (2006, April). *Core principles and essential components of RTI* [PowerPoint presentation]. Presentation at the Response-to-Intervention Symposium, Austin, TX. Retrieved from www.centeroninstruction.org/files/CorePrinciplesAndEssentialComponentsOfRTI.pdf

CHAPTER 5

Social Studies Education

Promoting and Developing Inclusive Perspectives

Bárbara C. Cruz

Social studies teacher education provides rich opportunities to discuss the issues of race, ethnicity, culture, and gender. Because I am a Latina professor in this field, students often view me as an embodiment of these sometimes controversial issues, and discussions routinely surface in class. Usually, students are respectful and merely curious—after all, in most of their courses they do not have a Latina professor as their instructor. In fact, the sobering statistics regarding Latina/os in academia are disheartening: only 1.2% of Latina/os in the United States earn professional and doctoral degrees (U.S. Bureau of the Census, 2007). Thus, it is not likely for college students to encounter many Latino/a professors in their coursework. Knowing I am a relative oddity for them, I allow and encourage them to ask me questions about my background, my education, and especially how culture and ethnicity intersects with each.

But I was not prepared for the virulent anti-immigration stance expressed by some of my students in a graduate course on Global and Multicultural Perspectives I was teaching one fall. Because (I am told) I have no detectable accent when I speak English, my students usually assume I am a 2nd- or 3rd-generation immigrant. I am, however, a 1st-generation immigrant who came to the United States at the age of nearly 5, after I had already started school in my native country. My parents were blue-collar workers who never did learn English very well, focusing instead on working multiple jobs and raising their family in their adopted country.

One day, we were discussing the landmark court case *Plyler v. Doe* (1982). I explained how, in a 5-to-4 decision, the Supreme Court ruled that under the Fourteenth Amendment a state cannot deny school enrollment to children of undocumented immigrants. The Court reasoned that undocumented immigrants and their children—although not citizens of the United States—are people "in any ordinary sense of the term" and, therefore, are protected by the Fourteenth Amendment of the U.S. Constitution.

One student raised his hand and blurted, "But it's not right that children who are born outside the U.S. and enter the country illegally with their parents be allowed to attend American public schools. Why should I have to pay for that?" A second student added, "Yeah, as citizens we are overtaxed already and people who are here illegally don't pay any taxes. So why should we educate their children in our schools that are overcrowded enough as it is?"

While it was certainly not the first time I had heard that position, it was the first time those sentiments had been expressed in my classroom by prospective teachers. And because the students' views had been articulated immediately after I had shared a story about being an English language learner myself, I couldn't help but feel personally attacked. In the past, I had experienced benefiting from the automatic "street cred" that being a person of color is sometimes afforded in the classroom when discussing diversity but had often escaped the stinging invidious flip side of the same coin (see Chapter 1).

I took a deep breath and knew it wouldn't be constructive to the discussion if I became defensive. So I distanced the comments from the students and replied, "Although I know that some people may claim immigrants don't pay taxes, studies have shown quite the opposite. If you can give me until next class session, I will gather more information on this, and we will revisit this issue then. And I invite you to do the same." This response did several things. First, by distancing the comments from the individual students, it didn't feel like I was assailing them personally. Second, it shifted the focus away from the moral implications of that position (certainly a legitimate concern, but one that is more difficult to manage with people who have staunchly held opinions) and centered instead on verifiable facts. By inviting them to look into the issue, I also shared the responsibility for learning with my students and kept the opportunity for discussion open. And perhaps most importantly, it bought me time to reflect and adequately prepare for a guided discussion.

At our next class meeting, I had gathered some of the most current census information about immigration and about how immigrants contribute to the U.S. economy and put the issue into historical perspective by using a political cartoon published in 1893 (see Figure 5.3). I cannot say that my meticulous presentation of facts, statistics, and government reports completely reversed my xenophobic students' position—there were still the questions of moral and ethical treatment of all students—but this strategy did help to diffuse the tension in the class and encouraged my students to consider more thoughtful, research-based approaches for issues of diversity. I also had to tell myself that the students' reactions were not necessarily an attack on me personally but a projection of their ignorance of the facts. Upon reflection, I realized that over time, I had developed what Gallavan (2000) calls "unique coping skills both personally and professionally" (p. 5). This chapter is an attempt to share some of the strategies I use to develop those skills.

DISCUSSING DIVERSITY IN THE SOCIAL STUDIES EDUCATION CLASSROOM

The National Council for the Social Studies (2001), the profession's flagship organization, asserts that "a primary goal of public education is to prepare students to be engaged and effective citizens" (para. 2). Yet many social studies teachers are unclear as to what degree issues concerning culture, ethnicity, socioeconomics, and other issues related to diversity are to be incorporated into the core mission of "help[ing] students develop the knowledge, skills, and values that will enable them to become effective citizens" (para. 6). In various and important ways, this lack of clarity is reflected in social studies classrooms across the nation, where teachers both intentionally and unintentionally shy away from diversity education. This disconnect often is also seen in preservice social studies teacher education, where the relationship between teaching in culturally diverse contexts and social studies teacher education is not always apparent (Castro, Field, Bauml, & Morowski, 2012).

Discussing issues of diversity in the social studies classroom should be a given, but many instructors purposefully avoid discussing these issues due to a myriad of reasons, including the following:

- Fear of change: Resistance to change by both K–12 teachers and school administrators and paradigm shifting in the classroom have been well documented (e.g., Evans, 2001; Payne, 2008; Schlecty, 1990); it is often safer (and easier) to continue the curricular and instructional status quo.
- Limited incentives: In higher education, faculty reward systems typically center around research, publication, and grant writing. Some institutions also highly value teaching; however, high course evaluations are generally sufficient to demonstrate instructional efficacy—infusing diversity discussions are not necessarily prized. And, based on my experience serving on faculty review committees and confirmed by research, sometimes diversity discussions can actually impact course evaluations negatively (Helms et al., 2003; Kelly-Woessner & Woessner, 2006).

- Limited class time: With so much material to cover, faculty report difficulty in finding enough time in a given course to thoroughly discuss assigned course content (Asimeng-Boahene & Klein, 2004). Discussing issues of diversity is often perceived as an add-on to the course syllabus.
- Lack of materials, equipment, and resources: Many faculty wishing to incorporate diversity issues into their courses often feel stymied by the relative lack of resources in their field (Gaudelli, 2001). In the social studies, while there are many worthwhile materials in the field of multicultural education, there is often a dearth in content areas, such as economics, government/civics, and geography. Further, some of the resources— for example, cross-cultural simulations—may be expensive, necessitate special equipment, or have special physical-space requirements.
- Increase in preparation time: Because there is a dearth of materials written expressively for university faculty, instructors who are committed to infusing diversity issues into their courses may find themselves spending a great deal of time searching for readings, creating appropriate learning activities, and modifying assessments.
- Difficult to use in large classes: Diversity issues—perhaps more than other topics—require sustained discussion and class involvement. While not impossible with large groups (Bonwell & Eison, 1991), instructors, especially those who are less experienced, may find it daunting to incorporate some of the strategies proposed by multicultural educators into very large classes.
- Diversity involves risk: Given the potential volatility of many issues related to diversity, some instructors may fear the loss of control in their classrooms. Might a student make a prejudiced statement in class? Could a discussion degenerate into hostile argumentation? Could students ask questions about which the instructor feels insecure or uninformed? The answer to all of these questions is, clearly, yes. As Gallavan (2000) points out, university courses that deal with multicultural education can present problems and challenges— including student resistance, hostility, anger, and opposition—that do not frequently surface in other college curricula.

However, a number of interventions and approaches exist that multicultural educators have found to be effective in mediating and mitigating the challenges associated with this field of study. All of the items in the above list, as well as the incident described in the opening vignette, demonstrate the complexity and challenge of this work, but also the necessity of pursing these conversations.

In my social studies education courses, I utilize specific activities and discussions to help my students develop diversity awareness and cross-cultural competence (see Figure 5.1). By "diversity awareness," I mean at a minimum a simple awareness of diversity that is imperative for contemporary educators— what diversity can encompass and the sheer range of ideas and practices to be found among various groups, both in the United States and around the world. This anthropological and sociological appreciation is an important first step

Figure 5.1. Activities for Supporting Diversity Awareness

Political Cartoons and Comic Strips

As accepted forms of social commentary, political cartoons can be effective mechanisms for discussing a wide range of diversity issues. Comic strips, too, can bring poignant levity to a class discussion and can spark a considered debate like no other medium. The Internet has made finding and using these visuals in the classroom easier than ever before.

Questioning and Discussion

Questioning and discussion are at the heart of the social studies classroom. Civil discourse is a necessary component of a participatory democracy, and the development of critical thinking and discussion skills are central to our field. While seizing unexpected teaching moments can yield rich classroom discussion, it is imperative that the instructor formulate some questions beforehand to help guide studious consideration in class.

Guided Imagery

This teaching strategy capitalizes on students' imagination and guides them mentally through an experience in order to better understand concepts. Imagining issues of diversity as they can unfold and impact people can be valuable in developing awareness and empathy.

Role-Playing

A role-playing exercise is an enactment or reenactment of a situation in which the players assume certain roles and are confronted with a problem involving a moral or value dilemma, one that usually requires players to make a decision. There may be more than one possible solution to the scenario, and the consequences that occur are not always predictable. Putting students in a position in which they must consider a difficult situation and then decide how they should act on it can be very instructive in their development as educators.

Simulations

Simulations are attempts to recreate certain aspects of reality for the purpose of gaining information, clarifying values, understanding other people, or developing a skill. Often, there are strict rules that must be followed, and in many simulation games there are winners and losers. Cross-cultural simulations such as BaFá BaFá and the Albatross (see the Resources section) can be very effective in developing perspective consciousness and cross-cultural awareness.

employed by many social studies educators to help develop understanding and empathy in their students. Developing cognitive empathy—that is, making the attempt to understand others' perspectives (Gurin, Nagda, & Zúñiga, 2013)—is a central goal in my courses, as is the development of cross-cultural competence. The latter encompasses the knowledge and skills necessary to relate to others in cross-cultural environments, an aptitude especially important for social studies educators. Fortunately, in social studies education there are a number of approaches and strategies that can further the examination of diversity issues and help prospective teachers develop diversity awareness and cross-cultural competence.

What follows is a selection of classroom activities that my colleagues and I have used in our social studies teacher preparation courses (Elementary Social Studies Teaching Methods, Middle School Social Studies Teaching Methods, Secondary Social Studies Teaching Methods, and Global and Multicultural Perspectives in Social Studies Education). In each case, caveats and potential problems are discussed so that instructors can determine the appropriateness of the activities for their specific teaching situations as well as possibly adapt them to better suit their needs. Generally speaking, the activities are presented from low-risk to high-risk—for both instructor and students.

SELECTED INSTRUCTIONAL ACTIVITIES

Diversity Bingo

Diversity Bingo is a popular and simple icebreaker that can highlight the diversity present in a given course or professional development setting. Essentially, the instructor creates a "bingo" game card that reflects the global and multicultural community in their locale (see the example I developed for our community of Tampa Bay, Florida, in Figure 5.2). Each student signs his or her name in the center box and must fill in the remaining boxes by collecting classmates' signatures. This activity has the po-

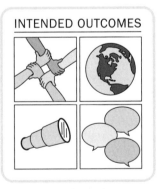

INTENDED OUTCOMES

tential to bring to light the amount of diversity that is present in a given community and in a specific classroom, along with various "advantages" of those who have diverse backgrounds (students who can speak another language, have traveled or lived elsewhere, or know about other cultures become very popular as they are sought out by their classmates to sign their bingo cards). After the exercise, the instructor can further help students reflect on diversity by posing these follow-up questions:

- For which boxes did you have the most difficulty in finding a signature?
- For which box was it easiest to obtain a signature?
- What was it like to have diversity valued and seen as an asset?
- How might this activity be modified for use in a K–12 setting?

Figure 5.2. Diversity Bingo

Tampa Bay: A Multicultural Community

Have you ever had Indian food?	Do you know who Zora Neale Hurston was?	Can you say "hello" and "peace" in Hebrew?	Have you ever attended a school outside the U.S.?	Can you name 5 countries in Asia?
Do you have relatives in another country?	Do you speak French or Haitian Creole?	Have you ever been to Mexico?	Do you know what couscous is?	Do you celebrate Hanukkah?
Have you visited Canada?	Have you been to a Native American ceremony?	FREE (Your Name Here) SPACE	Can you do any Latin American dance?	Were you born in another country?
Do you have a friend who celebrates Kwanza?	Have you ever lived in another country?	Can you name 5 islands in the Caribbean?	Can you speak Español fluently?	Has someone from another culture ever visited your home?
Do you have a friend with a Spanish surname?	Do you observe Ramadan?	Have you vacationed in another country?	Have you ever heard a kalimba?	Are you a native Floridian?

I have found this activity to be a very low-risk exercise suitable for the 1st or 2nd day of class or at the beginning of a professional development workshop. Participants get an opportunity to meet new people, learn new things about classmates they have already met, and stretch their legs as they move about the room collecting signatures. The follow-up discussion facilitates their reflection on diversity and gets them to start thinking about their K–12 students.

Historical Political Cartoons

Political cartoons are particularly effective in the social studies education classroom (see the Resources section for a list of helpful websites from which to gather comics and political cartoons). They can be used to introduce a topic, to delve further into a topic, or to bring closure to a presentation or discussion. Because the features of the public figures depicted in these comics are often caricatured and because the medium is so graphic, these visuals can clearly convey the controversy surrounding an issue and who is involved. By using humor or sarcasm, the political cartoonist attempts to change a viewer's opinion about an important issue. Because cartoons are commentaries, students usually should know something about the issue or topic before they are exposed to the cartoon. In using political cartoons, instructors should choose simple, uncomplicated cartoons that can help facilitate analysis and discussion.

INTENDED OUTCOMES

I usually follow a modified version of Bloom's (1956) taxonomy in posing questions that guide students in an analysis, adding queries that are specific to each cartoon. While there are other discussion and questioning models that could be employed, I have found that my preservice teachers can quickly learn and memorize the taxonomy and apply it easily to cartoons and other visuals. It is also convenient that the taxonomy mirrors the low-risk-to-high-risk strategy that I tend to favor and model in the classroom. Generally speaking, instructors can use the following format:

- ask students to identify standard symbols and central characters;
- if applicable, have students recognize the activity that is taking place in the scene;
- have students analyze the cartoonist's point-of-view;
- encourage students to determine the cartoonist's purpose;

- ask students to decide whether they agree or disagree with the cartoonist.

Note that using a questioning sequence that roughly follows Bloom's taxonomy, a system of classifying thinking skills used for creating learning objectives, can provide a natural connection for education majors. Some of my colleagues have also reported great success with having their students create their own cartoons on a given issue as a method of evaluation. For students who are not comfortable drawing, pairs or groups of students can work together so that each group includes a student who likes to draw.

Historical cartoons are especially appropriate for the social studies classroom, both providing a glimpse into the past and connecting the past to the present. And because the cartoon was published in the historical past, it can give us the opportunity to touch on contemporary issues in a roundabout way that may be less threatening. A good example of this is perhaps one of the most well-known political cartoons in social studies education, which appeared in *Puck* at the turn of the 20th century. It is titled "Looking Backward" (see Figure 5.3) and is very effective for teaching about immigration in U.S. history as well as touching on contemporary debates regarding immigration.

Figure 5.3. "Looking Backward," Joseph Keppler, *Puck*, 1893.

I use the following questions to guide a discussion of the cartoon:

- Who are the characters in the cartoon? Describe what they are wearing and what they look like.
- Where is the scene taking place? What visual cues did you use to make this determination?
- Why is the man in the middle pushing his hands out? What do you think this means?
- How many characters do you see in the cartoon? Who are the shadowy figures behind the men on the dock?
- What do you think the cartoonist is trying to say?
- Do you agree or disagree with the cartoonist? Justify your response.
- This cartoon was published at the turn of the 20th century. How might it be applicable today?

My students—all of them social science education majors—can easily identify the approximate time period during which the scene in the cartoon takes place. They often name Ellis Island as a possible location, with a new immigrant disembarking after a long overseas trip. The interesting observations begin to emerge as analysis continues. For one, when I ask "How many characters do you see in the cartoon?" most students reply, "Six." But I prod them to look more closely and soon someone will say "Eleven," counting the five shadowy figures in the background. Are the shadowy figures the rich men's ancestors? Or are they themselves years ago when they, too, might have immigrated to the United States? I ask if they have ever heard of the "close the door behind me" stance on immigration—that is, once I get through the immigration doors, close the door behind me so no one else can come in. I get them to consider if this cartoon reflects that stance. Invariably, students debate immigration policy—both historical and contemporary—clarifying and sometimes modifying their own values related to the issue.

To discuss race and the civil rights movement, I have used a cartoon by Herb Block from July 4, 1963 (see Figure 5.4), to discuss what societal conditions have changed and which need further improvement in the United States. Questions that guided analysis and discussion of this cartoon included the following:

- Who are the characters shown in the cartoon?
- Where is the scene taking place?
- What profession is the focus of the cartoon?
- What is the name of the hospital? What does that mean?
- What does the dialogue above the cartoon say? What "incurable skin condition" does the seated man have?

- What is the cartoonist trying to say?
- This cartoon was published in 1963. How are things either different or the same today?

I use this cartoon in my Secondary Social Studies Teaching Methods course; the last question in particular always leads to an important discussion in class about racism in society. Last year, a (White) student pointed out how, the year after the cartoon was published, the Civil Rights Act was passed, guaranteeing all citizens equal protection under the law in public places such as schools and the workplace. As he spoke, I noticed an exchange of knowing looks between an African American student and a Latino in class. I asked the class if anyone wanted to comment on the Civil Rights Act. When no one volunteered, I shared how, when I was in high school, my high school counselor gave me a stack of secretarial-school brochures to

Figure 5.4. "Sorry, but you have an incurable skin condition."

A 1963 Herblock Cartoon, © The Herb Block Foundation

peruse. Her expectations for me were so clear I even went so far as to check out books from the library on shorthand, typing, and stenography. A beloved teacher intervened and insisted I take the SAT, even paying for my test. Those scores, in turn, resulted in a college scholarship and eventually led to a career in academia. After I shared this story, one of the students of color raised his hand and shared with the class that just 2 years before, when he was in high school, his guidance counselor was suggesting that perhaps he should consider the local community college (rather than the university he was now attending). In his lived experience, he was still feeling the sting of racism and prejudice more than 40 years after the cartoon was published. A whole class discussion on institutional racism blossomed. At the end of the discussion, students concluded that while many positive changes and laws have been put into place, the struggle for equality continues. The combination of the political cartoon and the instructor's personal disclosure facilitated a potentially difficult discussion and connected the past to the present.

Experiential Learning

Experiential learning puts students at the center of the learning process so that they can make meaning from their direct experience. By definition, it is composed of instructional activities in which students are involved in *doing* and *thinking*. Experiential learning is especially useful in the examination of diversity issues because it affords learners the opportunity to use higher-order thinking skills and a variety of learning styles and to reflect on their own learning. Strategies such as guided imagery, role playing, and simulations can also access affective learning and often motivate students to learn more.

Cross-cultural simulations (see the Resources section) can be particularly effective in developing perspective consciousness and cross-cultural awareness (Delany-Barmann & Minner, 1996). About midway through the semester I conduct one such simulation, the Albatross, in my secondary social studies methods course. The exercise consists of asking students to participate in a "ceremony" being hosted by an Albatrossian couple (Gochenour, 1977). Students are asked to follow along as best they can—which is interesting to watch, as the Albatrossians communicate with only clicks, hums, and hisses. Afterward, the facilitators lead the class in a discussion about what they observed, what transpired, and what they learned about Albatrossian culture. Ultimately, the facilitators fill students in about the true nature of the culture, almost always the exact opposite of what students perceived.

The Albatross is a relatively simple simulation that requires two facilitators. Sometimes I serve as facilitator with another colleague; other times I ask two students from the class to serve that function. It takes only about 15 minutes to execute the simulation itself and another 30 to 45 minutes to conduct the discussion and debriefing. Like all simulations, the experiential learning activity will not lead to learning unless there is rich and deep discussion after students participate in the exercise.

I like using the Albatross simulation because it can be completely conducted within one class period—important modeling for preservice teachers. It is also a very forgiving simulation; although a suggested sequence is given, facilitators are free to improvise and it is not problematic if a step or two is omitted or forgotten. Other pluses are that this simulation is freely available in a number of print sources and on the web and that it can be conducted with simple items found at home.

For the social studies educators in my methods course, the exercise serves as a powerful reminder that what we perceive as reality and irrefutable truth is always affected by our cultural lenses. Students invariably make negative assumptions about the Albatrossians that are value laden and prove to be false. With very little prodding, they begin to question their interactions with other people and, especially, with their own students. This reflection and self-awareness is an important first step in developing a culturally sensitive pedagogical orientation.

A note to instructors who are reticent to conduct an actual simulation in their classrooms: Try to participate in a simulation conducted by a colleague first so you can be reassured that these exercises, with thoughtful planning, can be conducted in the classroom with few problems. Second, know that several simulations (including the Albatross) are available in video format on the Internet—that is, you can screen a simulation conducted elsewhere, learn vicariously through the film, and then follow up with a discussion in your class.

Showing a simulation on film to your class versus having them actually engage in the simulation is also an option. For example, Jane Elliott's famous "blue eye/brown eye experiment," while difficult to re-create, can provide the basis for important conversations related to diversity and pedagogy. *The Eye of the Storm* (ABC, 1970) is the original ABC documentary that chronicled Elliott's experiment. Many university libraries own the film and a subsequent program, *A Class Divided* (Peters, 1985), can be found online, along with a teaching guide (www.pbs.org/wgbh/pages/frontline/shows/divided). These can be used effectively in the college classroom to examine the realities of discrimination. *The Eye of the Storm* chronicles the experiences of actual students in the classroom of 3rd-grade teacher Jane Elliott, whose now famous simulation exercise shows how quickly children can succumb to discriminatory behavior. The film then shows how easily prejudicial attitudes can lead to frustration, broken friendships, and vicious behavior. Elliott's method is based on her belief that people can best be motivated to fight discrimination by experiencing it themselves, if only for a few hours in a controlled environment.

For those of us in social studies education, it is important to discuss Jane Elliott's professed methodology: She believes that it is not effective to intellectualize highly emotionally charged or challenging topics. Instead, she creates a situation in which participants experience discrimination themselves and, therefore, feel its effects emotionally, not intellectually. Instead of respecting students' existing knowledge, affirming their sense of self, et cetera, she uses participants' own emotions to make them feel discomfort, guilt, shame, embarrassment, and humiliation. The cognitive dissonance that ensues leads to critical self-reflection and, ultimately, growth.

So, while not all educators may want to re-create Elliott's simulation, watching the film and then following up with a well-guided discussion, prompted by questions such as the following, can achieve some of the same benefits vicariously:

- How was the exercise that Elliott designed a response to the children's question, "Why would anyone want to murder Martin Luther King, Jr.?" Did the "experiment" provide an answer to the question?
- What did the children's body language indicate about the impact of discrimination?
- How did the negative and positive labels placed on a group become self-fulfilling prophecies?
- What features did Elliott ascribe to the superior and inferior groups and how did those characteristics reflect stereotypes about Blacks and Whites?
- How did Elliott's discrimination create no-win situations for those placed in the inferior group? How did she selectively interpret behavior to confirm the stereotypes she had assigned?
- Is this simulation strategy appropriate for a secondary classroom? A middle school classroom? An elementary classroom?
- What sorts of precautions should a teacher take if she or he decides to conduct a potentially volatile simulation in his or her classroom?

As a follow-up, I have also shown portions of the *Frontline* program *A Class Divided* (Peters, 1985). Filmed 15 years after *Eye of the Storm*, this program explores what the children in Jane Elliott's daring classroom experiment learned about discrimination and how it still affects them today. This documentary reunites the teacher and her now-adult students to relate the enduring effects of the exercise and its impact on their lives.

CONCLUSION

Space limitations preclude me from describing the many approaches and exercises that social studies educators can utilize in their teaching methods courses, but hopefully those included herein will spark ideas for your own courses. Additional readings and resources can be found in the Resources appendix.

While infusing diversity issues into our curriculum carries some risk, I would argue that *not* including discussion of diversity carries an even greater one. Social studies education has, as a central mission, the development of a participatory democratic electorate. Becoming informed and thinking critically about these issues is essential to that aim.

The work of a multicultural educator is certainly not the path most easily followed. Perhaps the best attitude one can embrace is a variation of John F. Kennedy's observation that he was "an idealist without illusions" (O'Brien, 2006, p. 804). While we cannot hope to completely change every bigoted student who comes through our classroom lacking the professional dispositions and mindset needed to best teach and reach today's diverse K–12 student population, we can certainly aim to have all our students stretch their thinking and reflect on their own values and behavior and help those who refuse to establish the appropriate mindset to seek another profession. Especially because our students will become (or already are) practicing teachers, we owe it to *their* students to try.

REFERENCES

American Broadcasting Company (ABC). (1970). *The eye of the storm*. United States: Author.

Asimeng-Boahene, L., & Klein, A. M. (2004). Is the diversity issue a non-issue in mainstream academia? *Multicultural Education, 12*(1), 47–52.

Bloom, B. (1956). *Taxonomy of educational objectives*. New York, NY: David McKay.

Bonwell, C. C., & Eison, J. A. (1991). *Active learning: Creating excitement in the classroom*. San Francisco, CA: Jossey-Bass.

Castro, A. J., Field, S. L., Bauml, M., & Morowski, D. (2012). "I want a multicultural classroom": Preparing social studies teachers for culturally diverse classrooms. *The Social Studies, 103*(3), 97–106.

Delany-Barmann, G., & Minner, S. (1996). Cross-cultural workshops and simulations for teachers. *The Teacher Educator, 32*(1), 37–47.

Evans, R. (2001). *The human side of school change.* San Francisco, CA: Jossey-Bass.

Gallavan, N. P. (2000). Multicultural education at the academy: Teacher educators' challenges, conflicts, and coping skills. *Equity & Excellence in Education, 33*(3), 5–11.

Gaudelli, W. (2001). Reflections on multicultural education: A teacher's experience. *Multicultural Education, 8*(4), 35–37.

Gochenour, T. (1977). The albatross. In D. Batchelder & E. G. Warner (Eds.), *Beyond experience: The experiential approach to cross-cultural education* (pp. 119–127). Brattleboro, VT: The Experiment Press.

Gurin, P., Nagda, B. A., & Zúñiga, X. (2013). *Dialogue across difference: Practice, theory, and research on intergroup dialogue.* New York, NY: Russell Sage Foundation.

Helms, J. E., Malone, L. S., Henze, K., Satiani, A., Perry, J., & Warren, A. (2003). First annual diversity challenge: "How to survive teaching courses on race and culture." *Journal of Multicultural Counseling and Development, 31*(1), 3–11.

Kelly-Woessner, K., & Woessner, M. C. (2006). My professor is a partisan hack: How perceptions of a professor's political views affect student course evaluations. *Political Science and Politics, 39*(3), 495–501.

National Council for the Social Studies. (2001). *Creating effective citizens.* Silver Spring, MD: Author. Retrieved from www.socialstudies.org/positions/effectivecitizens

O'Brien, M. (2006). *John F. Kennedy: A biography.* New York, NY: St. Martin's Griffin.

Payne, C. M. (2008). *So much reform, so little change.* Cambridge, MA: Harvard Education Press.

Peters, W. (Producer & Director). (1985). *A class divided.* United States: WGBH Boston.

Public Broadcasting Service (PBS). (1985). A class divided. Arlington, VA: Author.

Plyler v. Doe. 457 U.S. 202 (1982).

Schlecty, P. C. (1990). *Schools for the twenty-first century: Leadership imperatives for educational reform.* San Francisco, CA: Jossey-Bass.

U.S. Bureau of the Census. (2007). *Educational attainment of the population 25 years and over, by citizenship, nativity and period of entry, age, sex, race, and Hispanic origin: 2006.* Washington, DC: U.S. Printing Office.

CHAPTER 6

Mathematics Education

Challenging Beliefs and Developing Teacher Knowledge Related to English Language Learners

Eugenia Vomvoridi-Ivanović and Kathryn B. Chval

Eugenia walked into her classroom on the first day of class and immediately noticed that the undergraduate elementary preservice teachers appeared to be a bit nervous. She smiled at them. They smiled back. A couple of students complimented her on her dress and her earrings or shoes. She debated with herself, "Should I really risk it? Will anyone get offended?" She plunged in with a very thick foreign accent: "Hello everyone and welcome to Math I, Teaching Mathematics in the Elementary School." She said her name the way it would be pronounced in her home country (Ev-ye-NEE-a) and asked the undergraduates to guess where she was from. Students started naming countries, eventually guessing correctly—Greece. She continued, "How long do you think I have lived in the United States?" Most students thought she had arrived recently. Suddenly, she began speaking in a mainstream Northern American accent. A sense of relief filled the room; some students exhaled "phew" while others started giggling. She began to challenge her students: "What assumptions did you make about me when I first walked into the classroom? When I began to speak with a foreign accent? How did those assumptions change after I removed the accent?" She also asked them to consider what assumptions they might make about their future students' mathematical backgrounds and abilities depending on how they look and how they speak. At the end of the period, a student approached the professor and stated, "I was so relieved when you started speaking normal! When I first heard you speak I got nervous because I thought you just got off the boat, and I thought what does she know about our educational system? I really thought

Talking Diversity with Teachers and Teacher Educators, edited by Bárbara C. Cruz, Cheryl R. Ellerbrock, Anete Vásquez, & Elaine V. Howes. Copyright © 2014 by Teachers College, Columbia University. All rights reserved. Prior to photocopying items for classroom use, please contact the Copyright Clearance Center, Customer Service, 222 Rosewood Dr., Danvers, MA 01923, USA, tel. (978) 750-8400, www.copyright.com.

this was going to be a very long semester trying to follow you in that accent. Phew. You almost got us there!" Eugenia realized her risk was worth it, and there was much work to be done.

As shown in this vignette, most people, including preservice teachers (PSTs), make assumptions about the knowledge and capabilities of others, depending on how they look, act, and speak. These assumptions, in turn, influence how PSTs interact with other people in general and ultimately how they will interact with their future students. More specifically, the vignette illustrates that PSTs make assumptions directly related to language and demonstrates the Naiveté/Pre-Awareness stage discussed in Chapter 1. As a result, it is important to determine the assumptions that PSTs make about English language learners (ELLs) and to challenge those assumptions so that PSTs are better prepared to teach mathematics to ELLs. In this chapter, we argue that conversations related to teaching ELLs are critical for preparing prospective mathematics teachers. Toward this end, we describe several approaches that we use in our courses in order to (a) identify and challenge our PSTs' assumptions and beliefs about teaching mathematics to ELLs and (b) help our PSTs develop certain knowledge and competencies for teaching mathematics to ELLs. Successfully implementing these approaches and facilitating productive discussions requires teacher educators who create and cultivate positive learning environments, as described in Chapter 2.

ENGLISH LANGUAGE LEARNERS AND MATHEMATICS TEACHING

Every year, large numbers of children move to the United States from other countries. The percentage of public school students in the United States who were being served in programs of language assistance (e.g., English as a Second Language, High Intensity Language Training, bilingual education) in 2010–11 was 10% (U.S. Department of Education National Center for Education Statistics [NCES], 2013), while in 2012, the percentage of 5- to 17-year-olds who spoke a language other than English at home was 21.1% (U.S. Census Bureau, 2012). Some U.S. classrooms have one isolated ELL, while others are composed of 100% ELLs. Unfortunately, most PSTs do not have the opportunity to learn how to meet the needs of ELLs in their content methods courses. Therefore, the purpose of this chapter is to provide some resources teacher educators can use in mathematics methods courses to help PSTs start thinking about how they can meet the needs of ELLs.

Some educators view mathematics as a *universal language* that is common to all other languages, or even that it is language free (Remillard &

Cahnmann, 2005). As a result, they assume that learning mathematics requires the ability to master a well-defined and *culture-free* body of knowledge (Boero, Douek, & Ferrari, 2002; Burton, 1994; Volmink, 1994). In other words, many still have the view that because mathematics is a universal language, all students, regardless of English proficiency, can grasp it. This dominant perspective in the United States portrays language in mathematics as consisting only of mathematical vocabulary, notation, metaphors and jargon, grammar and syntax—all in English. Unfortunately, this acceptance of the universality of mathematics has fostered little attention to students' cultural or linguistic backgrounds in the mathematics education community (Gutiérrez, 2002). As a result, in many cases, mathematics is the first content area that ELLs are assigned to learn in English (before other subjects such as science or social studies).

Recent curriculum and instructional recommendations, however, emphasize cognitively demanding mathematical learning tasks for all students, language-rich environments, and multiple modes of communication (Chval & Khisty, 2009; NCTM, 2000; Steinbring, Bartolini Bussi, & Sierpinska, 1998). In addition, researchers in bilingual education argue that the development of the second language needed for schooling can be better achieved when students use the target language in active and dialogic communication that is purposeful, such as negotiating meanings of mathematical problems or tasks (Mohan, 1990; Mohan & Slater, 2005). The nature of mathematical tasks and the talk focused on those tasks influence what students learn. Connolly (1989) explained that language plays a powerful role in "the production, as well as the presentation, of knowledge" in a mathematics or science classroom (pp. 2–3).

Although the importance of language and communication in learning mathematics has gained considerable attention in recent years, teacher preparation programs have not given sufficient attention to the interplay between language, culture and mathematics, and teaching and learning. In teacher education, typically, courses treat language teaching as a subject, and as a result it is separated from the content areas—if it is dealt with at all (Setati, 2005). This separation is evidenced by the absence of substantial language and discourse content in most mathematics teaching courses for PSTs. Moreover, the discourse around teacher knowledge centers on a monolingual perspective that does not explicitly identify what knowledge and competencies PSTs need in relation to ELLs' language and culture.

Shulman (1986) outlined a variety of knowledge bases that teachers need to develop, including content knowledge, pedagogical knowledge, pedagogical content knowledge (PCK), and curricular knowledge. Shulman argued that PCK includes the most useful forms of representation, the most powerful analogies, illustrations, examples, explanations, demonstrations, pedagogical techniques, and knowledge of what makes concepts. In conceptualizations of PCK, it is implicit that teachers should be able to effectively facilitate mathematical communication in the classroom as they draw on these different knowledge bases. Yet teachers are not always successful with facilitating mathematical discussions (Khisty & Chval, 2002). Therefore, conversations revolving around the development of PCK for PSTs must involve the critical aspects of language and culture. In other words, teachers must develop a deep knowledge of the linguistic and cultural demands that are unique to the teaching and learning of mathematics. This becomes more important when students speak (or are learning) more than one language (Valdés, Bunch, Snow, Lee, & Matos, 2005). Unfortunately, discussions in mathematics education have not given sufficient attention to developing teacher knowledge related to teaching ELLs, and this has direct implications for how mathematics teacher preparation is traditionally structured. As a result, in most U.S. teacher preparation programs, future teachers are not prepared to teach mathematics to ELLs. PSTs enter the profession with little knowledge about the needs, resources, and supports required to effectively teach mathematics to ELLs (Chval & Pinnow, 2010).

If we want to move toward preparing teachers to teach mathematics to ELLs, we need to improve mathematics teacher education programs and professional development so that they address misconceptions related to teaching mathematics to ELLs and to develop teacher knowledge related to teaching ELLs. The development of this knowledge should not be deferred to additional certification programs or professional development but rather needs to be initiated early in the preparation process (Chval & Pinnow, 2010). Teacher preparation programs should include experiences specifically aimed at addressing the often implicit assumptions, beliefs, and expectations that teachers have in regard to students from linguistically and culturally diverse backgrounds. Moreover, these experiences need to include opportunities to expose assumptions PSTs might hold about students based upon their ethnicity, race, and educational background so they can develop more critical and reflective pedagogy.

ACTIVITIES RELATED TO TEACHING MATHEMATICS TO ENGLISH LANGUAGE LEARNERS

We realize that much work needs to be done to explore ways to assess and challenge beliefs that PSTs have about ELLs and to conceptualize the knowledge base that PSTs should develop in mathematics methods courses as it relates to teaching mathematics to ELLs. The tasks that we describe below should not minimize the complexity of this work or suggest that a few activities will address the deficiencies identified above. However, these tasks and activities do represent images and examples of critical conversations that should take place in teacher preparation programs and courses. Specifically, we have included activities that (a) bring preservice teachers' beliefs about ELLs to the surface, (b) challenge these beliefs, and (c) help preservice teachers understand the complexities of language in instruction as it applies to all students and ELLs in particular.

Eliciting and Challenging PSTs' Beliefs

Prospective teachers enter methods courses and classroom field experiences with vivid images and strongly held beliefs about teaching mathematics that impact their professional growth. Therefore, mathematics teacher educators need tools to elicit PSTs' beliefs individually and collectively as well as to provoke PSTs to examine their own beliefs (Chval, Lannin, Arbaugh, & Bowzer, 2009), especially in relation to teaching ELLs. The opening vignette illustrated one approach that elicited PSTs' beliefs; however, this approach is not an option for monolingual mathematics teacher educators like one of the co-authors of this chapter, Kathryn. As a result, Kathryn distributes a handout with the following four questions at the beginning of the semester. She asks students to write responses without identifying their names.

INTENDED OUTCOMES

1. Imagine it is your first year of teaching. You have taken a position as a 3rd-grade teacher. One of your students has just moved to the United States from Central America. What do you think this child will need during mathematics instruction? How will you assess the child's needs? How will you support this student during mathematics?
2. Imagine it is your first year of teaching. You have taken a position as a 3rd-grade teacher. One of your students has just moved to the United States from China. What do you think this child will need during mathematics instruction? How will you assess the child's needs? How will you support this student during mathematics?
3. Do you anticipate that the needs would be different depending upon the continent or country of origin?
4. How comfortable would you feel about these two different situations?

Unfortunately, PSTs may make assumptions about the needs of these children based on their countries of origins. That is, the child from Central America will need remediation and the child from China will need enrichment in mathematics (Chval & Pinnow, 2010). Ultimately, both of these assumptions are problematic. For this particular exercise, Kathryn could have selected two specific countries, such as China and Mexico. However, she decided to select a large, diverse country from Asia (i.e., China) and a larger geographic region in another part of the world (i.e., Central America). This structure provides additional opportunities to discuss assumptions PSTs make about specific countries and continents.

Kathryn collects her students' written responses and compiles some of the ideas that surface. She then distributes a few samples in the following class to provoke discussion. For example, Table 6.1 shows the responses written by two PSTs.

Kathryn then facilitates a discussion related to the following questions:

- What do you notice about the responses in the table?
- What assumptions are apparent in the responses?
- How will you help ELLs participate productively in group settings?
- What will you do to prevent them from becoming isolated in the mathematics classroom?

As the PSTs discuss these questions, Kathryn emphasizes the assumptions they make about mathematical ability, based on very little information about the child. She also discusses how these assumptions influence teacher expectations in relation to specific children.

The research literature demonstrates the importance of eliciting and challenging PSTs' beliefs and perceptions related to teaching and learning (Chval et al., 2009). Once these beliefs become explicit, teachers and teacher educators

Table 6.1. Written Responses About the Needs of ELLs from Two PSTs

PST	About Child from Central America	About Child from China
#1	The child will need extra help and support during mathematics instruction.	The child will need deeper instruction and manipulatives to work out problems.
#2	The child will need one-on-one help and some translation & explanation.	The child will need me to explain the directions, but based on previous experiences, my Asian students are excellent in math.

must provide the necessary support and guidance as PSTs begin to wrestle with and further shape those beliefs.

Video Images that Challenge Beliefs

Images of and artifacts (i.e., student thinking and written work) produced by ELLs in mathematics classrooms can be effective tools for challenging PSTs' beliefs, especially videos and artifacts that display ELLs who are successful at learning mathematics and teachers who clearly have high expectations for their students. We use these videos and artifacts throughout the semester, yet it is critical to begin early on in the semester so that mathematics teacher educators have time throughout the semester to challenge beliefs that surface. We use the following example to illustrate the effectiveness of using video images to challenge PSTs' beliefs, rather than to suggest the use of a particular video.

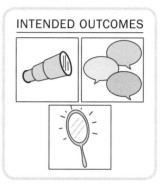

INTENDED OUTCOMES

Toward the beginning of the semester, we display a 10-minute video clip from a 5th-grade classroom. In this example, the teacher draws a figure on the board (see Figure 6.1).

She then asks the students to calculate the area and the perimeter of the figure using their calculators. Prior to introducing the video, we ask the PSTs to solve the problem using strategies that would be accessible to 5th-graders (they have not been introduced to formal algebra). Most of the PSTs have

Figure 6.1. Problem Posed to 5th-grade ELLs

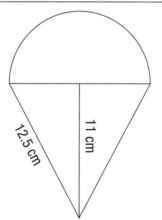

trouble solving the problem and cannot anticipate how 5th-graders would solve it. We then introduce the context of the classroom that will be displayed in the video. The students are all English language learners primarily from Mexico, and all of the children come from low-income households. Finally, we play the video. We watch as 5th-grade students work collaboratively to solve the problem in a short period of time. Two girls in the video then come to the board to write the calculator keystrokes they used to calculate the area as shown in Figure 6.2.

From observing the video, it is obvious that this problem is not challenging for these 5th-grade students. This is a worthwhile video to show PSTs because it highlights the fact that low-income, Latino/a ELLs can be successful at learning mathematics when given the opportunity and the support to do so.

To provide contrast to this example, we show transcripts from another classroom video. In this classroom, Janessa, a 4th-grade Latina, is positioned by her teacher as a student who needs help and one who needs to go at a slower pace. In one instance, the teacher asks Rob, a 4th-grade White male, to work with Janessa. The teacher says:

> So Rob, good job, now go a little slower. Work with the second one. [The teacher pulls Janessa's paper closer to Rob's.] Okay? All right? You're going to go *Janessa's* speed today, okay?

We also show video clips of Janessa as a silent spectator in the mathematics classroom who allows others to do her work for her, avoiding contact with her peers and teacher. These video clips are troubling for PSTs. We ask, "Would you want to elevate the status of some of your students above other students? Would you want children to feel afraid to participate in your classroom? Would you want children to feel unsuccessful in your classroom? Will you have low expectations for some of your students?" The PSTs want to answer "no" to all these questions, but they display worried looks. We ask, "How would you teach Janessa differently?" They return with a question, "How can I effectively

Figure 6.2. Student Solution to Area Problem

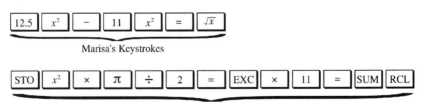

Marisa's Keystrokes

Violetta's Keystrokes

teach students like Janessa? I want to know." At that moment, the videos and transcripts have served their purpose.[1]

Written Images that Challenge Beliefs and Build Knowledge Related to Teaching ELLs

Mathematics teacher educators do not always have access to videos of ELLs, but they do have access to publications related to teaching mathematics to ELLs. Throughout the semester, we ask our PSTs to read articles about teaching ELLs that are written for teachers (e.g., Chval & Chávez, 2011/2012; Chval, Chávez, Pomerenke, & Reams, 2009). In addition, we use transcripts from research publications to facilitate discussions about teaching ELLs. For example, we ask our students to read and analyze transcripts from two elementary mathematics classrooms (see Figure 6.3; Khisty & Chval, 2002, p. 158). After PSTs read Transcript 1 and Transcript 2 from Ms. Martinez's classroom, they first individually think about and then discuss the following questions in their small groups:

1. What are examples of mathematical language that Ms. Martinez emphasizes?
2. What strategies does she use to help students build meaning for this mathematical language?

After the PSTs share their ideas with the whole class, they then read the transcript taken from Ms. Tapia's 2nd-grade mathematics classroom (see Figure 6.4.; Khisty & Chval, 2002, pp. 165–166), in which Ms. Tapia reads a literature book about sharing Ma's cookies. Each time the doorbell rings (represented by the phrase "ding dong") the children have to share the cookies with more people. After PSTs read the transcript from Ms. Tapia's classroom, they individually think about and then discuss the following questions in their small groups, and then debrief with the whole class:

1. What are examples of mathematical language that Ms. Tapia emphasizes?
2. What strategies does she use to help students build meaning for this mathematical language?
3. How do the mathematical discussions differ in these two classrooms?

Figure 6.3. Transcripts from Ms. Martinez's Classroom

T: Teacher
S: Student
CH: Choral response

Transcript 1 (from First Mathematics Class of the School Year)

T: *It has four sides.* You know what? I'm going to put the word "rectangle" into a *category*. And I am going to *call this category "quadrilaterals."*
[Teacher writes "quadrilaterals" on the board.]
T: Do you recognize or at least listen to the sound of the word and see if there is any part of this word that you recognize. "Qua—dri—lat—er—al." "Qua—dri—lat—er—al." "Qua—dri—lat—er—al." Cuadrado, right? What is a cuadrado?
S(1): A square.
S(2): A shape.
T: A shape that has?
S(3): Four sides.
T: A shape that has four sides. Look at your classroom. *Do you see a lot of shapes that are quadrilaterals?*

Transcript 2 (from 5th Day of School)

S(1): Multiplication.
T: Multiplication. We're not going to say *opposite. We're going to add a new word here.*
[Teacher writes "inverse" on the board.]
T: What's *the inverse* of multiplication?
[Pause]
S(1): Division.
T: What is the *inverse* of division?
CH: Multiplication.
T: *Good, you know another word.* Now let's look at another one. Everyone knows how to use the word "length." Everyone knows how to use the word "base" and the word "height."

The PSTs recognize that in one classroom the teacher, Ms. Martinez, uses sophisticated mathematical language with her 5th-grade Latino students. She assumes that ELLs can handle sophisticated language and she capitalizes on students' knowledge of Spanish to have them construct meaning for the word "quadrilateral." She also writes important mathematical terms on the board and refers to shapes in their classroom environment. However, in Ms. Tapia's classroom, the children's responses focus on numerical answers or nonmathematical aspects of the story (i.e., "ding dong") rather than on important mathematical ideas or language.

As videos and artifacts of classrooms became available on the commercial market, teacher educators began to utilize them in their courses for PSTs. Yet in most cases, these products did not involve examples of effective

Figure 6.4. Transcript from Ms. Tapia's Classroom

T: In the story, how many people are there . . . at the beginning, how many do you remember?

CH: Two.

T: You two will start off. How many cookies should we use? You choose. Choose some. [The students seem very confused by this question and do not respond.] Do you want twelve, six? How many cookies?

S(1): Seven?

T: Well, I think six. Let's start with six. Count out six [indicating the plastic chips in the middle of the group] and put them on your plates. [The two students who are to begin hesitate, but then, one selects six chips and puts them in a pile.] Grandmother has made six cookies . . . OK; put them on your plates like in the story. [The students silently each take one cookie at a time until all the cookies are distributed between the two of them.] Good. What happened? [No one answers.] What happened? Look at your plates.

S(2): Three cookies.

T: Good. You each have three cookies. Now what happens?

S(3): [One of the other students at the table answers.] Ding dong.

CH: Ding dong.

T: Come in. Two, no, one more come in. Now share the cookies again but for the three of you.

[One student hesitantly redistributes the cookies accordingly. No one talks as this goes on. This continues with the same type of dialogue between teacher and students as before, with six players with one cookie each.]

T: Now, what happens if there are six more people and six cookies? Twelve people altogether and six cookies. What will happen?

CH: Ding dong.

---

practice directly related to teaching ELLs. In the two sections above, we provided examples of videos and transcripts that can be used with PSTs. As additional videos and transcripts of classrooms involving ELLs become available, teacher educators should select and use appropriate examples of classroom images that specifically address issues related to language and culture in their courses.

Understanding the Complexities of Language in Mathematics Instruction: The Baseball Problem

Many PSTs enter our methods courses with very simplistic notions about the language demands in mathematics classrooms. In addition, their notion of mathematical language is reduced to mathematical terminology too often and, as a result, many PSTs assume that simply providing their students with a vocabulary list or definitions of mathematical terminology will suffice. In order to help PSTs understand the complexities of language in mathematics instruction, we use several activities, one of which is described below. Discussions around these activities also focus on other important notions, such as specialized vocabulary, discourse, conversational and academic language, as well as context. We use these activities in the middle of the semester, after PSTs have completed relevant readings on language, discourse, and register (see the Resources section).

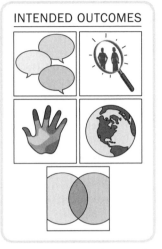

INTENDED OUTCOMES

The goal of this activity (see Razfar, 2012 and Vomvoridi-Ivanović & Razfar, 2013, for more details) is for PSTs to experience what many ELLs who have conversational fluency in English experience in the mathematics classroom. Specifically, PSTs discuss and solve a mathematics problem in the context of baseball. The mathematical skills required to solve the problem are simple. However, for students who are not familiar with baseball, it may be impossible for them to make sense of the problem. In other words, students will experience what it is like to have conversational fluency (the problem is in English) and know the mathematics content, but not be able to solve the problem because of not knowing the specialized language of baseball. Those students who are very knowledgeable about baseball and its language will see how difficult it is to have students who are not familiar with baseball jargon make sense of the problem.

Start by informing your students that they will solve a baseball problem working with peers who have similar knowledge about baseball. Ask students to self-select into one of three groups: Baseball Experts (very knowledgeable about baseball), Baseball Intermediates (some knowledge about baseball), and Baseball Novices (little or no knowledge of baseball). In this activity, "Baseball Language Learners" (BLLs) will consist of Baseball Intermediates and Baseball Novices.

Ask PSTs to work in their groups to define the following baseball terms: batting three hundred, ball, strike, diamond, base, steal, stealing home, hit and run, triple crown, run, out, balk, and save. Ask groups to share their definitions with the rest of the class, starting with the Novice group, followed by the Intermediate group, and ending with Expert group. This should spark some discussion about specialized language that often includes jargon and about the fact that the meaning of each word depends on the context. Have members from the Baseball Expert group explain what each term means in the context of baseball and write the agreed-upon definitions of these terms on the board.

The Novice group and, to a lesser extent, the Intermediate group members will still struggle with understanding what some of these terms mean. Then pose the following baseball problem: Hank Aaron, one of baseball's most prolific home-run hitters, had a career batting average of three-o-five (as .305 is verbalized orally). If he had 3,771 hits, how many at-bats did he have?

Ask PSTs to solve the problem collaboratively in their groups. As each group attempts to solve the problem, ask the two BLL groups to monitor the process of trying to understand the problem. What resources do they draw from to make sense of the problem? Also, ask the Baseball Expert group to think about how they would help the BLL groups make sense of the problem.

Begin a discussion when the Baseball Experts finish solving the problem. Ask the Baseball Novices to share the process they went through as they tried to make sense of and solve the problem. Then ask the Baseball Intermediates to share their process. The assumption is that the two BLL groups will not have reached an appropriate solution for the problem. (If Baseball Intermediates have a correct solution, then do not ask them share it at this time.) Discuss the following as a whole class:

- Why was it not productive to simply go over key baseball terms (vocabulary) at the beginning? How did this approach differ from what Ms. Martinez did with the term "quadrilateral"?
- Identify the baseball-specific language in the problem.

Now, rearrange the groups. Have students form groups with at least one Baseball Expert and one BLL. Ask the Baseball Experts to assist the BLLs in understanding and solving the problem. The assumption is that the Baseball Experts will try to explain the problem using various aids, such as visual and/or physical representations.

Facilitate a whole-class discussion in which the groups share their solutions and the methods the Baseball Experts employed to assist the BLLs. Also have the BLLs express whether, after having received assistance from the Baseball Experts, they fully understand the problem and its solution and whether they feel confident that they could solve a similar baseball problem. Finally, discuss lessons learned from this experience, particularly as they relate to ELLs. Emphasize the fact that Ms. Martinez did not begin with a definition of "quadrilateral." Instead, she used the students' home language and visual examples in the classroom to help students build meaning for quadrilaterals. In addition, students had previous experiences with shapes. Yet with the baseball example, some PSTs had limited knowledge and experience with baseball, and they were not given access to this context through the use of visuals or prior knowledge. Finally, make connections with relevant readings, such as Bresser (2003); Coggins, Kravin, Coates, and Carroll (2007); and Moschkovich (1999). Possible discussion questions include:

1. Why is conversational language important and where does it fall short when you are trying to make sense of the problem?
2. Is knowledge of baseball jargon sufficient for understanding the problem? Why or why not?
3. What would it take for BLLs to become proficient in the language of baseball?
4. What are different ways that students could interpret .305 in the Hank Aaron problem?
5. What kinds of insights have you gained from this experience that relate to the teaching and learning of mathematics for ELLs?

These prompts generate very rich discussions around language, culture, context, mathematics, and ELLs. PSTs, for example, notice that in this problem .305 means 30.5%. This can bring up the point that mathematical meaning is situated in the context and "universal" mathematical representations such as 100 mean different things in the context of baseball or in the context of a number system with bases other than 10, for example.

CONCLUSION

What we have included in this chapter reflects a work in progress. More research is needed on ways to assess and challenge beliefs that PSTs have about ELLs and the field of mathematics teacher education needs to continue to conceptualize and articulate the knowledge base that PSTs should develop in mathematics methods courses as it relates to teaching mathematics to ELLs.

Finally, mathematics teacher educators need professional development that will help them incorporate the issues discussed in this chapter in their mathematics methods courses. In addition, the field needs more resources so that PSTs can view images, from video or field experiences, of effective mathematical learning environments that serve ELLs. In other words, the field is in desperate need of good models for teaching mathematics to ELLs and ways to share these models with preservice teachers.

NOTE

1. We recognize that these video clips are not widely available to mathematics teacher educators at this time. Although, with funding from the National Science Foundation,

Kathryn is in the process of creating written and video cases involving ELLs for teacher educators to use with PSTs as well as practicing teachers. Teacher educators may want to videotape effective teachers of ELLs in their communities.

ACKNOWLEDGMENT

This material is based on work supported by the National Science Foundation under grant number DRL-0844556. Any opinions, findings, and conclusions or recommendations expressed in this material are those of the authors and do not necessarily reflect the views of the National Science Foundation.

REFERENCES

Boero, P., Douek, N., & Ferrari, P. L. (2002). Developing mastery of natural language: Approaches to the theoretical aspects of mathematics. In L. D. English (Ed.), *Handbook of international research in mathematics education* (pp. 241–268). Mahwah, NJ: Lawrence Erlbaum.

Bresser, R. (2003). Helping English language learners develop computational fluency. *Teaching Children Mathematics, 9*(6), 294–299.

Burton, L. (1994). Whose culture includes mathematics? In S. Lerman (Ed.), *Cultural perspectives on the mathematics classroom* (pp. 69–83). Boston, MA: Kluwer.

Chval, K. B., & Chávez, Ó. (2011/2012). Designing mathematics lessons for English language learners. *Teaching Mathematics in the Middle School, 17*(5), 261–265.

Chval, K. B., & Khisty, L. (2009). Latino students, writing, and mathematics: A case study of successful teaching and learning. In R. Barwell (Ed.), *Multilingualism in mathematics classrooms: Global perspectives.* (pp. 128–144). Clevedon, England: Multilingual Matters.

Chval, K. B., & Pinnow, R. (2010). Preservice teachers' assumptions about Latino/a English language learners. *Journal of Teaching for Excellence and Equity in Mathematics, 2*(1), 6–12.

Chval, K. B., Chávez, Ó., Pomerenke, S., & Reams, K. (2009). Enhancing mathematics lessons to support all students. In D. Y. White & J. S. Silva (Eds.), *Mathematics for every student: Responding to diversity PK–5.* (pp. 43–52). Reston, VA: National Council of Teachers of Mathematics.

Chval, K. B., Lannin, J., Arbaugh, F., & Bowzer, A. (2009). Classroom videos and prospective teachers. *Teaching Children Mathematics, 16*(2), 98–105.

Coggins, D., Kravin, D., Coates, G. D., & Carroll, M. D. (2007). *English language learners in the mathematics classroom.* Thousand Oaks, CA: Corwin.

Connolly, P. (1989). Writing and the ecology of learning. In P. Connolly & T. Vilardi (Eds.), *Writing to learn mathematics and science* (pp. 1–14). New York, NY: Teachers College Press.

Gutiérrez, R. (2002). Beyond essentialism: The complexity of language in teaching mathematics to Latino students. *American Educational Research Journal, 39*(4), 1047–1088.

Khisty, L. L., & Chval, K. B. (2002). Pedagogic discourse and equity in mathematics: When teachers' talk matters. *Mathematics Education Research Journal, 14*(3), 154–168.

Mohan, B. (1990). LEP students and the integration of language and content: Knowledge structures and tasks. In J. Gomez (Ed.), *Proceedings of the First Research Symposium on Limited English Proficient Student Issues* (pp. 113–160). Washington, DC: Office for Bilingual Education and Minority Language Affairs.

Mohan, B., & Slater, T. (2005). A functional perspective on the critical "theory/practice" relation in teaching language and science. *Linguistics and Education, 16*, 151–172.

Moschkovich, J. N. (1999). Understanding the needs of Latino students in reform-oriented mathematics classrooms. In L. Ortiz-Franco, N. G. Hernández, & Y. De La Cruz (Eds.), *Changing the faces of mathematics: Perspectives on Latinos* (pp. 23–33). Reston, VA: National Council of Teachers of Mathematics.

National Council of Teachers of Mathematics (NCTM). (2000). *Principles and standards for school mathematics.* Reston, VA: Author.

Razfar, A. (2012). Discoursing mathematically: Using discourse analysis to develop a sociocritical perspective of mathematics education. *The Mathematics Educator, 22*(1), 39–62.

Remillard, J. T., & Cahnmann, M. (2005). Researching mathematics teaching in bilingual-bicultural classrooms. In T. L. McCarty (Ed.), *Language, literacy, and power in schooling,* (pp. 169–188) Mahwah, NJ: Lawrence Erlbaum.

Setati, M. (2005). Learning and teaching mathematics in a primary multilingual classroom. *Journal for Research in Mathematics Education, 36*(5), 447–466.

Shulman, L. S. (1986). Those who understand: Knowledge growth in teaching. *Educational Researcher, 15*(2), 4–14.

Steinbring, H., Bartolini Bussi, M., & Sierpinska, A. (1998). *Language and communication in the mathematics classroom.* Reston, VA: National Council of Teachers of Mathematics.

U.S. Census Bureau. (2012). *Statistical abstract of the United States: 2012.* Retrieved from www.census.gov/population/www/socdemo/school.html

U.S. Department of Education National Center for Education Statistics. (2013). *The Condition of Education 2013.* Retrieved from nces.ed.gov/programs/coe/

Valdés, G., Bunch, G., Snow, C., Lee, C., & Matos, L. (2005). Enhancing the development of students' language(s). In L. Darling-Hammond & J. Bradsford (Ed.), *Preparing teachers for a changing world: What teachers should learn and be able to do* (pp. 126–168). San Francisco, CA: Jossey-Bass.

Volmink, J. (1994). Mathematics by all. In S. Lerman (Ed.), *Cultural perspectives on the mathematics classroom* (pp. 51–67). Boston, MA: Kluwer.

Vomvoridi-Ivanović, E., & Razfar, A. (2013). In the shoes of English language learners: Helping preservice teachers understand some complexities of language in mathematics instruction through a baseball activity. *Journal of Teaching for Excellence and Equity in Mathematics, 15*(1), 7–15.

CHAPTER 7

Science Education

Exploring Diverse Visions of Science and Scientists

Elaine V. Howes and Miyoun Lim

Students' and teachers' beliefs about science and the people who do science strongly influence their eagerness to engage with scientific processes and science content. That is why so much of our teaching and research, and therefore this chapter, has a biographical theme: biographies of scientists, autobiographical approaches to students' experiences with science, and cultural experiences and knowledge of students' lives form the core of this chapter. We begin with our own brief "science" biographies:

Elaine: I began my scientific work partly as rebellion (I can do this, even though I'm a woman!) but mostly due to curiosity about the natural world. Although I am embarrassed to say so now, I must admit that, for a while, I felt special among women, because I succeeded in science. I was unaware of the privileges enjoyed that allowed this success and unaware that I was perpetuating sexist attitudes by celebrating my own perceived exceptionality among women. Nonetheless, after a few years in laboratory science, I decided to go into teaching—where I believed I would have more opportunities to share fascinating scientific concepts, along with the very human, socially grounded development of these concepts with my students. It was due to this choice that I encountered studies based in feminist theory (e.g., Ehrenreich & English, 1978; Hubbard, 1990; Keller, 1996) and other cultural and historical perspectives (e.g., Conner, 2005; Gould, 1996). Through reading and discussion with other women, I learned that my sometimes uncomfortable position as a woman in science is shaped by privileges assigned to me as a White, middle-class, heterosexual academic and, concomitantly, by visions of women as unfit for full participation in scientific activity.

Miyoun: I first encountered biology as an academic discipline in middle school and fell in love with it. I grew up dreaming about becoming a scientist. I have been very fortunate and privileged to have teachers and parents who have inspired, encouraged, and nurtured me, which made it possible to overcome or ignore sociocultural challenges that many young women encounter while pursuing a dream of becoming a scientist. My continued interdisciplinary academic experiences across biology, environmental studies, and education have assisted me in developing a critical understanding of science education within social, cultural, and political contexts. Furthermore, my time as an Asian (I was referred to as "Asian"; my specific nationality as a Korean was not recognized) professor in a southern U.S. university setting provided me with experiences and examples of the continuing racism of American society.

To summarize: Both of us are women in science education but from different cultural and national backgrounds. We have both experienced exclusion and privilege simultaneously, although in very different ways. We aim through uses of biography and autobiography in our teacher education work to help our students become teachers who recognize the human diversity of the scientific world and, especially, to value (and use in their teaching) the parallel rich diversity of the students with whom they work.

SCIENCE EDUCATION AND DIVERSITY EDUCATION

Students often come into science education with stereotypical visions of who can do science (Finson, 2002; McAdam, 1990; Rahm, 2007). Although education students learn about various cultures, ways of speaking, and attitudes toward schooling in "diversity" courses, they do not necessarily learn how these apply to teaching and learning science (Mensah, 2009; Patchen & Cox-Petersen, 2008; Southerland & Gess-Newsome, 1999). Furthermore, science educators tend not to work closely with other instructors in their students' programs, particularly in elementary science education, where science education specialists often teach elementary science education as a "service course" outside of their own department. This all-too-familiar separation between science education and the rest of students' education reinforces the mythical separation of the practice of science from the rest of society.

We know that students and their teachers have visions of science and of scientists that do not include a diverse array of cultures, classes, and linguistic groups but instead represent science as a mysterious endeavor practiced by people (mostly White men) who exist and work separately from our complex society (Finson, 2002; McAdam, 1990; Rahm, 2007). By the time students have reached a teacher preparation program, "accumulated images of science have become deeply ingrained as educational beliefs about what science education 'should be'" (Levitt, 2001, p. 4). We also know that preservice education students, along with many practicing teachers, believe science teaching should be student centered and welcoming to all students (Deng, Chen, Tsai, & Chai, 2011; Howes, 2001; Levitt, 2001). The assignments described here support education students' desires to make science engaging and relevant to their students' knowledge and interests, as student-centered teaching strives to do, while also helping our students (and, by extension, their students) to re-envision stereotypical images of science and scientists.

We hope to help preservice and inservice teacher education students move toward an understanding of science as a human enterprise, with all of the good and the not-so-good that it implies. Our goal is to support both PSTs and practicing teachers in learning to respond actively and productively when they hear themselves or any of their students say, "I am not," "she or he is not," or "they are not" good at science. Thus, we hope to interrupt the historical dialogue that imagines successful scientists as primarily White, unusually bright, and male. To this end, we have developed activities that purposefully replace stereotypical visions of scientists with real people and help students rethink what counts as science. These activities are designed to be easily adaptable for K–12 classrooms, with the common goal of "challenging the stereotype of scientists" (Roth, 2010, personal communication).

ASSIGNMENTS AND ACTIVITIES: CHALLENGING THE STEREOTYPES OF SCIENCE AND SCIENTISTS

Our science education courses do not consist wholly of the assignments in this chapter. We have chosen the four assignments that best represent our belief that biography, autobiography, and cultural roots matter in science education: Becoming a Scientist, Photonarratives: Science in My Life, Gathering Cultural and Scientific Knowledge, and Medical Ethnography. Each assignment or activity description is followed by a brief reflection. The chapter ends with a summary in which we share our ideas about the role of activities like these in developing science education that serves all children better.

Becoming a Scientist

The role-playing assignment described here is designed to inspire preservice teachers (PSTs) to consider the questions, "Who does science?" and concurrently, "What is science?" (Howes & Cruz, 2009). The Becoming a

Scientist assignment is not intended to provide any one vision of science, but to help PSTs see that science is and has been practiced in many different ways by many different kinds of people. In this process, they may recognize their own biases concerning who does science and, in turn, help their own students challenge these biases and stereotypes. The Becoming a Scientist assignment proceeds through several stages, described below.

INTENDED OUTCOMES

Draw a Scientist. On the first day of class, PSTs "draw a scientist." This is not an unusual or novel teacher education project and has, in fact, been successfully utilized by a number of science educators (Finson, 2002). What is unique about this version is that PSTs first draw what comes to mind immediately, without censoring, when they hear the word "scientist"; and then count the numbers of people of color, women, and men represented in the totality of the class's drawings. As a class, students then construct descriptions of what their scientists look like, materials their scientists are using, and where their scientists are working. The drawings and the discussions show that the large majority of students depict scientists as antisocial, White, hyper-intellectual, and male (and mostly dressed in the science uniform of white lab coats and pocket protectors). The places in which these cold and weird humans conduct their work are also cold and weird: all hard edges and shiny equipment, mysterious cabinets and refrigerators holding dangerous chemicals and engineered life. PSTs' drawings and their analyses of them provide a distillation of the usually hidden, but always powerful images that these education students hold of professional science and its practitioners.

Who Does Science? Based in these tabulations and descriptions, we continue the discussion focusing on where these visions of scientists originate, how they are represented in the society at large, and how they might affect K–12 students' perceptions of science. After this in-depth discussion of students' drawings of scientists, the class brainstorms a list of all of the scientists they can think of. After the usual suspects are on the board (e.g., Galileo, Darwin, Newton, and eventually George Washington Carver and Marie Curie), students are encouraged to push the boundaries of what counts as science—to name people they think could be considered scientists, even if they are not in the textbooks and do not have PhDs. Then cooks (e.g., Emeril Lagasse, Anton Uhl, even Julia Child), television shows and personalities (e.g., *MythBusters*, *Stormchasers*, Steve Irwin), and friends and relatives begin to make it onto the board. In addition, given more time (and some noticing that even within our list of real scientists, the numbers of people of color and of women are pretty scant), students name Louis Latimer, Benjamin Banneker, Jane Goodall, Rosalind Franklin, and other people who have been successful in traditionally scientific and technological fields who do not come to mind immediately when they think "scientist."

The next step of the assignment is for students to find a scientist and "become that scientist," in preparation for our Becoming a Scientist seminar (see Figure 7.1). The rationale for the next step comes from what students have already noted: that stereotypical images of science are all around us, and yet, with a little bit of work, we can name and learn about all kinds of people who do science, traditionally defined or otherwise.[1]

Figure 7.1. Becoming a Scientist

A part of learning how to teach science is finding out what scientists are like and how they go about doing their work. We have already spent some time working with the ideas that come to mind most quickly when we ask ourselves the question, "Who does science?" Now it's time to explore this question a little more deeply and, in the process, challenge those stereotypical images and develop images of scientists and science that expand our visions of what science and scientists have been and could be.

Another aspect of this assignment is to explore a way to help kids—all kids—connect to science. Lisa Delpit (1992) borrows the phrase "in their blood" from Jaime Escalante to indicate how we must recognize the heritage that all children bring with them to the classroom:

> If we know the intellectual legacies of our students, we will gain insight into how to teach them. For instance, Jaime Escalante repeatedly calls upon the Latin American heritage of his poor Latino students as he successfully teaches them advanced calculus. . . . "You have to learn math, math is in your blood! The Mayans discovered zero!" . . . Teachers . . . must also learn about the brilliance the students bring with them "in their blood." (p. 248)

The Assignment

Study up on a scientist, and come to class prepared to be that scientist. We'll have a mini-seminar, in which each scientist explains her or his work and then lets us know how she or he would answer the question, "What is science?" Also write something, in your scientist's voice, indicating how your scientist would respond to the question, "What is science?" This chart should help you focus and clarify the question of "What is science?" because it forces you to think of short, clear descriptions. It may also be something that you will choose to use in your own teaching with children. (It's been done before!) Don't forget to include your source.

Explore the library or other resources to find a scientist who appeals to you. Use biographies written for adults or biographies written for children. Use long pieces (whole books); medium-sized pieces (chapters); or short pieces (magazine articles and websites). *Make sure to choose scientists who break the stereotypical mold, or people who have traditionally been shut out of science.* Infer from what you read what this scientist would say to the question, "What is science?"

The more surprising kinds of scientists you can find, the more interesting our seminar on "What is science?" will be!

Becoming a Scientist Seminar. On the day of the Becoming a Scientist seminar, students, in groups, begin the role-playing portion of the activity. Using their scientists' voices, they provide a brief biography, a description of their scientists' work, and a statement of how their scientists would respond to the question "What is science?" After all PSTs in the small group have introduced their scientists, the group fulfills the next step of the assignment, which is to prepare a presentation for a fictional elementary school, expressing to the teachers and administrators at that school their beliefs about science and science education (see Figure 7.2). In this presentation, they maintain their scientists' identities and speak from their scientists' perspectives.

Reflection: Becoming a Scientist. As science teacher educators committed to creating an educational system that serves all children well, part of our work is to help students learn about scientists who have contributed to the field in both traditional and untraditional ways. This is where Becoming a Scientist comes in. When students have the opportunity to explore

Figure 7.2. Becoming a Scientist Seminar

You have been called together as a group of respected scientists to help us think about science teaching at Gopher Tortoise Elementary School. You will be split up into teams. Each team is charged with giving advice to the teachers and administrators of Gopher Tortoise Elementary School on creating instruction that represents the best approaches to teaching science, from your perspectives as successful scientists.

1. First, for your team's discussion
   a. Each person, one at a time, describe her or his life and work. This person should then respond to the question, "What is science?" Try to limit each person to 5 minutes.
   b. Come to consensus—this is not a list of ideas, but *a consensus*—on the 3 questions below.
   c. Prepare to share your consensus responses with the faculty and staff of Gopher Tortoise Elementary School.
2. Then, prepare a presentation to the faculty and staff of the school. Use newsprint, overheads, skits, or songs to support your presentations. We just ask that you be clear and dignified, as befits the situation. Please respond to the following questions in your presentation:
   a. How do you want children to define science?
   b. What kinds of people do you want children to see as doing science and being scientists?
   c. What suggestions do you have for teachers and administrators who want to help kids develop these ways of thinking about and doing science?

Thank you very much for sharing your time, energy, and expertise with the educators at Gopher Tortoise Elementary School!

a variety of scientists with little constraint and choose the ones they find most interesting, they will gain something that is unattainable when they are told which scientists are important to study. This is especially pertinent for prospective and practicing teachers who do not feel confident in the field of science. In addition, due to its role-playing structure, students can step out of their own shoes and develop a moderate affinity with a person who chose a life in science. PSTs learn not only about scientists' lives but about the scientific knowledge they work with and generate. Even if they choose "one of the usual suspects"—that is, one of those White, male scientists who comes so immediately to mind—PSTs regularly find surprises that help the stereotypes dissolve. For instance, Albert Einstein's IQ was "low," and he was labeled in his elementary school as being lacking in normal intelligence. What would students make of the contradiction of this reality and the mythology surrounding this iconic figure? This example and others like it, in which people who have become scientists were not recognized as gifted and possibly even considered "at risk" in school, might be used to help PSTs have high expectations for *all* of their students in science.

The scientists that PSTs choose to "become" can also provide the impetus for impromptu discussions about gender, ethnicity, and the purposes to which science is put in our society. For example, several African American women PSTs over the years have chosen Madam C. J. Walker for the scientist they become for the seminar. During one class session, several African American women not only focused on the fact that Walker was the first African American woman millionaire, and active in the Harlem Renaissance, but also thanked her profusely for the development of hair-straightening products. It is mostly African American women who straighten their hair—not African American men. Women of all cultures in the United States spend inordinate amounts of time, energy, money, and psychological pain in keeping up appearances. In addition, cosmetic industries employ many scientists. What human potential has been lost or utilized in these efforts? What does this situation have to do with science and science education? Some girls might be attracted to chemistry through beauty products—is this a way to reinforce gendered norms of beauty or could it be a way to open up interests in chemistry? Questions like these can bring to light possibilities for attracting all students to science, while also encouraging PSTs to learn about the socially constructed activities and knowledge that make up contemporary Western science. For example, sometimes PSTs are angry when they find out that there are so many accomplished women scientists, engineers, inventors, and astronauts of whom they have never even heard. We hope that this anger will help fuel their commitment to making sure that their own students do not leave school with images of science that exclude so many.

Photonarratives: Science in My Life

For photonarrative assignments, students produce personal visual narratives about science using photographic images; they then create narratives to accompany their photographs, thus providing for themselves and others unique and rich texts for analysis. The creation of photonarratives may be put to good use at all levels (K–12, college, and postgraduate) to help students develop a sense of their own beliefs about "what counts" as science, as well as how it should be taught. Coupled with rich and

critical discussions, photonarratives provide opportunities to articulate ideas about science that are not immediately obvious, nor easy to share with others. Importantly, photonarratives provide windows into students' lives and interests and thus may support culturally responsive pedagogy by helping teachers place science content in a context that matters to their students. The use of photonarratives in a preservice methods course and in a graduate course for practicing teachers is described below.

Photonarratives in Preservice Science Teacher Education. In a preservice science methods course, PSTs create photonarratives that reflect their own ideas and experiences with science. The assignment requires PSTs to bring together the distinct but connected aspects of their understanding of science by portraying their visions of what science is as well as illustrating their own relationships with science in their lives. They take photographs and write narratives that represent these two perspectives. Then they share them with the rest of the class. Thus the whole class can discuss real and unique stories that illuminate the different ways that we envision and connect (or not) to science, science learning, and science teaching. To push PSTs' learning further, questions to facilitate their thinking from a teacher's perspective include:

- What does this mean about you as a science teacher?
- How do you want your own students to create relationships to science (as it is or as it could be)?
- What can you learn about your students through having *them* do simple photonarratives?

Photonarratives in Graduate-Level Teacher Education. The second way to use the photonarrative assignment is more appropriate for students who are

already teaching (masters and doctoral level). The assignment is multilayered and complex (see Figure 7.3).

Figure 7.3. Photonarratives Assignment Description

Photonarratives Project (Part I)

Create your photonarrative focusing on the following steps and questions:

1. Take pictures of "science": What is science? When you think of science, what images come to mind? Take a few pictures to show your ideas or understanding of what science is.
2. Take pictures that represent "science in my life": What does science mean to you? What is your relationship with science? What science do you have in your life? What science do you do? Take some pictures to show your relationship with science.
3. Take pictures of "my science teaching": What "science" do you teach? How do you frame science in your teaching? What kinds of science teacher are you? Take some pictures that can capture your science teaching.

You do not need to take numerous pictures (3–5 pictures for each category is enough). But it is critical that you provide narratives for each picture. PowerPoint is the format I expect, but feel free to make your presentation a slide show. In that case, you will need to provide a written script.

Photonarratives Project (Part II)

You will create another photonarrative with one or more of your students.

1. Recruit one or more of your students to help you with your assignment. Ask the student(s) to take 3 to 5 pictures that show understanding of science and to provide accompanying narratives.
2. Once a student completes the first task, ask that student to engage in the second task: Ask the student to carry a camera for a day or two to take 15 to 20 pictures of the science that exists in his or her life (at home, in her or his neighborhood and community) and the kinds of science in which he or she engages. Ask the student to respond to the question, What science do you have in your life? What science do you do?

Photonarratives Project (Part III)

Write up your analysis and reflection of your students' photonarratives (500–800 words). Prepare a presentation to share your key findings and reflections with the class. Use the following questions to frame your presentation:

1. What did you learn from your students' photonarratives? What kinds of relationship with science do you see in your own and in your students' photonarratives? Do you see any similarities and/or differences?
2. Reflect on your findings and identify pedagogical possibilities and implications from the narratives. How could what you learned inform your science teaching?

First, science teachers create their own photonarratives; second, the teachers' own students develop photonarratives; and third, the teachers make sense of their students' photonarratives in the context of their teaching. Science teachers address questions such as those in Part III of the assignment to work toward further understanding of their students' thinking about themselves and science.

Reflection: Photonarratives. Two narratives regularly appear in teachers' work on this assignment. One of these narratives tries to validate prescribed definitions of science. For example, one teacher took pictures of various lab equipment and another photographed a student mixing vinegar and baking soda (to display a chemical reaction). In this light, these teachers' photonarratives are driven by the desire to "get the right answer"—as one teacher said, "I was trying to make sure everyone was aware that I truly understand 'science.'" Teachers also noted that their *students'* photonarratives revealed stereotypical and limited views of science. One teacher wrote that her "students would refer to definitions and vocabulary when describing science in their life instead of taking a personal view of what science was to them. . . . I fear that my students may see science as a collection of formulas, equations, and laws from a textbook, not as something they shape for their own use or define for themselves." However, there were also examples of these teachers' students showing more personal and authentic connections to science. One chose to share a picture of a syringe with a medicine bottle, explaining how she gives her father an injection of Vitamin B-12 every day; another provided several images of her Chinese cooking to show her fascination with the kitchen.

As the latter examples indicate, photonarratives can provide teachers with material to work from when striving to attend to their K–12 students' particular personal and cultural lenses in the science classroom. As teacher educators, we can model teachers' roles as moderator and translator between students' worlds and the world of science and bring our own students' lives into the center of our science teaching.

ASSIGNMENTS AND ACTIVITIES:
LANGUAGE, CULTURE, AND SCIENTIFIC CONTENT

Similar to the field of mathematics (Vomvoridi-Ivanović & Chval, this volume), science is often thought of as a universal language that needs no translation. However, we take advantage of the fact that as science teacher educators, we are expected to model reform-based ways of teaching science, with the twin goals that PSTs will learn good science pedagogy and some science content along the way. This section summarizes two approaches we have taken to this challenge, while infusing language and culture throughout in order to make clear that "good science teaching" means teaching with cultural and language diversity in mind.

"Gathering" Cultural and Scientific Knowledge

This simple activity is embedded in a series of activities that are meant to help PSTs learn the basics of plant reproduction. It has two main objectives: (1) provide PSTs with an example of how to show respect for and interest in their students' language and culture within a science teaching context and (2) help PSTs learn the scientific definition of "fruit" as the part of the plant that is or has the seeds. The parts of the plant and their roles in plant life are commonly taught at all levels in elementary

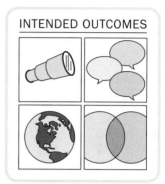

INTENDED OUTCOMES

school; the topic is a natural one to use to help students develop their science knowledge for teaching, while also encouraging them to take advantage of the knowledge that many children bring from their home cultures to the classroom.

The activity is introduced with the children's book *Gathering the Sun: An Alphabet in Spanish and English* (Ada, 1997). This book is written from the perspective of a young girl in a Latino migrant farming family; each letter begins a poem (in both Spanish and English versions) that describes the fields, flowers, fruit, family, and larger social and political context ("C" is for "Chávez"; "H" is for "honor") of the child's life. In areas with large Spanish-speaking migrant populations, this book could be particularly powerful. It portrays migrant farmworkers in a positive light, and this may help to enlighten those outside of Latino culture, as well as help those within it feel recognized and valued in the classroom.

In preparing to read the book to the class, all students are emailed[2] and asked to volunteer to partner with someone to read the English and the Spanish portions to the class. These two volunteers then read to the class, and we follow up with a discussion of language and culture in the science classroom. The point of this discussion is to help education students see the knowledge about the natural world children from families who work on the land can bring to science class—to view these children's experiences as strengths rather than deficits (Ladson-Billings, 2009). This discussion could be broadened to include (1) the knowledge that all children who work alongside adults could bring to science if encouraged and (2) the knowledge and community-based skills that teachers and teacher candidates themselves can bring to science teaching. This last can be very powerful for people who are new to teaching, new to science, and new to academia because they are first-generation college attenders. It is a beginning effort to make students who feel like outsiders to science feel instead *central* to science education.

The second part of class on this day is spent with a laboratory experience focusing on observation and on communicating one's ideas both in small groups and to the whole class, followed by an Internet assignment. Several (at least ten) food items are set around the classroom; these are all things that in everyday parlance we would call fruits, vegetables, or nuts. Next to each food item is a piece of paper with its English name and its Spanish name (sometimes there is more than one Spanish name—a learning objective in itself—since there are regional differences in the Spanish that is spoken in the Western hemisphere). There is also a space on the paper for PSTs to write the name of the food item in a language other than English or Spanish, if they know it. An interesting challenge for the teacher educator is to find a variety of culturally important fruits and vegetables (not just apples, tomatoes, peanuts, and other foods that are familiar to White middle-class students)—this can provide students with the opportunity to explain to others (including their teacher) how these foods are grown, procured, used, and prepared.

Medical Ethnography

The assignment above was designed for elementary science methods students. A more sophisticated way to approach language and culture in science education (recommended for graduate-level students; described in depth in Torres-Guzmán & Howes, 2009) is outlined briefly here. Students choose a health issue of interest to them (e.g., digestive problems or diabetes). They then research the treatments for these conditions from a Western scientific medical perspective: What are the causes of  these conditions? What are the treatments? They also research the causes and the treatments of these conditions from a traditional healing perspective. Students may even encounter differences among how nations approach healing—for example, how to treat a baby's very high fever. In the United States, tepid baths are prescribed; in Japan, the infant is swaddled in blankets. Both work to bring the fever down, even though the treatments seem contradictory.

This assignment is especially rich if the student population has strong family ties to grandparents and other relatives who have direct experiences with traditional healing. The writing and discussions that come out of this assignment are complex and socially situated, rather than textbook based: Western science, healing of all sorts, wonderful stories, and explanations from "elders" all come into the mix. It is important—and actually not very difficult, given the power of the traditional healers' beliefs and healing approaches, many of which involve plants—not to give the impression that Western medicine has all of the answers, or that traditional ways of healing have no merit. This is a good time in the history of scientific medicine to help students think about traditional and modern ways of healing, as the knowledge-sharing between the two is gaining traction.

Reflection: Language, Culture, and Science Content. How can these assignments help future teachers develop a sensitivity to cultural and language diversity? In addition to students learning the science of plants, it shows that the simple act of reading in another language, or that asking one's grandmother about how to treat diabetes, is a way of showing respect and honoring a culture's traditions. These traditions, in some ways, are different from the Western scientific tradition of knowledge generation and transmission. For instance, the girl in *Gathering the Sun* has learned about how plants grow and produce fruit by working directly with the plants; her knowledge is truly "hands-on" and not solely drawn from textbook drawings of plant life cycles. In fact, this is an area in which children who work alongside adults will excel. In reference to the Medical Ethnography assignment, several students reported on the use of the nopal plant to treat diabetes; one student's grandmother scolded her family for choosing a high-fat, unhealthful U.S. diet rather than traditional Mexican foods. Thus PSTs as well as practicing teachers may learn to value the knowledge that their own students bring with them—the "funds of knowledge" (Gonzalez, Moll, & Amanti, 2005) that all students bring with them from their homes and communities. Teachers are thus provided with the opportunity to help children value outside-of-school knowledge concerning the natural world. Furthermore, teachers have the interesting challenge of planning to use that knowledge to help make school science accessible and interesting to all children.

CONCLUSION

There is a theme running through all three of these assignments—that of biography. This is no accident. A central stereotypical mythical aspect of science is that it is without human affect and value and disconnected from social life—it seems to exist in a vacuum, too difficult or unattractive for regular people (especially women and people of color or lower SES) to enter. This powerful vision alienates many from the pursuit of science. Thus, all of these activities serve the dual purposes of learning to see science as a human, social practice (with all of the richness and complexity that that adds) and of learning to see oneself as a (potential) scientist. This "demystifying" project has both more- and less-modest aims. More modest is to help K–12 students believe that they can do science and thus hopefully succeed in school science as it stands. Less modest is to revolutionize the relationships among science, school science, and children's cultures such that science education itself adapts to the children it serves.

Despite the movements for civil rights, gender equality, and other social movements that have brought a measure of equity to our society, science still is generally perceived as the work of extra-intelligent, geeky, and usually White men. It is imperative that school science teaching deal regularly and openly with this misperception. Preservice teachers are consistent in their stated belief that everyone can do science and that they hope to help all of their students believe so as well.

These assignments do not carry with them any guarantees that PSTs, inservice teachers, or K–12 students will learn that all kinds of people have been, are, and can be scientists,[3] nor that language and cultural diversity can be a strength rather than a deficit in science learning. If nothing else, however, the assignments are ways to open up conversations about what science is and who does it. Assignments such as these need to permeate our science education curriculum. With all the technique in the world, teachers who do not believe that all of their children can succeed in science and continue on into lives of science learning and practice will not make a dent in the harmful stereotypes that continue to misrepresent the people who contribute to our nation's scientific efforts. In addition, opening up "what counts" as science creates multiple pathways into canonical scientific knowledge: The serious gardener may be curious about plant growth and soil life; the cook, about chemistry; the mechanic, about physics. Including multiple and diverse models of "who can be a scientist" and how science is done may help us to expand scientific options and opportunities for our teacher education students and, in turn, for the diverse students with whom they will work.

NOTES

1. For secondary education students, whose content knowledge should be stronger than that of elementary education students, this assignment includes the further requirement that the work of the scientist under study be explained in more detail and be tied

into what science came before and after and how this scientist's work is represented (and therefore could be taught in the classroom in a biographical/historical context) in local and national standards documents.

2. One experience led to the choice to email rather than to ask in person: A student whom Elaine knew to be a very strong Spanish speaker appeared embarrassed and withdrew when I asked her publically if she would like to read the Spanish half of the book. Elaine realized (with the help of Bárbara Cruz) that the student might not be certain of her academic Spanish; in addition, she realized that she might be pointing out this student as "different," making her into a representative of a group rather than treating her as an individual. At no time has there been a dearth of volunteers to read the book (some of them with stronger Spanish, *and* stronger English, than others!). If there are multiple volunteers, they take turns reading the book.

3. Historically, Western science has been built upon the knowledge and the creations of workers, merchants, herbalists, and health-care givers. Modern science "arose" from "the people's'" work (Conner, 2005; Ehrenrich & English, 1978) and, although we can't see it now, it is undoubtedly reliant upon the labor, the dollars, and the thinking of people who do not have PhDs and who are not considered scientists.

REFERENCES

Ada, A. F. (1997). *Gathering the sun: An alphabet in Spanish and English* (S. Silva, illustrator). New York, NY: Rayo.

Conner, C. D. (2005). A people's history of science: Miners, midwives, and "low mechanicks." New York, NY: Nation Books.

Delpit, L. D. (1992). Education in a multicultural society: Our future's greatest challenge. *Journal of Negro Education, 61*(3), 237–249.

Deng, F., Chen, D.-T., Tsai, C.-C., & Chai, C. S. (2011). Students' views of the nature of science: A critical review of research. *Science Education, 95*: 961–999. doi:10.1002/sce.20460

Ehrenreich, B., & English, D. (1978). *For her own good: 150 years of the experts' advice to women.* New York, NY: Anchor Books.

Finson, K. D. (2002). Drawing a scientist: What we do and do not know after fifty years of drawings. *School Science and Mathematics, 102*(7), 335–345.

Gonzalez, N., Moll, L. C., & Amanti, C. (Eds.). (2005). *Funds of knowledge: Theorizing practices in households, communities, and classrooms.* New York, NY: Routledge.

Gould, S. J. (1996). The mismeasure of man (2nd ed.). New York, NY: W. W. Norton.

Howes, E. V. (2001). Visions of "science for all" in the elementary classroom. In A. Calabrese Barton & M. D. Osborne (Eds.), *Teaching science in diverse settings: Marginalized discourses and classroom practice* (pp. 129–157). New York, NY: Peter Lang.

Howes, E. V., & Cruz, B. (2009). Role-playing in science education: An effective strategy for developing multiple perspectives. *Journal of Elementary Science Education, 21*(3), 33–46.

Hubbard, R. (1990). *The politics of women's biology.* New Brunswick, NJ: Rutgers University Press.

Keller, E. F. (1996). *Reflections on gender and science* (10th anniversary ed.). New Haven, CT: Yale University Press.

Ladson-Billings, G. (2009). *The dreamkeepers: Successful teachers of African American Children*. San Francisco, CA: Jossey-Bass.

Levitt, K. E. (2001). An analysis of elementary teachers' beliefs regarding the teaching and learning of science. *Science Education, 86,* 1–22.

McAdam, J. E. (1990). The persistent stereotype: Children's images of scientists. *Physics Education, 25,* 102–105.

Mensah, F. M. (2009). Confronting assumptions, biases, and stereotypes in preservice teachers' conceptualizations of science teaching through the use of book club. *Journal of Research in Science Teaching, 46,* 1041–1066.

Patchen, T., & Cox-Petersen, A. (2008). Constructing cultural relevance in science: A case study of two elementary teachers. *Science Education, 92,* 994–1014.

Rahm, J. (2007). Youths' and scientists' authoring of and positioning within science and scientists' work. *Cultural Studies of Science Education, 1,* 517–544.

Southerland, S. A., & Gess-Newsome, J. (1999). Inclusive science teaching as shaped by images of teaching, learning, and knowledge. *Science Education, 83,* 131–150.

Torres-Guzmán, M., & Howes, E. V. (2009). Experimenting in teams and tongues: Team teaching a bilingual science education course. In K. R. Bruna & K. Gomez (Eds.), *Talking science, writing science: The work of language in multicultural classrooms* (pp. 317–339). New York, NY: Routledge.

CHAPTER 8

ESOL Education

Empowering Preservice Teachers to Advocate for English Language Learners

Deoksoon Kim and Sylvia Celedón-Pattichis

Teachers must learn to advocate for English language learners (ELLs) from varied cultural, language, and socioeconomic backgrounds. Sylvia Celedón-Pattichis typically begins her ESOL methods courses, which emphasize working with culturally and linguistically diverse students, by sharing her own personal story as an English language learner. Here is how she begins:

My personal story goes something like this . . . My name is Sylvia Celedón-Pattichis. I was born in the small town of Saliñeno, Texas, and raised in Miguel Alemán Tamaulipas, México, from birth to age eight. I went to school up to third grade in México. My Spanish literacy and mathematics skills were at high proficiency levels. When I was in fourth grade, my parents obtained their visa to move to California. It was the first time I was exposed to other cultures. There were Asian, African American, and White students. In my school in México I had been used to seeing only Mexican students. I was placed in an ESL classroom without native language support to learn English.

After spending one year in California, we moved to Rio Grande City, Texas. My ESL label followed me until ninth grade, when I was fortunate to have Mrs. Barbara Osuna, a White female teacher who taught ESL and College Preparatory courses in English. She was an advocate for me and broke the ESL label by providing me with the opportunity to try College Prep English. It was that simple yet powerful move that allowed me to take college preparatory courses throughout high school and become the first in my family to graduate.

I then set my sights on the University of Texas at Austin. My father had wanted me to stay close to home, so the University of Texas at Pan American seemed a better choice. I was also the oldest in the family and my siblings and I had been helping the family economically by playing an instrument in my father's conjunto (musical band).

Mr. Sabas Osuna, who is married to Mrs. Barbara Osuna, had been my pre-algebra teacher in ninth grade and my calculus teacher in twelfth grade. He helped me and other students create positive dispositions toward mathematics learning. Caring about our success transferred to actions like his visiting my father at home and convincing him that it was okay to let me go to the University of Texas at Austin. He assured him that I would do well. My father was concerned about the financial aspect; he had no money to put me through college. Mrs. Osuna, who was a counselor during my senior year, offered to help submit all the financial application materials needed. With the help of teachers, friends, and family, I was able to enroll at UT Austin, complete my undergraduate degree, and become a high school mathematics teacher at Rio Grande City High School, the same school I had attended.

After Sylvia shares her own personal story, she tells preservice teachers they can ask questions about what she presented to them. One issue they are always interested in knowing more about is the tracking of ELLs in lower levels of content area courses, such as mathematics. Sylvia tells them that for ELLs, it is an endless cycle (Valdés, 2001) unless a teacher or someone else intervenes and advocates in the placement process. Counselors often place ELLs in different courses based on their English language proficiency rather than on their potential in a content area such as mathematics (Celedón-Pattichis, 2004). These placements often go unchallenged, as parents from other countries may hold educators in high regard and respect any decisions they make. Parents are also figuring out how to navigate the educational system in the United States.

Sylvia also asks the preservice teachers (PSTs) questions of her own, stimulating a discussion by asking the following:

- Given that many ELLs may look, think, and talk differently than the mainstream population, what can you do to ease their transition to a different school culture?
- How might you advocate for ELLs who are academically prepared to perform at more-advanced levels in content areas but might still be at beginning levels of English language development?
- What role do you envision as a teacher in forming relationships to help guide families to gain access to colleges and universities?

Sylvia uses these questions and her own case study of being an ELL as a way to illustrate to preservice teachers how they themselves can empower and advance the education of ELLs. As her story as an ELL indicates, a White teacher was the one who initially made a huge impact for her by opening a pathway to college preparatory courses. In addition, a Latino teacher influenced her decision to become a mathematics educator. These experiences challenge the misconception that White teachers do not make an impact in communities of color (see, e.g., Ladson-Billings, 2009, for a discussion on how White teachers make a difference in the education of African Americans) and also highlight how teachers of color can influence and advocate for ELLs (see also de Oliveira & Athanases, 2007) as they pursue postsecondary studies.

ACTIVITIES TO EMPOWER FOR ADVOCACY

Cultural Identity Activity

After Sylvia shares her own story as an ELL and her educational journey, she then engages preservice teachers in a cultural identity activity.[1] The purpose of the activity is to have preservice teachers reflect on their own cultural and linguistic backgrounds. During a 10-minute activity, students draw a visual representation that addresses the following:

INTENDED OUTCOMES

- Describe your cultural identity (e.g., race, class, culture, gender, sexual orientation, language, religion).
- Describe a critical moment/incident in which your cultural identity was *affirmed*.
- Describe a critical moment/incident in which your cultural identity was *questioned*.
- Describe a critical moment/incident in which your cultural identity *impacted your development* as a teacher.

Sylvia's own case study covers the first and last points of this activity (see Figure 8.1). She usually draws a map of Texas and the border with Mexico as a visual representation of her cultural identity since that is the region in which she grew up. She also shares that her cultural identity was affirmed when she was a graduate student in the doctoral program and she was a member of the Bilingual Education Student Organization (BESO) at the

Figure 8.1. Cultural Identity Visual Representation

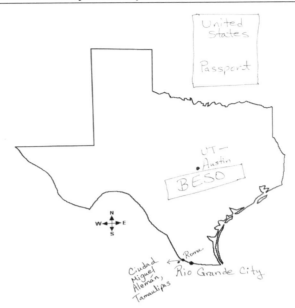

University of Texas at Austin. Her identity was affirmed because there were students in this particular organization with the same goals of promoting biliteracy for all students. Her cultural identity was questioned when she was trying to obtain her passport for the first time. The issue was that the staff could not obtain confirmation on her U.S. citizenship through the official, computerized system because she had been born with a midwife right along the border in Texas.

The cultural identity activity creates a space for students to share their own experiences with classmates. It also provides a lens from which to understand what impacted their interest in becoming an educator.

Before preservice teachers share their own cultural visual representations, we review the following guidelines for listening to one another's stories (see also Chapter 2):

- Value experience and opinion.
- Be mindful of verbal and nonverbal actions (e.g., tone, gestures, facial expressions).
- Listen actively.
- Be mindful of your own thoughts, feelings, and emotions.
- Leave room for others' thoughts, feelings, and emotions.
- Respect confidentiality.

- Respect the learning process (i.e., continual, takes time, different for everyone).
- Be accepting of silences.

After presenting these guidelines, Sylvia also asks preservice teachers if there is anything else that should be added to these guidelines. Students are also asked to take notes of similar experiences, so that as a class themes can be created that run across stories. In sharing their stories, some preservice teachers often comment on the hardships they faced when they came to this country undocumented, which presents a different experience from Sylvia's. Others discuss how their identities were questioned. For example, one preservice teacher mentioned that in Kansas people frequently asked if she was American. She is from Puerto Rico and is of mixed African and Latina/o heritage; however, some people did not consider her to have an American identity because they did not consider Puerto Rico to be part of the United States.

Perhaps the most important discussion emerges as some preservice teachers notice that others' cultural identities have never been questioned before, so we discuss as a class why that might be so. For example, some White students in class often comment, "I do not have a cultural identity," and those who do claim to have a cultural identity state, "People have never questioned who I am. The assumption is that I am American because I am White." There are also some students of mixed heritage (Latina/o and White) who state, "Because I can pass as White, my identity is never questioned." Issues of race enter the conversation, and the fact that there is unearned privilege (McIntosh, 2003) also emerges as a theme as each preservice teacher shares his or her cultural identity. The conversation usually comes full circle with Sylvia's vignette and raising the following question: How can preservice teachers use their own privilege to make changes in the education of ELLs and all students?

English Language Learner Case Studies

The case-study pedagogy engages students and teachers in a dialogue with real-life situations in school settings. It can include engaged discussion, the principle of artistry, principles of appropriate attitudes, principles of scholarship, and principles of teaching as social art (Barnes, Christensen, & Hansen, 1994). By creating a case study, preservice teachers learn about an ELL's linguistic and cultural background, the educational setting in which the

INTENDED OUTCOMES

ELL is situated, as well as challenges and opportunities ELLs face in their schooling. They also have an opportunity to offer reflections and recommendations. In conducting and discussing each ELL case study, preservice teachers note potential pedagogical problems, ethics and equity concerns, and relevant policy issues. Educators then take these into consideration when formulating recommendations, thus facilitating ELLs' progress. ESOL resource teachers are often asked to conduct this sort of holistic assessment of an English language student and present their findings to mainstream teachers and administrators at the school. Case study methodology thus has the potential to serve as a form of authentic assessment for future ESOL educators.

In Deoksoon Kim's ESOL methods course, her students conduct a case study of one ELL during the semester, and they podcast and blog about that case study. Preservice teachers post their ELL case studies in the form of a written report, a podcast of an ELL interview segment and a reading sample, and scanned samples of the ELL's writing. Preservice teachers share their case studies with classmates and engage in an ongoing dialogue on a protected electronic platform. For this core project, preservice teachers evaluate the ELL's second language (L2) reading and literacy development, provide reflective questions and recommendations to teachers, and share their work with peers utilizing Web 2.0 tools.

Before the preservice teachers create their case studies, they read and discuss various published cases. An assigned reading contains 13 case studies (Erben & Zoran, 2005). Each case study provides a unique view of an English language learner from a different country and with a different cultural background and language development. More case studies are available for University of South Florida students on the university's closed iTunes U.

Existing case studies provide good resources for PSTs to reflect on how an ELL from a different culture experiences school and social settings. Preservice teachers should be well grounded in the principles and theories of second language acquisition and literacy. Preservice teachers should also practice analyzing interviews and reading samples using miscue analysis (Goodman, Watson, & Burke, 2005) and think-aloud protocols. Identifying the main points of the case study helps preservice teachers scaffold their own case studies.

Once preservice teachers have read several case studies and understand data collection and data analysis, they find an ELL for their own case study. The process consists of five activities: conducting and writing the ELL case study, blogging the case study, podcasting the audio files, inviting dialogue, and assessing students' English language development.

Writing the ELL Case Study. Data for the case study is assembled by interviewing the ELL, conducting classroom observations, and collecting reading

and writing samples. Preservice teachers then prepare a case study report in six phases: analyzing social background, assessing linguistic development, analyzing multiple data sets, writing the case study, creating reflective questions, and providing implications and suggestions for teachers. Based on the case study experience, preservice teachers create reflection questions for the general audience who will be reading the case studies, particularly their colleagues, administrators, and the ELLs' parents.

Blogging the ELL Case Study. After preservice teachers write the ELL case study and prepare the report for posting, they post the written portion of the case study on the class's secure website, including artifacts and observations collected during the interviews. Incorporating Web 2.0 technology such as blogging and podcasting helps bring the ELLs' voices to the audience so that they can understand the study in a holistic way. It also facilitates sharing the case studies with colleagues, administrators, and the ELLs' parents—in a form that can improve understanding of and advocacy for the ELLs.

The preservice teachers may use a site such as Blogger (www.blogger.com) or USF Blog (blog.usf.edu) or post their case study on the website directly. It is important to make the site private so that only members and those who are invited can view it.

Podcasting the Audio Files. Podcasting is a more recent and rapidly developing instructional technology that allows teachers or students to share their work with others (Kim, 2011; Richardson, 2006). This technology allows the audience to subscribe to digitally recorded files and send their own multimedia files to others via Really Simple Syndication (RSS), a Web-feed format that makes new information readily accessible (Richardson, 2006). Podcasting is thus a potentially transformative information-delivery system for educational settings that facilitates direct personal connections and the sharing of case studies (Campbell, 2005).

Podcasting ELLs' interview segments and reading samples allows the audience to listen to the ELLs' own voices. These voices enhance the case study and illustrate the ELLs' language development. Podcasted reading and writing samples give the audience a real sense of the ELL, and they allow preservice teachers to foreground selected aspects of the reading and writing data. Blog sites, Ning, Google sites, and others can be used for blogging and podcasting.

Inviting Dialogue. All PSTs are invited to review their classmates' ELL case studies and add their feedback and comments, either directly on the blog or at the location where the ELL case study is posted. Peers are encouraged to share critical insights on two or more studies and connect to their own thinking about teaching ELLs. Sharing their ELL case studies in this way enhances their learning and helps create a learning community.

Assessment. In assessing preservice teachers' ELL case studies, two main parts of the project are reviewed: the content of the case study and the instructional technology used. See Figure 8.2 for the rubric used to assess the ELL case studies.

Preservice teachers report that the case study assignment is helpful in a number of ways. They learn more about the various challenges ELLs face in schools and in society. As one preservice teacher noted, "It gave me a lot more insight into the great challenges that she [the ELL] had. So it helped me to be a better teacher for my future ELLs." Other students appreciated the authentic nature of the assignment: "I think that the 'hands-on' style of learning really helps me retain information." By conducting case studies, preservice teachers can improve their understanding of the complexities of teaching ELLs. They not only enhance their knowledge and experiences, but also reflect upon their learning process throughout the project.

CONCLUSION

Future ESOL teachers need to understand that they will serve as advocates for their ELLs—sometimes as their only advocate. The Cultural Identity Activity not only helps preservice teachers understand their own cultural identity, but it also positions them to support and advocate for their students. Completing an ELL case study can also give PSTs the knowledge and skills necessary to ensure that their English learners' needs are addressed. Silvina, one of the preservice teachers who conducted an ELL case study, said,

> I thought it was a great experience. I liked discussing with her [the ELL], having conversation with her about her background and how she came to be in the U.S., the different difficulties and challenges that she's having. Learning her second language learning development and cultural experiences were eye-opening to me. As a native American person who hasn't had those experiences, it gave me a lot more insight into the great challenges that she had. So it helped me to be a better teacher for my future ELLs.

Both of these assignments are important steps that can help preservice teachers take on the mantle of advocacy.

Figure 8.2. Case study rubric

	Poor	Adequate	Target	Possible Points out of 20
Writing and Presentation of Content (societal, linguistic, background, language analysis, problems, perspectives, and solution)	• Presentation of the study was disorganized. • One or more components of the content were missing. • The analysis of the study was superficial. • There were spelling and grammatical errors.	• Presentation of the study was organized. • All components were included in order. • The analysis of the study was developed adequately. • Proper grammar and spelling were used.	• Presentation of the study was clearly organized and easy to follow. • The analysis of the study was thoughtful and articulated useful implications. • There were no spelling or grammatical errors. • The level of writing was appropriate and formal.	
Assessment/Data Analysis (focus on reading and writing): Miscue analysis and/or think-aloud protocol	• The preservice teacher used limited assessments and conducted superficial data analysis.	• The preservice teacher used various assessments and conducted adequate data analysis.	• The preservice teacher used various assessments, conducted in-depth data analysis, and developed implications. • Analysis was thoughtful, complete, and insightful.	
Creation of transcription and discussion questions	• Less than 5 minutes of transcription and discussion questions were created.	• Around 5 minutes of transcription and discussion questions were created.	• Well over 5 minutes of transcription and outstanding discussion questions are created. • Discussion questions are complete, appropriate to the analysis, and detailed in their treatment of the issues.	
Podcasting (interview segments and reading segments)	• Preservice teacher conducted live interview but did not upload the podcast.	• The podcast is uploaded but contains a minimal amount of audio.	• The podcast is complete and uploaded to the correct forum. It is clear and understandable.	
Blogging and uploading of materials	• The study has been uploaded. Materials contain very limited parts of the study.	• The study has been developed using various materials in an adequate manner.	• The study has been uploaded using various materials and developed completely, insightfully, and creatively.	
Overall Scores and Comments				

NOTE

1. Dr. Julia Aguirre developed this activity and the guidelines that follow. She teaches at the University of Washington at Tacoma.

REFERENCES

Barnes, L. B., Christensen, C. R., & Hansen, A. J. (1994). *Teaching and the case method: Text, cases, and readings.* Boston, MA: Harvard Business School Press.

Campbell, G. (2005). There's something in the air: Podcasting in education. *Educause Review, 40*(6), 33–46.

Celedón-Pattichis, S. (2004). Rethinking policies and procedures for placing English language learners in mathematics. *NABE Journal of Research and Practice, 2*(1), 176–192.

De Oliveira, L. C., & Athanases, S. Z. (2007). Graduates' reports of advocating for English language learners. *Journal of Teacher Education, 58*(3), 202–215.

Erben, A., & Zoran, A. (2005). Case study pedagogy for preservice teachers working with English language learners: Studies from reflective practice. In J. Govonni (Ed.), *Perspectives on teaching K–12 English language learners* (pp. 121–142). Thousand Oaks, CA: Sage.

Goodman, Y., Watson, D., & Burke, C. (2005). *Reading miscue inventory: From evaluation to instruction.* Katonah, NY: Richard C. Owen.

Kim, D. (2011). Incorporating podcasting and blogging into a core task for ESOL teacher candidates. *Computers and Education, 56*(3), 632–641.

Ladson-Billings, G. (2009). *The dreamkeepers: Successful teachers of African American children.* San Francisco, CA: Jossey-Bass.

McIntosh, P. (2003). White privilege and male privilege: A personal account of coming to see correspondences through work in women's studies. In M. S. Kimmel & A. B. Ferber (Eds.), *A reader: Privilege* (pp. 147–160). Boulder, CO: Westview Press.

Richardson, W. (2006). Making waves [Electronic version]. *School Library Journal, 52*(10), 54–56.

Valdés, G. (2001). *Learning and not learning English: Latino students in American schools.* New York, NY: Teachers College Press.

CHAPTER 9

(Foreign) Language Education

Lessons from a Journey in Rethinking "Diversity" and Thinking About Privilege[1]

Adam Schwartz

For an overconfident minute there, I thought we were really onto something. My first session of Secondary Methods in Foreign Language Education seemed promising. After welcoming my new students with a bit of streaming bilingual music, we followed with the requisite introductions and syllabus review, and I decided to present the class with a series of images as a way of introducing the idea of linguistic landscape. In theory, linguistic landscape is simple: Language is all around us, literally, visually, and from one moment to the next. (cf. Leeman & Modan, 2009). Multiple languages, styles, and scripts greet our eyes, stimulate our senses, and shape the way we inhabit and experience our lived realities.

After a brief introduction to this concept, I presented two photographs to the class, one at a time, both of storefronts featuring multilingual signage. I gave students a moment to take in the visuals and take notes on their initial reactions. The first photo was of a colorfully painted service station in Austin, Texas, a locally owned business called Leal's Tire Shop (see Figure 9.1).

The second photograph was from my own collection; taken at night, it features the glowing signage of Main Deli on Montreal's Boulevard Saint-Laurent (see Figure 9.2).

I asked: "What are you reading?" "Who in the photograph is reading this?" "Why are these 'landscapes' designed in the way they appear here?" Finally, "Where do you think this is?" Not one of my students identified the locations of these photographs right away. After a few questions, a future French teacher located Main Deli correctly; Montreal, in fact, was a city he had once visited. He didn't decode the faux Hebrew script as such; one student guessed Arabic and another thought it was of East Indian origin. I offered a chart of the alef-bet

(Hebrew alphabet) to allow students to make the connections visually (The *I* and *N* in "MAIN" are graphically identical to the symbols used to convey letters *vav* [ו] and *alef* [א] in Hebrew). Leal's seemed a lost cause, although a future Spanish teacher swore she had seen this (or a similar?) business in a nearby town here in Florida.[2]

This icebreaker felt great. Students were raising and answering their own questions and defending their claims with impassioned arguments explaining why Leal's could be in Puerto Rico ("After all, they use English there!") and how the deli looked like New York City, but had to be in Paris. Students were justifying linguistic landscapes in ways that reaffirmed the ways in which they saw, thought, and imagined their multilingual worlds. We took a break and then tackled the readings for the day, one of them appropriately titled "When Methodology Fails" (Reagan & Osborn, 2002).

The preceding vignette captures my state of mind at the close of my first year (which coincided with the close of my first methods class) as an assistant professor of Foreign Language Education. As I reflect on this a few years later, I review my experience in both personal and professional contexts. I begin this discussion, then, by sharing how I came to be an educator of prospective (foreign) language teachers.

Figure 9.1. Leal's Tire Shop, Austin, Texas (2004)

Photo: Mai Kuha

Figure 9.2. Main Deli, Montreal, Quebec, Canada (2006)

Photo: Adam Schwartz

CRITICAL PEDAGOGY:
TEACHING LANGUAGE TEACHERS ABOUT PRIVILEGE

As a Spanish language speaker who grew up in a monolingual English home, I identify with Spanish learners who come from similar sociolinguistic backgrounds. I have benefitted handsomely from the privileges of being White, male, and a native speaker of a relatively standard variety of U.S. English. I appreciate how learning a second language highlights attitudes and ideologies about what it means to speak a language "well." Just like several of my students, I studied a grammatically standard, monolingual, and Eurocentric variety of Spanish that could allow me to "pass for a native," no matter where in the Spanish-speaking world I might find myself. That said, I am fascinated with how a privileged stance shapes students' identities as language learners and how students' performances of these identities reflect their relationship to the larger societal order. For instance, I wonder how student motivation and achievement in Spanish classes is influenced by their complex physical appearance: "looking" White, Latina/o, male, female, wealthy, poor, American, or "foreign."

To support education students in recognizing how privilege affects their thinking about language teaching, I invite them to consider the statement, "Not all bilingualisms are created equal." Native speakers of English learning Spanish are rarely aware of the overt criticisms that riddle native Spanish speakers of color who are learning English. This contradiction in expectations is governed by larger policies and ideologies that uphold standard English as a mainstream "American" language (Lippi-Green, 1997/2012). In order to illustrate this ideologically to students, I find it necessary to implicate my own privileges honestly to my students, often within the first few weeks of class. I explain that while I've not once been expected to speak Spanish while showing my face anywhere north of the U.S.-Mexico borderlands (classrooms are exceptions to that rule), I'm regularly congratulated on my ability to do so seemingly "like a native."

To provide another example of the privileges with which one is born (e.g., Whiteness, maleness, and high social and class capital), I also share the story of my college roommate Paul. Born to a Mexican mother and an Italian father, Paul is blond and light-skinned and fits the All-American boy phenotype even more than I, and certainly more so than his older, darker siblings. Raised solely by his bilingual mother in Southern California, Paul and his brothers grew up speaking both Spanish and English at home, with friends, and at school. From an early age, Paul was regularly asked by teachers and other adults to translate messages directed to his older brothers or mother. By virtue of arbitrary luck, really—his appearance and theirs—it was assumed that he spoke English fluently and that his "family" could not. Paul's bilingualism is also *additive*, while that of his siblings and mother is more often *subtractive*. Paul's brothers and mother—along with their linguistic abilities and intelligence—will be questioned in ways that Paul or I have never experienced; that is, we've never been questioned in our ability to *understand* and *comprehend* others. And in this sense, it becomes clear when and how language use becomes an icon of racial identification (cf. Urcuioli, 1996, 2011).

Such inequalities of who gets to use and benefit from "good" or "bad" language and how—this all underlies how we teach "foreign" languages in the United States, and to whom. Discourses of low expectations and high rewards are foundational to the institutionalization of *elective* Spanish language in K–16 curricula as enrichment (Bale, 2011; Leeman, 2007), where the opposite is true in *circumstantial* second language education.[3] For students who find themselves assigned to the latter camp, success often involves rapid immersion into English-only classrooms, "so that multilingual learners can quickly be absorbed into regular district programs and become invisible in policy and practice" (Mitchell, 2012, p. 6).

This language-as-problem versus language-as-resource double standard (Ruiz, 1984) extends to language use locally, nationally, and internationally. Ways of speaking are highly politicized and racialized among varieties of any language, whether we dismiss African American English as improper and uneducated, or essentialize peninsular Spanish as stuffy and imperialist. How can these realities inform how we teach Spanish and other languages? How can we encourage language education less as mastery of a monolingual foreign code and instead encourage a mastery of bilingualism *itself* as a necessary entrée into a more critical understanding of race, privilege, gender, voice, and access in our own local, culturally diverse communities here in the United States? Additionally, how do we mindfully educate teachers when they are entering fields where their own titles—teachers of *foreign* languages—may reference the aforementioned inequalities of race, privilege, voice, and access? These are questions I wish I had successfully unpacked with the preservice teachers in the Methods of Teaching Foreign Languages class. In the remainder of this chapter, I will explain what I have learned and the assignments and activities that I have designed to address education students' needs while also teaching about privilege and inequities in foreign language education. Admittedly, I don't claim to have simple answers to the above questions—nor a clean template with which another language teacher educator might follow to achieve those results. Answering these questions requires continuous dialogue with cohorts upon cohorts of preservice teachers (not to mention with colleagues, friends, and oneself), and that's a wealth of experience I simply cannot yet claim. However, I gladly share how these questions have allowed me and my students to think and rethink "diversity" since teaching that first Methods course.

"GOOD LANGUAGE LEARNERS" AND CRITICAL PEDAGOGY

I am a practitioner of critical pedagogy in language teacher education. Leeman (2005) concisely articulates *visibility, voice, agency,* and *activism* as central to what is termed *critical language pedagogy*:

> Critical language pedagogy demands that educators see language—like education—as a site of struggle,[4] and that together with our students, we explore its sociopolitical implications in the production of knowledge, culture and identities. Central to critical approaches to language pedagogy, then, are the dialogic examination and questioning of sociopolitical hierarchies—and in particular the role of language in those hierarchies, the promotion of student voice and agency, and the commitment to democratic social change. (p. 36)

Given this, I encourage students to see their bilingualism as a tool in making the world a better place, one conscious and critical of inequality in its multiple forms (Kramsch, 1997; Leeman, Rabin, & Román-Mendoza, 2011). Yet thinking critically about how we learn to use language is something many future teachers do not expect to encounter. Many education students have achieved a "good language learner identity" (Norton & Toohey, 2001; Pomerantz, 2008) by proficiently mastering a textbook-centered curriculum of vocabulary quizzes, grammar translation exercises, and oral presentations. They have not been encouraged to rethink "diversity" or critically examine connections among culture, privilege, and oppression. Robinson (1978) described this foreign language curricular agenda as a "magic-carpet-ride-to-another-culture syndrome," where a survey of folklore, history literature, and conversational pragmatics is perpetually linked to understanding language as bounded to foreign, geographical locales outside of the United States. Foreign language education is predicated on the notion that local linguistic diversity—and by extension, local bilingual voices—are not worth acknowledgment, or at worst, simply don't exist (Leeman & Martínez, 2007). We fail to help students see and challenge how language organizes and is organized by social and racial divisions that contribute to the maintenance of oppressive social structures, while allowing us to feel at home—to be "Americans" here in the United States.

In addition to teaching a methods course for preservice teachers, I teach a required preservice-level course called Current Trends. This course, as the title implies, introduces PSTs to recent research and practice in the field. The activities in the following section are used in both courses.

ACTIVITIES: DIVERSITY AS PROCESS

Many preservice (foreign) language teachers enter professional education because of a deep love and enjoyment of language learning and *identifying* bilingually. They enjoy the prospect of teaching others a second language in order to help their own students reap these rewards. However, preservice teachers' (PSTs) needs are diverse on both personal and professional levels. For one, a methods classroom will need to accommodate PSTs' interests in a variety of languages (Spanish, French, Chinese, Arabic, and even Latin). PSTs also come to our classrooms with diverse life experiences and wildly different orientations to a profession of which they may or may not be familiar. Teaching these PSTs has taught me a great deal about diverse populations of teachers and how they imagine *themselves* as language educators. Methods inspired me to teach critical language education by modeling critical pedagogy in my own instruction. The remainder of this chapter describes assignments that I have developed and used to support students in "becoming critical" (Carr & Kemmis, 1986).

Doing the Groundwork

Preservice teachers may feel more secure and ready to explore critical pedagogy after they have the opportunity to create a repertoire of teaching strategies that focus on multiple language learning techniques. For this purpose, I assign *Techniques and Principles in Language Teaching* (Larsen-Freedman & Anderson, 2011), an accessible handbook-style volume. Each chapter (an exploration of an individual method) concludes with a critical discussion of the effectiveness and disadvantages to a given approach, thus contributing to Larsen-Freeman and Anderson's (2011) contention that "teacher educators can help teachers become . . . clear on where they stand [and thus] choose to teach differently than the way they were taught" (p. xi). The Larsen-Freedman and Anderson text offers an authoritative foundation for the co-construction of knowledge and support of the idea that students can learn to be professional advocates for socially responsive curriculum.

INTENDED OUTCOMES

Students are invited to spend the first week scanning and reviewing chapters that cover methods with which they are most familiar (e.g., the Grammar-Translation Method, the Direct Method, and the Audio-Lingual Method). Then we explore methods based in communicative competence (Canale & Swain, 1980; Hymes, 1971),[5] including Communicative Language Teaching, Content-Based Instruction, and Task-Based Language Teaching. At this point, students make their first written contribution to an online discussion board, for all class members to see and comment upon. Each post is anchored by a keyword of a student's choosing: a particular "loaded" concept or phrase from or related to the Larsen-Freedman and Anderson chapters that struck the student's interest (some popular choices were "authenticity," "indigenous," and "identity"). Students define and connect their term to one of the communicative methods they had studied in the Larsen-Freedman and Anderson volume in an original, practical way relating to instruction. This proves difficult for many, but when students are asked to articulate the connection, they appear to take their time in formulating arguments online and pay attention to cues from other classmates' posts. Here, I am able to observe patterns in students' selections and respond to their needs and interests appropriately.

Future posts (due every other week) feature this same pattern, as students choose and connect new keywords of relevance to their professional interest and engage in commentary with their classmates—we call this a Discussion Cycle. Luckily some students naturally gravitate toward terms that require prior notions of diversity to be challenge and reconstructed. Other activities on the schedule (interviews with local language teachers about what they would explore in a methods class knowing what they know now) aim to enhance this process of knowledge production and turn any keyword exploration into a socially responsive exercise.

Recognizing and Interrogating Privilege

INTENDED OUTCOMES

I share a narrative of my early experience teaching middle school Spanish in an effort to demonstrate how complex and often problematic language ideologies (informing my own biases as a teacher, at times) shape the realities in which we teach a "foreign" language. In this short case study, entitled "Fred, Pedro, Peter, and Mike," I appear as "Fred," although I purposely wait to disclose this connection until the end. Through pointed reflection questions, participants explore how attitudes and ideologies about the languages we learn (and those we speak "natively") emerge as inherently personal and local . . . and hardly *foreign* (See Figure 9.3).

Responding to and Engaging with Practicing Teachers' Expertise

INTENDED OUTCOMES

According to hooks (2010), self-reflection is essential to critical pedagogy at any level. For language teachers, this might be best realized in mentorship with a seasoned (or more novice!) educator currently working in a local K–12 classroom. This assignment is designed to help PSTs engage critically with an educator and his or her lived experiences in a classroom environment. Students' work is scaffolded with an interview template (see Figure 9.4).

Asking teachers to contribute their own keywords, just as students had, is to not only validate the exercise as relevant outside the university context but to empower PSTs to respond to

Figure 9.3. Sample Case Study

"Fred, Pedro, Peter and Mike": A Case Study

Fred is an in-service language teacher at a local charter middle school in urban Arizona. In his mid-20s, Fred is a native English-speaking White male who has spent most of his life learning and speaking Spanish, both socially and academically. He self-identifies as bilingual, and since graduating from college, has taught Spanish in various settings. At the middle school, he's been hired to not only teach Spanish, but to design and implement an exciting new language program in which all students will participate. Beginner-level classes will be required for 6th, 7th and 8th graders. He's enjoyed the challenge, and by and large Fred gets great support from his colleagues and parents.

A few of his students come from Spanish-speaking families, and as such, their proficiency and literacy skills in Spanish vary, although all are native English speakers. One student, Peter (Fred enjoys using names in Spanish with his students, and so Peter is affectionately called "Pedro") can understand and produce very little Spanish; he's a third-generation Mexican American who hasn't necessarily been encouraged to identify as such. While his Spanish-speaking grandmother disagrees, it seems that his father, Miguel (A military veteran who insists on being called *Mike*), is a strict disciplinarian who has instilled in Peter to take pride in being an "American who happens to be of Mexican heritage."

After noting some behavioral problems with Peter in class, coupled with recent failing vocabulary quiz scores, Fred decides to phone Mike to discuss the situation. After Fred invites Mike to join him in designing a plan for his son's improvement, Mike accepts the offer half-heartedly. He agrees to work with Peter on his "discipline," but uses the moment to express his distaste with the Spanish curriculum Fred has designed, questioning the value of the vocabulary quizzes in the first place. "I can understand learning a few key conversational phrases," Mike says. "But we live in America. Peter needs to focus on mastering English first."

Fred is speechless. He's not sure what to say to Peter's father, and never thought a conversation with a parent would ever turn in such a politicized direction. It's certainly not what he had in mind when he "signed up" to become a Spanish teacher.

Questions for Discussion

1. Read and re-read the passage carefully. What about this story surprises you? What resonates with you? Do you identify with any of the "players" in this story? Do you find any of their actions problematic? Who and why?
2. Choose a phrase or comment that reflects the language ideologies to which Mike and Fred subscribe. Explain what your phrase articulates directly and indirectly, and how it informs what either Mike or Fred feel is in Peter's best interests as a student and Spanish speaker.
3. How do racial, ethnic, and linguistic identities play a part in this case? Be specific.
4. Why is it significant that such a "politicized" conversation doesn't reflect what Fred had in mind when he "signed up" to teach Spanish? What does that phrase mean to you, anyway? And, why is it significant that what Fred may have "signed up" for went challenged here?
5. Is this case relevant to you as a teacher? Why or why not?

Figure 9.4. Current Trends Interview Template

Interviewer's name: _____

Teacher's name: _____

Years teaching in current school (including this year): _____

Total years of teaching experience (including this year): _____

Current school and level of instruction (elementary, middle, high, university, etc.):
_____

Courses currently teaching: _____

Previous language teaching history (include levels and courses taught):
_____

After years of experience teaching _____ language at the _____ level(s), consider what you've learned about language education. If you were in my shoes, and back in school taking a Current Trends techniques/principles course, what three concepts would you want to study and why? Choose any three. The "term" can be one word or a particular phrase.

Key Term/Concept 1: _____

Key Term/Concept 2: _____

Key Term/Concept 3: _____

Please elaborate on your definition of these terms, and be as specific as possible. What do these terms "look like" in the classroom and in the lives of your students, for instance?

Elaboration on 1: _____

Elaboration on 2: _____

Elaboration on 3: _____

How did you select these terms? Why do you feel that a study of these terms is so relevant to your teaching career and mine?

Answer for 1: _____

Answer for 2: _____

Answer for 3: _____

unimagined, real-life teacher concerns. PSTs can be asked to consider questions such as the following:

- What did you learn about this teacher and his or her ideas about "trendy" terms or ideas in language teaching? What are three "findings" upon reflecting on your interview results?
- Although "diversity" may not have been discussed in your interview overtly, how were ideas of diversity (linguistic, cultural, sociopolitical—i.e., additive and subtractive bilingualism) constructed in your teacher's conversations about his or her students and classroom?
- What in this interview did you appreciate learning, and why? What challenged you? What did you disagree with, and why?

In addition, a teacher-colleague eclipses the role of textbook or college-based instructor. The teacher interview, when followed with a shared and critical dialogue in the classroom (e.g., visually mapping out keywords from interviews, identifying and analyzing patterns or rifts in responses between teachers of different languages, etc.), may allow students to reconstruct their ideas about diversity in K–12 classrooms and move away from definitions that posit difference as a deficit.

Photographs as Transformative Texts

In this activity, I encourage PSTs to complete a photo-diary assignment that could easily be assigned to their own students. Helen Terry (a Spanish teacher and doctoral student who was researching culturally responsive Spanish language education) has tried this assignment with her own beginner-level classes. Helen and I contend that this photo-diary work[6] engages all members of a language classroom to recognize multilingual community voices as culturally and historically authorita-

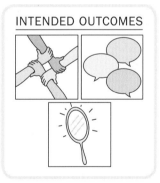

INTENDED OUTCOMES

tive (Terry & Schwartz, 2013). To fulfill the assignment, students respond to questions with their own photographs and then reflect upon these unique "texts" and respond to their classmates' contributions through both their own authored texts and photos. Terry's simple yet pointed questions elicit diverse attitudes toward language standardization (her specific exercise included *"¿Quién habla el 'español verdadero'?"*/"Who speaks 'real Spanish'?"), identify and locate community bilingualism (*"¿Dónde se habla español en tu comunidad?"*/"Where is Spanish spoken in your community?"), and complicate relationships between language, culture, and identity (*"¿Qué es la cultura hispanohablante?"*/"What is Spanish-speaking culture?"). Students may submit their responses in all forms, from photos of family members and coworkers to snapshots of restaurants and trilingual newspapers (a local publication, *La Gaceta,* prints in English, Spanish, and Italian).

In a college-level course, asking students to take photographs and then offer written reflection empowers them all to reconsider language instruction as not just an act of teaching language, but teaching *about* the nature of language. In so doing, this co-constructed learning becomes inclusive of critical counternarratives (Solórzano & Yosso, 2002) to "standard" expectations for learning Spanish, French, Chinese, or Arabic. Learners not only use the photos and written word to practice narration and composition, they also use a second language to reflect crucially on the socially constructed hierarchies of language use in their daily lives (Leeman & Martínez, 2007; Martínez, 2003).

UNDOING THE "FOREIGN" IN (FOREIGN) LANGUAGE EDUCATION: RECONSIDERING WHAT LANGUAGE "LOOKS LIKE" LOCALLY

This section does not describe a specific activity or assignment. Instead, it lays out a rationale for the argument that teacher educators should set up courses so that classroom communities are "critically engaging in and demonstrating values and classroom practices that can counteract the limited knowledge and normative practices so common in schools today" (Swartz, 2009, p. 1044). In order to interrogate the inequity inherent in typical school practices, coursework must unpack the assumptions and ideologies to which preservice and inservice teachers alike are expected to subscribe. Language and culture isn't just "ours" (students' and teachers') for the taking; these aren't simply targets for which "good teaching" aims. Critical educators must actively fight to end the oppressive traditions of exploiting, exoticizing, and stereotyping of cultural practices that make us consider a language "foreign." We may do this by facilitating systematic participation of local bilingual voices (from family members, community organizers, etc.) in our courses, in order to bring in the assumptions and ideologies of the speakers of non-English languages, to make language *un*-foreign through the inclusion of the voices of community members as holders of cultural expertise. These conversations can support language teachers in participating with community members to ensure first-language maintenance and to pre-serve diverse linguistic and cultural heritages.

CONCLUSION

Foreign Language methodology courses present unique challenges for practitioners of critical pedagogy. As an educator *and* a student of the social sciences, I'm of the belief that methods should and can change according to sociopolitical and local contexts. In addition, teachers should be critical consumers of the methods that are institutionalized as "normal." This involves encouraging critical inquiry that is interdisciplinary in nature and indeed necessitates a constant rethinking of "what we signed up for" when thinking about our roles as language educators. This rethinking is particularly needed in light of the schizophrenic policies that govern language use in the United States. To that end, I invite my colleagues and their students alike to visit and comment on the hard work my students have put forth in their quest to problematize and critically situate "Current Trends" keywords in today's language classrooms. Their Wikipedia-style entries on terms such as *identity, motivation, communi-ty*, and *intercultural speakers* can be found at languageeducation.pbworks.com.

NOTES

1. Gracias y saludos a mis amigos y colegas Bárbara Cruz y Juan Antonio Trujillo, with whom I enjoy sharing inspired dialogue and debate. Their wisdom helped tremen-dously to improve portions of this chapter.

2. At the time of this writing, I was teaching at a large research university in Florida.

3. Valdés (1992) explains this distinction: "Elective bilinguals become bilingual as in-dividuals. The group to which they belong has little to do with their decision to become speakers of another language. Circumstantial bilinguals, on the other hand, are generally members of a group of individuals who as a group must become bilingual in order to par-ticipate in the society that surrounds them" (p. 39).

4. Speaking as an African American woman, bell hooks (1995) also defines "language as struggle" in her own relationship with Black English and its (and by extension her) re-lationship to standard, Anglophone English. Reflecting on a poem by the late Adrienne Rich, hooks writes, "I know that it is not the English language that hurts me, but what the oppressors do with it, how they shape it to become a territory that limits and defines, how they make it a weapon that can shame, humiliate, colonize. Gloria Anzaldúa reminds us of this pain in *Borderlands/La Frontera* [1987] when she asserts, 'So, if you want to really hurt me, talk badly about my language'" (hooks, 1995, p. 296).

5. Communicative competence continues to be maintained as a central hallmark of language proficiency (Savignon, 1997) and has thus been endorsed programmatically by

the Modern Language Association (MLA), ACTFL/NCATE standards for teacher education, and the postsecondary Association of Departments of Foreign Languages (ADFL).

6. This multimodal approach to community engagement stems from photovoice, a participatory research technique (Booth & Booth, 2003; Graziano & Litton, 2007; Wang, 1999).

REFERENCES

Anzaldúa, G. (1987). *Borderlands/La Frontera: The new mestiza.* San Francisco, CA: Spinsters/Aunt Lute.

Bale, J. (2011). Tongue-tied: Imperialism and second language education in the United States. *Critical Education, 2*(8). Retrieved from ojs.library.ubc.ca/index.php/criticaled

Booth, T., & Booth, W. (2003). In the frame: Photovoice and mothers with learning difficulties. *Disability & Society, 18*(4), 431–442.

Canale, M., & Swain, M. (1980). Theoretical bases of communicative approaches to second language teaching and testing. *Applied Linguistics, 1*, 1–147.

Carr, W., & Kemmis, S. (1986). *Becoming critical: Education knowledge and action research.* New York, NY: Falmer.

Graziano, K. J., & Litton, E. F. (2007). First year teachers and diversity: Teacher research through photography. *Issues in Teacher Education, 16*(1), 7–19.

hooks, b. (1995). Killing rage, ending racism. New York, NY: Henry Holt.

hooks, b. (2010). *Teaching critical thinking: Practical wisdom.* New York, NY: Routledge.

Hymes, D. (1971). Competence and performance in linguistic theory. In R. Huxley & E. Ingram (Eds.), *Language acquisition: Models and methods* (pp. 3–28). London, England: Academic Press.

Kramsch, C. (1997). The privilege of the nonnative speaker. *PMLA, 112*(3), 359–369.

Larsen-Freeman, D., & Anderson, M. (2011). *Techniques and principles in language teaching* (3rd ed.). Oxford, U.K.: Oxford University Press.

Leeman, J. (2005). Engaging critical pedagogy: Spanish for native speakers. *Foreign Language Annals, 38*(1), 35–45.

Leeman, J. (2007). The value of Spanish: Shifting ideologies in United States language teaching. *ADFL Bulletin, 38*(1–2), 32–39.

Leeman, J., & Martínez, G. (2007). From identity to commodity: Ideologies of Spanish in heritage language textbooks. *Critical Inquiry in Language Studies, 4*(1), 35–65.

Leeman, J., & Modan, G. (2009). Commodified language in Chinatown: A contextualized approach to linguistic landscape. *Journal of Sociolinguistics, 13*(3), 332–362.

Leeman, J., Rabin, L., & Román-Mendoza, E. (2011). Identity and activism in heritage language education. *Modern Language Journal, 95*(4), 481–495.

Lippi-Green, R. (2012). *English with an accent.* New York, NY: Routledge. (Original work published 1997)

Martínez, G. (2003). Classroom based dialect awareness in heritage language instruction: A critical applied linguistic approach. *Heritage Language Journal, 1*(1). Retrieved from www.heritagelanguages.org

Mitchell, K. (2012). English is not *all* that matters in the education of secondary multilingual learners and their teachers. *International Journal of Multicultural Education, 14*(1), 1–21.

Norton, B., & Toohey, K. (2001). Changing perspectives on good language learners. *TESOL Quarterly, 35*(2), 307–322.

Pomerantz, A. (2008). "Tú necesitas preguntar en español": Negotiating good language learner identity in a Spanish classroom. *Journal of Language, Identity and Education, 7,* 253–271.

Reagan, T. G., & Osborn, T. A. (2002). *The foreign language educator in society.* Mahwah, NJ: Lawrence Erlbaum.

Robinson, G. L. (1978). The magic-carpet-ride-to-another-culture syndrome: An international perspective. *Foreign Language Annals, 11*(2), 135–146.

Ruiz, R. (1984). Orientations in language planning. *NABE Journal, 8*(2), 15–34.

Savignon, S. (1997). Communicative competence: Theory and classroom practice (2nd ed.). New York, NY: McGraw-Hill.

Solórzano, D., & Yosso, T. (2002). Critical race methodology: Counter-storytelling as analytical framework for education research. *Qualitative Inquiry, 8*(1), 23–44.

Swartz, E. (2009). Diversity: Gatekeeping knowledge and maintaining inequalities. *Review of Educational Research, 79*(2), 1044–1083.

Terry, H., & Schwartz, A. (2013, March). *"Esta fotographia es de mis abuelos": Participatory research as critical pedagogy in a L2 Spanish course.* Paper presented at the XXIV Conference on Spanish in the U.S. & VIV Spanish in Contact with Other Languages, McAllen, TX.

Urcuioli, B. (1996). *Exposing prejudice: Puerto Rican experiences of language, race, and class.* Boulder, CO: Westview Press.

Urcuioli, B. (2011). Discussion essay: Semiotic properties of racializing discourses. *Journal of Linguistic Anthropology, 21*(S1), E113–E122.

Valdés, G. (1992). Bilingual minorities and language issues in writing: Toward profession-wide responses to a new challenge. *Written Communication, 9,* 85–136,

Wang, C. C. (1999). Photovoice: A participatory action research strategy applied to women's health. *Journal of Women's Health, 8*(2), 185–192.

CHAPTER 10

Exceptional Student Education

Utilizing the Arts to Facilitate Inclusive Environments

Patricia Alvarez McHatton and Roseanne K. Vallice

A colleague and the first author of this chapter were conducting a project investigating the experiences of and attitudes about differently positioned students. We use the term "differently positioned" to refer to diverse populations of students (with regard to the following categories: achievement, disabilities, culture, language, ethnicity, socioeconomic status, sexual orientation, and gender) who are alternately positioned within schools and communities from their dominant culture peers. The following excerpt is from a group interview conducted with gifted high school students. Their comments relate to their perceptions regarding the physical environment of the school (emphasis added in italics).

Student A: I don't think they should have like I know that there is a 6th-grade[1] hallway and that's for like the *physically retarded* kids but our lockers are there and *some of us can't emotionally handle that* like the first couple of days I'd come home crying like I can't be around *those type of people*. So I think they should have a building just for our lockers. It's like I'm the one walking behind the kid with crutches and he walks like in slow motion but *I feel bad for him* but then again I can't like get to class and I can't get past him and I have to hold the door open for him and *it's sad and inconvenient*.
Student B: And I've been nearly run over by wheelchairs thousands of times. They race around.
Student C: It's worse than *actual* people like I got pushed really hard today.
Student D: I think that we would be better if the physically and mentally handicapped people were *in their own like completely removed area*. And have like their own stuff. So we wouldn't have to like . . .

I remember the first time I read through the transcript. While the students' comments signify a privileged existence, I found myself asking how students with disabilities were perceived by the teachers and other adults in that setting. As someone who spends a great deal of time in schools, I see the failure by adults to act when students call each other "faggot" or "retard," and I am reminded of a presentation by Rothenberg (2006) in which she stated, "What you don't say will still be heard." The students' responses suggest a setting in which silence is thunderous.

The comments made by these high school students are not unlike some of the comments we have heard from general education preservice teachers who are completing the one course they take that pertains to addressing students with disabilities (Integrating Exceptional Students in General Education Settings). Most believe they won't have "those kinds of kids" in their classroom; "that's what the special education teacher is for." At the end of this particular course, all realize that they will have students with disabilities in their classroom, and while special educators will be there to support them, they are not there to serve as a mediator between the general educator and the student. Rather, they are there to assist by providing instructional strategies that meet the needs of the wide range of students that will be in the general education setting. In addition, the role of the special education teacher is also to assist the general educator with appropriate accommodations to ensure maximum access to the curriculum by students with disabilities.

In this chapter, we address the concept of difference and how perceptions of difference can cause stigmatization and discrimination for students with disabilities within the classroom, as well as for families of students with disabilities, as they attempt to maneuver the educational system. Further, we provide instructional strategies, activities, and resources used in our course to address the notion of difference with teacher candidates and engage them in an introspective journey through which they examine their personal biases and beliefs.

Current reform efforts, including No Child Left Behind (NCLB) and the Individuals with Disabilities Education Improvement Act (IDEA) 1997 and 2004, have resulted in increased accountability for the educational outcomes of students both without and with disabilities. The U.S. Department of Education (2012) reports that 57.2% of students with disabilities spend approximately 80% or more of the day in general education settings. Implications of this finding are significant for all teachers but perhaps most specifically for general education teachers, who may lack the foundational understanding of the various disability categories, associated characteristics, and how these characteristics are manifested in the classroom. Furthermore, many of these students, who learn in different ways, may require accommodations that at times run contrary to many teachers' personal views regarding student performance both academically and behaviorally. For example, the use of a calculator may be necessary for students with learning disabilities who have difficulty memorizing the multiplication tables as a result of challenges with retrieving information due to memory deficits. This differentiation brings into question the concept of fairness. Many preservice and inservice teachers define "fair" as all students getting the same thing versus providing for individual needs to ensure equal access to instruction. In other words, the notion of fairness supersedes the need for equity (i.e., ensuring access and opportunity to a high-quality education for all students). Inherent in this reality is what Minow (1990) refers to as the dilemma of difference, which suggests that identification of a difference (i.e., disability) may lead to stigmatization and discrimination. Yet failure to identify a difference may do likewise, because it does not allow for the needs of the individual to be addressed, thereby diminishing his or her opportunities for success. The questions, "Different from whom?" and "What is the difference that is being highlighted?" are equally important in this process of differentiation of individuals. In addition, society consistently refers to the term "disability" when describing a differently abled individual. In reality an individual who is differently abled is able to live, achieve, and succeed in various ways—clearly not "disabled." We have chosen to focus on the assets these individuals possess rather than the challenges they may face and will use the term "differently abled" throughout most of this chapter.

When discussing individuals who are differently abled, we must consider that the concept of disability is multifaceted. For example, disabilities can be defined as either visible or invisible. Visible disabilities alert us to the fact that the person has a condition that affects the manner in which he or she may perform (e.g., Down's syndrome, cerebral palsy, physical impairments). Responses to visible disabilities often render the individual who is differently abled as invisible due to our own discomfort and biases in interacting with this person. Conversely, invisible disabilities, those that reside within, often render the individual visible in that the lack of academic achievement and/or emotionality displayed is often viewed from a deficit perspective. For example, many teachers may lower expectations, believing that a student with a learning disability will be unable to perform at the same level as their nonidentified peers. Students with behavior disorders may also be disproportionately segregated or disciplined due to overreactions and/or assumptions about them. For students with invisible disabilities, the lack of a physical marker signaling the need for support affects how or even if teachers respond to their academic and social-emotional needs.

Like their children, parents of children with a disability are also often viewed from a deficit perspective, and their behaviors are often labeled as such.

Parents of children with disabilities have been described as neurotic, dysfunctional, and overprotective; or have been accused of being in denial (Ferguson, 2002; Harry, 1997). In addition, service providers lament the lack of parental involvement and passivity while engaging in practices that undermine parental involvement and encourage compliance (Harry, 1992). There are multiple barriers faced by parents of children with disabilities in general and by cultural- and linguistic-minority parents of children with a disability in particular. These barriers point to service providers lacking the cultural competency necessary in collaborating with diverse families. Most service providers belong to the dominant culture and fail to understand the cultural perspectives of the children and families they serve. The intersection of culture, ethnicity, and disability is often overlooked as well (McHatton, 2004). Addressing culturally and linguistically diverse families within the context of exceptionality is essential given the continued disproportionality that exists in special education (Artiles & Bal, 2008). Students of color in general and African American males in particular are overrepresented in disability categories but underrepresented in gifted and talented programs.

Based on the issues described above, teacher educators must engage preservice and inservice teachers in substantive dialogue that facilitates self-reflection. Self-reflection can disclose how teacher candidates feel and respond to visible and/or invisible disabilities as well as how they perceive individuals who are differently abled. Many teacher candidates are not aware of their own biases until they begin this process of self-reflection. Facilitating an exploration of worldviews and personal ideologies by teacher candidates will assist instructors in providing developmentally appropriate instructional activities that will foster growth and understanding of differences.

The following activities can be used in a variety of courses and are structured to engage participants in an introspective journey that entails an analysis of self while exploring the other. Activities are grouped into the following five categories: fostering dialogue, self-reflection, visible disabilities, perceptions of differences, and families. An essential component of all of these activities is the instructor. Prior to using any of these activities in your course, it is imperative that you, as the instructor, have engaged in an introspective journey, examined and understood your own biases, and engaged in professional development to enhance your own understanding of difference. We, as teachers, often spend a great deal of time and effort addressing our students' biases; an equal amount of attention needs to be self-directed. Helping students evolve requires open dialogue. Be prepared for the unexpected, be cognizant of your own responses, and be sure that you are comfortable with discomfort, as this is necessary for change—any change—to occur.

As discussed in Chapter 2, fostering a safe, caring, and civil learning environment where students are comfortable sharing their beliefs and questions is essential for critical dialogue to ensue. The activities in this section are designed to take place at various points during the semester. Some (e.g., Keeping It Real) are better suited for the beginning of the semester. Others (e.g., The Kallikak Family) would be best suited after you have had sufficient time to get to know your students and have developed a safe classroom environment. Each activity allows students to reflect on themselves and their preconceived ideas and beliefs and to reconnect with their own experiences and identities. All serve to help build community and get students to think critically about unquestioned beliefs.

FOSTERING DIALOGUE

Keeping it Real

This activity is based on an excerpt from *The Velveteen Rabbit* (Williams, 1922). We recommend using it at the beginning of the semester. The *Velveteen Rabbit* is a story about the power of love and being accepted for who you truly are. The activity is from the website Group Dynamics and Community Building (www.community4me.com/Velvetveen.html), which provides a variety of resources on group building (Hampton, 2013). The excerpt highlights a conversation between the Velveteen Rabbit and the Skin Horse about what it means to be real. We use the activity on the first day of class as a way to discuss how we each define "real" and to gain commitment from the group for honest dialogue. To conduct this activity, you will need the story excerpt, discussion questions, chart paper, and markers.

INTENDED OUTCOMES

Read the excerpt aloud to the class. Ask students to respond individually in writing to the question, What does it mean to be real? (approximately 5 minutes). In small groups, students share their responses and develop a group response on the chart paper (approximately 15 minutes). Groups post and share their documents. After all the groups have shared their responses, generate continued discussion with the following guiding questions:

- What were the similarities and differences among the responses to the question, "What does it mean to be real?"

- What are some concerns we may have with "keeping it real"?
- How can we foster an environment in which we all feel able to "keep it real"?
- What is the ultimate goal of "keeping it real"?

SELF-REFLECTION

I Come From . . .

This activity can be done at the beginning of the semester. It is adapted from George Ella Lyons's (1999) poem "Where I'm From," which can easily be found online. We first used it in response to an experience we had where students were exploring contemporary culture and its impact on schools. Our previously tight-knit group became defensive and argumentative as discussions of power and privilege were drawn across ethnic lines. Through our discussions, we realized we were all dealing with three selves: one holding onto where we came from, one living in the present, and finally, the one we wanted to be. The "I come from . . ." poem provides a mechanism for students to reconnect with their experiences from early childhood and consider how those influence their current beliefs.

INTENDED OUTCOMES

Provide teacher candidates with a sheet of paper containing the following questions, with these instructions—Reflect on your childhood and list words and phrases that answer these questions:

- What was in your backyard?
- What did your kitchen look like? What was in it?
- What smells were a part of your home life?
- What kinds of sounds did you hear in your house/neighborhood?
- What kinds of foods did you eat?
- What are the names of some of the well-known people in your neighborhood?
- What are some of the sayings or reprimands that were often repeated in your home?

Instruct students to write a poem using the information they compiled. They should begin each stanza with the stem, "I come from . . ." After the teacher candidates complete their poems, ask teacher candidates to volunteer to share them. Once all volunteers have shared their poems, engage teacher candidates in a discussion of how their personal experiences growing up may affect how they interact with students and families.

Short Story: Country of the Blind

"Country of the Blind" (2014/1904) is a short story by H.G. Wells. This activity can be done at any point throughout the semester, although it may work best near the beginning as it provides a mechanism for teacher candidates to deconstruct the concept of disability. The story can be accessed online via www.on-line-literature.com/wellshg/3. It tells the tale of Nunez, a mountaineer who fell into the "unknown side of the mountain" (para. 1) during a climb. He found himself in the Country of the Blind, in which all inhabitants are blind from birth. Joyous that he was alive, he felt further blessed, believing that "in the Country of the Blind the one-eyed man is king" (para. 19). He soon realizes the disadvantage he is placed in as the only sighted person in this country. His continued ranting about what he *sees* is met with concern and distaste by the community members, who believe he is crazy. Soon, Nunez falls in love and is faced with the dilemma of either having his eyes removed in order to gain the elders' blessing on the pending nuptials or leaving the community. Ultimately, he decides that he cannot do without his eyesight and leaves the valley in hopes of returning to his birthplace.

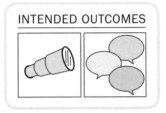

INTENDED OUTCOMES

This story demonstrates the social construction of disability and how the environment can be modified to significantly diminish difficulties for individuals who are differently abled. In this case, Nunez was viewed as an outsider and as the individual who encountered the most difficulties, though in our society, he would be considered "normal." For this activity, you will need copies of the story or the link to the story, activation questions, chart paper, and markers.

Engage teacher candidates in a Think-Pair-Share activity, in which they first individually reflect on the activation questions found below. They then discuss and record on chart paper a summary of their responses to the questions as a group. Finally, each group shares their answers and you facilitate the discussion by asking:

- What is normal?
- What is not?
- Who decides?

- How is the decision made?
- Who has the power to influence the decision?

Have teacher candidates read the story prior to the next class session. At the next class session, have them revisit their previous responses and discuss whether their perceptions have changed as a result of reading the story and, if so, how.

VISIBLE DISABILITIES

Film: *Freaks*

The movie *Freaks* was released in 1932 (Esper & Browning) and at that time was considered a horror movie. The film is available from various vendors, including Amazon, Netflix, and possibly the media center in your university library. We recommend that this film be used sometime during the middle of the semester after ensur-

INTENDED OUTCOMES

ing a safe environment in which participants are comfortable with and willing to engage in substantive and difficult dialogue. The story is set in a circus with the majority of the characters comprising of sideshow "freaks." The main character, Hans, is a little person who is in love with a high-wire trapeze artist, Cleopatra, who is able-bodied and personifies beauty. Cleopatra realizes Hans stands to earn a large sum of money and, as a result, decides to marry him. Her plan is to kill him so she may inherit his fortune. Although she is "normal" and thus considered an outsider, the "freaks" decide to accept her as one of them, based on her relationship with Hans. Once they learn of her desire to do away with Hans, the tight-knit community decides to take revenge on her while also preventing Hans's death. As a result of the attack, Cleopatra becomes disfigured and spends the rest of her life in a sideshow as "the human duck," with webbed hands and lower extremities that are permanently tarred and feathered.

To implement this activity, you will need a copy of the film and the guiding questions provided in Table 10.1. Prior to showing the movie, students are provided some background information on the film (Powell, 1932/2010), including reactions from viewers and consequences for the director (i.e., difficulties obtaining future work) and the studio that produced the film (i.e., it was forced to cut several scenes due to the strong reaction from audiences after the initial screening of the film). After viewing the film, have teacher candidates debrief through a series of guiding questions that are related to societal and cultural perspectives as well as the film itself (see Table 10.1).

Table 10.1. Guiding Questions for the film *Freaks*.

Domain	Guiding Questions
The Film	• How are people with exceptionalities portrayed? • How are they treated by people without exceptionalities and by those with exceptionalities? • What does this portrayal say to society?
Societal Perspectives	• How does society view the characters? • What has contributed to society's view of the characters? • How does this view affect the individuals?
Cultural Perspectives	• How do the cultural groups of the characters affect how they view themselves? • How do the cultural groups of the characters affect how society views them?
Summary	• Based on what you have learned, how does the portrayal of people with disabilities/exceptionalities lead to prejudice and discrimination? • What can be done about this?

Documentary: *I'm Tyler*

I'm Tyler is a documentary film available online at www.Imtyler.org (Greene, 2006). The video may be downloaded or obtained (with or without a donation) from the website and can be shown toward the middle of the semester. The video begins with a White, able-bodied teenager describing his school life and extra-curricular activities, which exemplify the general expectations of what the life of a successful high school student looks like. The character describes his academic success, his participation in the school band, and his engagement in after-school activities (i.e., karate, Boy Scouts, and baseball). Once the audience is informed of all his successes, the character discloses the fact that this life does not actually belong to him but rather to Tyler, who is diagnosed with cerebral palsy. His speech is difficult to understand, and his muscle control is erratic. Tyler begins talking about the people in his life who support and believe in him, while sharing some of his accomplishments and the accommodations that are necessary for participation in certain activities given his disability.

INTENDED OUTCOMES

The purpose of this activity is to uncover personal biases by having teacher candidates reflect on their acceptance of the able-bodied actor versus Tyler, someone with a visible disability, who is fully able to succeed in both academics and extracurricular pursuits. After viewing the video, have teaching candidates engage in a quick writing activity that provides them with an opportunity to express emotions and responses to the video and list any questions that resulted from the viewing. This quick writing usually takes about 5 to 8 minutes after which we engage teacher candidates in a discussion about the video and their responses. During open discussion, most teacher candidates disclose that once they realized that Tyler has a disability, they questioned how well and fully he could really participate in such activities. The discussion uncovers the assumptions we make regarding what people with visible disabilities can and cannot do. The issue of limitations placed on individuals with disabilities resulting from stereotypical views invariably arises.

Film: *The Diving Bell and the Butterfly*

The Diving Bell and the Butterfly (Kennedy, Kilik, & Schnabel, 2007) tells the story of *Elle* editor Jean-Dominique Bauby, who had a stroke at the age of 42. The film is available from Netflix and possibly also the media center at your university library. As with the film *Freaks*, we recommend that it be viewed to-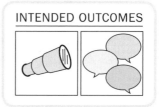ward the middle of the semester after ensuring a safe environment in which participants are comfortable with and willing to engage in substantive and difficult dialogue. As a result of the stroke, Bauby is diagnosed with locked-in syndrome. This syndrome renders him completely paralyzed with the exception of the muscles that control his left eye, which he uses to communicate by blinking the alphabet. Although his body is immobile, his mind is lucid, and he uses the remaining 4 months of his life to write his memoirs. The body entrapment Bauby experienced is cleverly portrayed in the film by having the first 25 minutes of the film viewed through Bauby's eyes. In other words, Bauby's view is the camera's frame; you do not see his face until much later in the film. Through this perspective you are able to see the reactions of the medical community and his family and the manner in which others react to his condition, all while having an insider's view by being privy to Bauby's thoughts, feelings, and reactions.

The film introduces students to possibilities that remain despite barriers that may come with being differently abled. There is also an attempt to personalize the issue of disabilities in the way the story is told. The suddenness of the event that leaves Bauby immobile is important in that it leads students to consider and reflect on the idea that at any moment events can occur to anyone, including themselves, that can render them differently abled. Also, through this film the students come to see the importance of self-determination for people who are differently abled. Ultimately, self-determination and the ways in which we develop self-determination become a pivotal topic in discussing disability.

Prior to students viewing the film, the plot is summarized by the instructor without disclosing the ending. Students are made aware of the awards and nominations received by the movie (see www.imdb.com/title/tt0401383/awards). After viewing the film, students are asked for general reactions to the film. Using Think-Pair-Share, in which students first think about the questions, then discuss them with a partner, and finally share them with a small group (3–4 students), students discuss and respond to four guiding questions:

- Did Jean-Dominique Bauby demonstrate self-determined characteristics throughout his life? Explain your answer.
- How did Jean-Dominique Bauby view himself and his disability?
- How was his identity formed/transformed?
- What transitions did the character experience in accepting or not accepting his disabling condition?

We close the activity with a mini-lecture on self-determination (e.g., definition, essential characteristics, and components of self-determination).

PERCEPTIONS OF DIFFERENCE

Preservice teachers are not always aware that their own backgrounds and experiences shape how they perceive other people, including students. They may believe that purely behavioral analyses of students disallow for personal influences on decisions regarding how children are treated. This activity helps PSTs to recognize their own personal perceptions of difference and thus become more conscious of their personal beliefs and their effects on their students.

Revealing Personal Perceptions of Difference

This is a forced-choice activity (Butler & Mayhew, 2004) whereby teacher candidates must select which students they would remove from their classroom. The purpose is to engage them in a concrete activity that highlights their individual perceptions regarding differently positioned students and requires them to ver-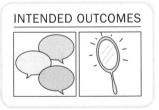

INTENDED OUTCOMES

balize the rationale for their choices. This activity may be better suited for early in the semester, in order to gauge teacher candidates' perceptions of differently abled students. To complete this activity, you will need enough decks of playing cards to provide each group with 4 sets of 25 cards representing students (i.e., a deck contains 52 cards, so you will need to tabulate the total number of cards needed based on the number of groups you have), a student information sheet (see below), and guiding questions.

Place teacher candidates into groups of five. Four will be teachers and one will serve as an instructional coach. Give each of the 4 teachers 25 cards that will represent students having the characteristics found in Table 10.2. Provide the following information:

> It is the beginning of the school year at Sunshine Elementary School. You and the other teachers in your team meet with a counselor to get the class rosters of your new students. Your team will be teaching the 5th graders. Each of you has been assigned 25 students having the characteristics found in the chart (see Table 10.2), but due to the class-size reduction amendment, you need to reduce your rolls by 5 students each.

Give students approximately 15 minutes to complete this task. Once all of the students to be reassigned have been selected, they are grouped together and set aside to form another group of 20 students.

Table 10.2. Sunshine Elementary School

Card	Description
Hearts	Innovative Learners*
Diamonds	Dynamic Learners*
Spades	Common Sense Learners*
Clubs	Analytic Learners*
Aces	Gifted Students
King of Diamonds and King of Spades	Students with Physical Impairments
King of Hearts and King of Clubs	Students with E/BD
Queens	Students with Learning Disabilities
Jack of Hearts and Jack of Diamonds	Students with Intellectual Disabilities and Developmental Delays
8s	Students who are English Language Learners
9s	Students who have low reading skills
10s	Students with ADHD
2s through 7s	Typical Students

*These designations refer to McCarthy's (1980) 4MAT system on learning styles. Refer to www.aboutlearning.com for additional information.

Teacher candidates work in their teams to plan for their new classes. They will need to note plans for seating arrangements, class rules, and routines and to answer the following questions:

- What kinds of grouping arrangements will you have?
- Do you feel that this particular group of students will pose any special problems for you?
- How will you handle the diversity of this group?
- Do you have any questions or concerns regarding your group of students?

Have someone call your cell phone at a predetermined time (or use some other audible signal). The district superintendent is calling to say that, due to budget cuts, all coaches will have to return to the classroom. The coaches are assigned the 20 students that the team reassigned. The groups are instructed to work together to assist the coach as she or he completes the previous activity. This should take approximately 15 minutes. Debrief by having students respond to the following questions:

- How did the activity make you feel?
- Whom did you reassign?
- Why did you select those students?
- What was the most difficult part of the activity?
- How did you feel when you knew your colleague was going to have the kids that you reassigned?
- How would you feel if you were the coach?
- What was the process that you used to select students?
- If the first 5 "types" of students were removed (hearts, diamonds, spades, clubs, and aces), which students would you have selected then, and why?

FAMILIES

My Child and Me: Traversing the Educational Terrain

Family members of individuals who are differently abled frequently encounter challenges as they attempt to maneuver through the educational system. Many parents and guardians are unfamiliar with their rights under IDEA 2004 due to the extensive educational jargon and/or lack of explanation and clarification at their child's initial staffing and Individualized Education Program

(IEP) meetings. Further, many may have had negative schooling experiences that affect their ability to seek the appropriate services for their children. Helping teacher candidates understand experiences by families of children with disabilities is necessary in order to help them understand how they can assist and respond to families' needs.

INTENDED OUTCOMES

This activity can be done at any point throughout the semester and can be completed either by having teacher candidates independently read the article "My Child and Me: Traversing the Educational Terrain" (McHatton & Shaunessy, 2006) or by performing the material in two voices. We recommend performing the piece in two voices,[2] as this provides a more authentic understanding of the issues faced by families of children with disabilities.

The paper is based on a series of interviews with parents of children with disabilities regarding their experiences with the education system. The findings are provided as a succession of found poems, a type of poem created by taking words, phrases, and sometimes whole passages from other sources, such as the interviews. The found poems represent a composite of the experiences shared by the participants along with reflections from the two researchers. We have observed that having the piece performed rather than simply read engages students on a deeper level. Upon completion, teacher candidates complete a quick-write activity describing their responses. Allow the writing to continue until the majority of participants have stopped writing. Give a 2-minute warning, so those who are still writing can end their sentence. We then discuss the emotions elicited by the piece and the issues that emerged from the collective experiences denoted in the piece. We close by addressing any additional questions and comments from the group.

The Kallikaks

The story of the Kallikak[3] family traces the lineage of Deborah Kallikak, a patient at the Research Laboratory of the Training School for Feeble-Minded Girls and Boys (Esping & Plucker, 2002). Henry Goddard, a psychologist and eugenicist, was the director of the school. Deborah was one of his patients and the focus of one his studies, in which he examined the cause of "feeble-mindedness,"

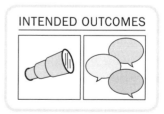

INTENDED OUTCOMES

a term used to describe an individual with intellectual disabilities, which is now considered to be derogatory. According to Goddard, Deborah's "feeble-mindedness" was a direct result of heredity. Her great-great-grandfather, Martin Kallikak, Jr., was the son of a "feeble-minded" barmaid and a "normal" male (Kallikak, Sr.). Investigating the Kallikak lineage led Goddard to determine that Martin Kallikak, Jr., had 480 descendants and of that 143 were feeble-minded and 46 were normal (Goddard, 1912). Further, all of the men and women from the Kallikak side (normal) were citizens in good standing. However, from the barmaid's side, many of the descendants were feeble-minded, criminals, and poor. Goddard argued that feeble-mindedness was genetic and believed that his findings in this study supported his theory. Initially, he supported the process of sterilization so these "diseases" could be permanently eliminated.

Part 1 of this activity can be completed toward the end of the semester. Download the story of the Kallikak family, available from the website Human Intelligence, at the University of Indiana (www.intelltheory.com/kallikak.shtml). Divide the document into two sections. The first section should include the Introduction, Goddard's Research, the Kallikak Family, Deborah Kallikak, Goddard's Recommendations, and Consequences of the Kallikak Family Study. The second section should include Controversial Photos, Goddard's Regrets, and References. Have teacher candidates read the first section in class, and then randomly assign students to two groups (Affirmative and Negative). Groups will debate the following statement: "Individuals with intellectual disabilities should be sterilized." Both groups will have 6 minutes to prepare their initial arguments. The Affirmative group has 3 minutes to present their opinion. The Negative group has 4 minutes to prepare for their cross-examination and 3 minutes to cross-examine the Affirmative group. Be sure to clearly state that the cross-examination can only address issues identified by the Affirmative group speaker(s). This process is repeated with the Negative group presenting their opinion and the Affirmative group cross-examining. After both groups have presented and cross-examined the opposing group, both sides have 4 minutes to prepare their rebuttals, which entails addressing and responding to weaknesses identified by the opposing group. Each group is given 2 minutes to deliver their rebuttal. Repeat this process, if necessary; otherwise, debrief the activity through discussion.

For part 2 of this activity, provide teacher candidates with the second section of the Kallikak Family story. Engage teacher candidates in a dialogue on the effect of Goddard's research and his subsequent change of mind. End the activity with a discussion on current events that may resemble what transpired with the Kallikak family and implications for students with and without disabilities.

CONCLUSION

Each of the activities here has been used multiple times and in multiple settings. Yet with each implementation, we learn something new about ourselves and our students. As with many things, with each rereading or reviewing, something previously hidden emerges. One cannot (and should not) definitively try to predict what "previously hidden" knowledge will "emerge." As teacher educators who lead difficult discussions, we need to be prepared for the unexpected. Outlining some experienced/anticipated outcomes defeats this important message. Likewise, teacher candidates' responses sometimes elicit emotions in us that were hidden, demonstrating the power of hegemony in maintaining the status quo and reinforcing the fact that the quest for cultural competency is a never-ending journey.

NOTES

1. The transcript is verbatim. These were high school students, and no middle school students attended the school. The reference to a 6th-grade hallway is interesting, as it may indicate how they perceive students with intellectual disabilities.
2. Contact the first author of this chapter for specifics if you wish to perform the piece.
3. Pseudonym created by Henry Goddard.

REFERENCES

Artiles, A. J., & Bal, A. (2008). The next generation of disproportionality research: Toward a comparative model in the study of equity in ability differences. *Journal of Special Education, 42*(4), 4–14.

Butler, F., & Mayhew, J. (2004, November). *Let's do it again! Using activities to teach preservice general educators.* Paper presented at Teacher Education Division (TED) of the Council for Exceptional Children 27th Annual Conference, Albuquerque, NM.

Esper, D. (Producer), & Browning, T. (Director). (1932). *Freaks* [Motion picture]. United States: MGM.

Esping, A., & Plucker, J. (2002). *The Kallikak family.* Retrieved from www.intelltheory.com/kallikak.shtml

Ferguson, P. M. (2002). A place in the family: An historical interpretation of research on parental reactions to having a child with a disability. *Journal of Special Education, 36*(3), 124–130.

Goddard, H. H. (1912). *The Kallikak family: A study in the heredity of feeble-mindedness.* New York, NY: Macmillan.

Greene, T. (2006). *I'm Tyler* [DVD]. Retrieved from www.imtyler.org

Hampton, J., (2013). Group dynamics and community building. Retrieved from www.community4me.com/Velvetveen.html

Harry, B. (1992). *Cultural diversity, families, and the special education system: Communication and empowerment.* New York, NY: Teachers College Press.

Harry, B. (1997). Applications and misapplications of ecological principles in working with families from diverse cultural backgrounds. In J. L. Paul, M. Churton, W. C. Morse, A. J. Duchnowski, B. Epanchin, P. G. Osne, & R. L. Smith (Eds.), *Special Education Practice* (pp. 156–170). Pacific Grove, CA: Brooks/Cole.

Kennedy, K., & Kilik, J. (Producers), & Schnabel, J. (Director). (2007). *The diving bell and the butterfly* [Motion picture]. France: Canal+, Kennedy Marshall Company, France 3 Cinéma.

Lyons, G. E. (1999). *Where I'm from, where poems come from.* Spring, TX: Absey.

McCarthy, B. (1980). *The 4MAT system.* Oakbrook, IL: Excel.

McHatton, P. A. (2004). Stigma and discrimination of Mexican and Puerto Rican single mothers of young children with disabilities: Interaction of culture and disability (Doctoral dissertation). Retrieved from Dissertations & Theses @ University of South Florida—FCLA. (Publication No. AAT 3121027).

McHatton, P. A., & Shaunessy, E. (2006, November 27). My child and me: Traversing the educational terrain. *Teachers College Record.* Retrieved from www.tcrecord.org

Minow, M. (1990). *Making all the difference: Inclusion, exclusion, and American law.* Ithaca, NY: Cornell University Press.

Powell, S. (2010). *Freaks* [Review]. Retrieved from classic-horror.com/reviews/freaks_1932

Rothenberg, P. (February, 2006). *Multicultural curriculum transformation: Beyond tacos and egg rolls.* Paper presented at the Globalization Speakers Series and Peace Through Diversity Lecture Series at the University of South Florida, Tampa, FL.

U.S. Department of Education. (2012). *31st Annual Report to Congress on the implementation of the Individuals with Disabilities Education Act, 2009.* Washington, DC: Author.

Wells, H. G. (2014). *The country of the blind.* Retrieved from www.online-literature.com/wellshg/3/ (Original work published 1904)

Williams, M. (1922). *The velveteen rabbit.* Garden City, NY: Doubleday.

Resources

Elaine V. Howes

This appendix provides an annotated list of resources for teaching about diversity in the college classroom. This section provides readers with an extensive and targeted bibliography of online resources, audiovisual materials, readings, and organizations that we believe are useful for subject-area specialists as well as generalists. Resources are organized by both issue and content area. In the case of Internet resources, three criteria were applied for inclusion: durability, self-renewal, and credibility.

ONLINE RESOURCES

General Diversity

ColorLines: News for Action. This website is a good resource for discussion of contemporary issues. colorlines.com

Difficult Dialogues Initiative: Promoting Pluralism and Academic Freedom on Campus. This program is designed to promote academic freedom and religious, cultural, and political pluralism on college and university campuses in the United States. www.difficultdialogues.org/projects/

Diversity in the Classroom. This excellent collection of articles, student writing, and classroom activities is designed to further social justice in our schools, focused on language arts teaching. www.gvsu.edu/ftlc/diversity-in-the-classroom-12.htm

Group Dynamics and Community Building by Jerry Hampton. This website provides a variety of resources on group building. McHatton and Vallice, in Chapter 10, use the excerpt from *The Velveteen Rabbit* (Williams, 1922) that highlights a conversation between the Velveteen Rabbit and the Skin Horse about what it means to be real. www.community4me.com/Velvetveen.html

StoryCorps. This resource provides powerful stories and interviews that educators may use in their own classrooms as well as lesson plans for teaching interviewing and storytelling skills. The Unheard Voices section provides curriculum to help educators integrate LGBT history and issues into their instruction. storycorps.org

English for Speakers of Other Languages

The Cognitive Academic Language Learning Approach (CALLA). Serving as a resource for the CALLA approach, the site also includes strategies for ELL student success. Handouts, events, projects, and references are provided. calla.ws

Cambridge English Teaching Support. The site provides lesson plans, worksheets, classroom activities, and teaching ideas for ESOL teachers. www.teachers.cambridgeesol.org/ts/teachingresources

Center for Applied Linguistics. This website includes different topics related to students learning English as a second language. www.cal.org/topics/ell

Center for the Mathematics Education of Latinas/os (CEMELA). This website provides research-based practices that connect the teaching of mathematics to Latina/o students' sociocultural contexts. cemela.math.arizona.edu

¡Colorín Colorado! This website offers a variety of resources on topics related to creating welcoming and supportive environments for ELLs and their families and suggests how to facilitate learning. www.colorincolorado.org/atoz

EFL Playhouse. This website provides various resources such as chants, worksheets, songs, games, interactive quizzes, and other materials particularly for young children. www.esl4kids.net

ESL Library. This website provides a variety of ESL lesson plans for teachers. www.esl-library.com/lessons.php

ESOL Tapestry. This organization supports the infusion of ESOL into teacher education programs. The site offers an expert series presented by professionals in the field of teaching English to speakers of other languages (TESOL) and contains lectures in video format, journal articles, and book titles. tapestry.usf.edu

Oxford Seminars. This website contains a free comprehensive collection of ESL teaching resources for English language teachers working around the world. www.oxfordseminars.com/esl-teaching-resources/

OWL Purdue Online Writing Lab: ESL Teacher Resources. This website provides both theoretical and practical professional resources. The list includes links to organizations, a list of journals in the field of TESOL, and a selection of online teaching and reference materials. Each link provides extensive information about further resources in the ESL community. owl.english.purdue.edu/owl/resource/586/1

Teaching Channel. This site has a few video clips that focus on connecting the Common Core State Standards to the teaching of ELLs. www.teachingchannel.org/

TESOL Resource Center. This site contains lesson plans, teaching tips, activities, assessment tools, and other resources in the field of teaching English to speakers of other languages (TESOL). Teachers can submit their own resources to share with other professionals in the field. www.tesol.org/connect/tesol-resource-center/

Understanding Language. This website has different resources that exemplify high-quality teaching for ELLs across English language arts, mathematics, and science. The resource also corresponds to the Common Core State Standards for English language arts and mathematics and to the Next Generation Science Standards. ell.stanford.edu

Exceptional Student Education

The Country of the Blind. This short story by H. G. Wells (1904) demonstrates the social construction of disability and how the environment can be modified to significantly diminish difficulties for individuals who are differently abled. For the online text, visit *The Literature Network.* www.online-literature.com/wellshg/3

The IRIS Center. This resource is a technical assistance center funded by the Office of Special Education Programs. It provides free resources for students with disabilities, including a searchable database on films addressing disability. iris.peabody.vanderbilt.edu/resource_TOOL_film/film.html

The Kallikak family. This story traces the lineage of Deborah Kallikak, a patient at the Research Laboratory of the Training School at Vineland, New Jersey, for Feeble-Minded Girls and Boys. Henry Goddard, a psychologist and eugenicist, was the director of the school and believed that Deborah's so-called feeble-mindedness was a direct result of heredity. www.intelltheory.com/kallikak.shtml

About Learning: Helping Teachers and Students with Learning That Matters. This substantial website represents a firm that supports educational organizations in creating "high performance learning." Most pertinent to this volume is Bernice McCarthy's 4MAT system, which includes her work on different types of learners—innovative learners, dynamic learners, commonsense learners, and analytic learners. www.aboutlearning.com

Foreign Language Education

Current Trends in Second/Foreign Language Education. This site is updated yearly with original work from different cohorts of pre- and inservice language teachers participating in courses taught by Adam Schwartz. languageeducation.pbworks.com

Links to Linguistically Significant Images. Mai Kuha's (Ball State University) beautiful collection of photos is a rich resource for supporting students' learning about linguistic landscapes. mkuha.iweb.bsu.edu/lgphoto/lgphotos.html

Spanish in Texas Project. This University of Texas project is a dynamic effort to localize Spanish and Spanish-English bilingualism in Texas. The project is based in the principle that "Spanish is not a foreign language in Texas." spanishintexas.org

American Tongues. This is a dated but highly relevant documentary on the diversity of American Englishes and "accented" English in the United States that is very pertinent to discussions on additive and subtractive bilingualism. www.pbs.org/pov/americantongues

Do You Speak American? More recent than *American Tongues*, this PBS documentary illuminates the diversity of American Englishes and "accented" English in the United States. www.pbs.org/speak

Dialect Diversity and ESOL. Dr. Walt Wolfram's online resource about linguistic diversity includes a video lecture, outline, viewing questions, and topic resources; it is relevant for any language teacher (English and second/foreign). tapestry.usf.edu/Wolfram/index.html

Stephen Fry Takes a Firm Stance on Grammar. He Doesn't Go the Way You'd Think. The comedian, author, and film director Stephen Fry uses words (literally) in this YouTube video to make fun of prescriptivism. He has other colorful material on YouTube and elsewhere. www.upworthy.com/stephen-fry-takes-a-firm-stance -on-grammar-he-doesnt-go-the-way-youd-think-2

The Freire Project. This site provides a rich source for critical pedagogy: readings and teacher resources, news and announcements, documentaries and interviews, and an area for blogging. www.freireproject.org

Mathematics Education

Teaching for Excellence and Equity in Mathematics (TEEM). This journal is published at least once per year. Members have online access to the current issue, while previous issues are available to the public. www.todos-math.org/teem

TODOS: Mathematics for All. This website presents the work of the TODOS organization, which aims to develop and implement equitable and rigorous mathematics education for all students. The site provides a series of webinars and other resources. www.todos-math.org.

Science Education

What Does It Mean to Be Human? This rich Smithsonian National Museum of Natural History website provides short video clips and text presenting the scientific consensus that we are all one species. It is useful for sparking discussions on why racial categories exist in our society, even though they have no basis in respectable science. The education page includes a teacher forum and lesson plans. humanorigins.si.edu/

National Center for Case Study Teaching in Science. This site provides an easily searchable database for educational case studies concerning a large diversity of cultural groups (including Native American, African American, Latino, and women). sciencecases.lib.buffalo.edu/cs/collection

Next Generation Science Standards Case Studies. Created to Accompany *NGSS Appendix D: All Standards, All Students*, these lengthy vignettes illustrate the implementation of the *NGSS.* Case studies are entitled "Economically Disadvantaged," "Race and Ethnicity," "Students with Disabilities," "English Language Learners," "Girls," "Alternative Education," and "Gifted and Talented Students." www.nextgenscience.org/appendix-d-case-studies

Race: The Power of an Illusion. This is an excellent website that includes online activities to help students question their own beliefs about race and learn the science behind the "illusion" of race. The site is a companion to the PBS video series *Race: The Power of an Illusion.* www.pbs.org/race/000_General/000_00-Home.htm (see YouTube for clips from the documentary: www.youtube.com/watch?v=V9YMCKp5myI)

SACNAS Biography Project. Developed by the Society for Advancement of Chicanos and Native Americans in Science, this website provides attractively presented biographies of Chicano/Latino and Native American scientists. It is explicitly designed for educational purposes. www.sacnas.org/biography/default.asp

Science Update: Spotlight on African American Scientists. The stories on this website are told from the perspectives of individual scientists and accompanied by photographs of African American scientists (many of them women) at work and by recent studies conducted by each scientist. www.scienceupdate.com/spotlights/african-american-scientists

Social Studies Education/Political Cartoons

Association of American Editorial Cartoonists. The site provides background on the cartoon, lesson plans, and worksheets for students. nieonline.com/aaec/cftc.cfm

Cartoon Archives. Editorial cartoons are organized on this website by subject matter. www.pritchettcartoons.com/archives.htm

Daryl Cagle's The Cagle Post Cartoons and Commentary. This site includes editorial cartoons, a best cartoon of the day feature, and a search tool to find specific topics or issues. The Teacher Guide has lesson plans using the cartoons across the curriculum. www.cagle.com/

Gocomics. This site provides a comprehensive and up-to-date collection of the best editorial cartoonists on the Internet. www.gocomics.com/explore/editorials

Herblock's History. The venerable political cartoonist's works are included in this collection, organized by topic. www.loc.gov/rr/print/swann/herblock/cartoon.html

The New York Times on the Web: Cartoons. A great variety of recent cartoons are stored here, including Trudeau's *Doonesbury* and other nationally syndicated cartoonists. www.nytimes.com/diversions/cartoons

NewsDirectory.com. This collection contains newspapers and magazines from around the world, including political cartoons appropriate for use in the classroom. www.ecola.com

The Opper Project. This online collection contains historic editorial cartoons covers over 100 years of American history; it is organized topically with associated lesson plans. hti.osu.edu/opper

University of Pennsylvania Library: Political Cartoons. This site provides a comprehensive list of links to a variety of political cartoon sites. www.library.upenn.edu/resources/subject/social/communication/politicalcartoons.html

AUDIOVISUAL MATERIALS

Note: The films and videos listed here are generally available from YouTube, Amazon, Netflix, or your university's library.

General Diversity

Avatar follows the story of U.S. Marine Jake Sully, who has complete paralysis in the lower half of his body. Despite his disability, he has chosen to protect the world of Pandora against its enemies. Cameron, J., & Landau, J. (Producers), & Cameron, J. (Director). (2009). USA: Twentieth Century Fox.

Ben X. Ben is a student with Autism who is constantly bullied in school. In order to escape, he immerses himself in the world of virtual video games and befriends a young female who helps him to heal from the challenges at school. Bos, B., Bouckaert, P., Provoost, E., de Rooij, M., & Veenendaal, S. (Producers), & Balthazar, N. (Director). (2007). Belgium: MMG Film & TV Production.

Center for Persons with Disabilities. This video clip reminds individuals to first see a person's ability and not the disability. www.youtube.com/watch?v=AW-L8o-fLpQ

Children of a Lesser God is the story of James, a speech teacher, who falls in love with Sarah, a student who studies at a school for the deaf. Palmer, P. J., & Sugarman, B. (Producers), & Haines, R. (Director). (1986). USA: Paramount Pictures.

Disability Means Possibility. This video clip reminds individuals to see the person first instead of the disability. www.youtube.com/watch?v=uhKMouRaWcY

The Diving Bell and the Butterfly tells the story of *Elle* editor Jean-Dominique Bauby, who had a stroke at the age of 42. The film introduces students to possibilities that remain despite barriers that may come with being differently abled. Kennedy, K., & Kilik, J. (Producers), & Schnabel, J. (Director). (2007). France: Canal+, Kennedy Marshall Company, France 3 Cinéma.

Freaks was released in 1932 and was considered a horror movie. It depicts how individuals with and without exceptionalities were treated in society. Esper, D. (Producer), & Browning, T. (Director). (1932). USA: MGM.

I Believe in Me. Do You Believe in Me? Nine-year-old Dalton Sherman addresses a crowd of 20,000 teachers and staff from the Dallas Independent School District by posing the question, "Do you believe in me?" http://www.schooltube.com/video/345da8d157134ec5a8f7/

I'm Tyler is a documentary about a young man diagnosed with cerebral palsy who discusses the people in his life who support and believe in him, as well as his accomplishments and the accommodations necessary for his participation in certain activities given his disability. www.imtyler.org

Including Samuel is a documentary that follows Dan Habib and his son Samuel, who is diagnosed with cerebral palsy. The film includes the stories of four other individuals with disabilities. Habib, D. (Director, Producer), & Desgres, R. (Editor). (2009). www.includingsamuel.com

Misunderstood Minds Searching for Success in Schools follows five families and shares their challenges and experiences with learning differences. Kirk, M. (Director). (2004). shop.pbs.org/products/A5391

Riding the Bus with My Sister tells the story of two sisters, Rachel and Beth; Beth has an intellectual disability. Upon the passing of their father, Rachel takes on the role of Beth's caregiver and is given the opportunity to learn more about Beth's life. Saito, S. (Producer), & Huston, A. (Director). (2005). USA: Blue Ridge Motion Pictures.

Three Faces of Eve follows Eve White, a woman suffering from multiple personality disorder, and explores how her doctor attempts to help her. Johnson, N. (Producer & Director). (1957). USA: Twentieth Century Fox Film Corporation.

Tim Wise on White Privilege: Racism, White Denial, and the Costs of Inequality. This lecture by the author of *White Like Me: Reflections on Race from a Privileged Son*

provides a personal and challenging vision of White privilege. www.timwise.org/2008/05/full-tim-wise-on-white-privilege-racism-white-denial-and-the-cost-of-inequality-2007/

Victor Villaseñor: Genius in All of Us. Victor Villaseñor shares his personal and educational experiences growing up as a Mexican American and as an individual with learning disabilities. (2008). www.youtube.com/watch?v=2BseETeAN2M

What Ever Happened to Baby Jane? This film chronicles the lives of Blanche and Jane Hudson. Blanche, confined to a wheelchair, is under the care of her sister, who mistreats her and is beginning to show signs of dementia. Aldrich, R. (Producer & Director). (1962). USA: Warner Brothers.

What's Disability to Me. This series of short videos, produced by the World Health Organization, features individuals from around the world living with a disability. (2011). www.who.int/disabilities/world_report/2011/videos/en

What's Eating Gilbert Grape? This film chronicles the fictional family of the Grapes. Gilbert Grape has assumed the patriarchal role and cares for his sisters, Ellen and Amy; his mother, who is morbidly obese; and his brother, Arnie, who has an intellectual disability. The film highlights the challenges Gilbert experiences when caring for his family as well as attempting to live his own life. Matalon, D., Ohlsson, B., & Teper, M. (Producers), & Hallström, L. (Director). (1993). USA: Paramount Pictures.

Science Education

At Last! LEGO Creates a Female Scientist Minifigure. Yes, LEGO has finally come out with a woman scientist figure. The fact that it took so long, that there is only one, and that she represents a stereotypical scientist (aside from her gender) provides great fodder for discussion in this article. (2013). www.today.com/moms/last-lego-creates-female-scientist-minifigure-8C11083650

READINGS

General Diversity: Books

Berlak, A., & Moyenda, S. (2001). *Taking it personally: Racism in the classroom from kindergarten to college.* Philadelphia, PA: Temple University Press. From a research-based standpoint, the authors relate their personal experiences and learning concerning "race consciousness" and education, with an eye on one's obligations to one's students.

Boykin, W. A., & Noguera, P. (2011). *Creating the opportunity to learn: Moving from research to practice to close the achievement gap.* Alexandria, VA: ASCD. This book presents a comprehensive view of the achievement gap and advocates for strategies that contribute to the success of all children.

Cleveland, D. (2004). *A long way to go: Conversations about race by African American faculty and graduate students. Higher Education* (Vol. 14.). New York, NY: Peter

Lang. This collection of writings focuses on the experiences of African American graduate students and faculty.

Corbett, D., Wilson, B., & Williams, B. (2002). *Effort and excellence in urban classrooms: Expecting—and getting—success with all students.* New York, NY: Teachers College Press. From the lens of students, teachers, and parents, this book discusses how schools worked to close the performance gap for urban, low-income students.

Crawford, J. (2000). *At war with diversity: U.S. language policy in an age of anxiety.* Clevedon, England: Multilingual Matters. Essays critically relate the history and contemporary influences of antibilingual movements on U.S. educational policy; includes description of resistance to English-only educational trends.

Delpit, L. (1995). *Other people's children: Cultural conflict in the classroom.* New York, NY: New Press. Presents ideas of how teachers in the classroom can become cultural transmitters for all their children.

Delpit, L., & Kilgour Dowdy, J. (2002). *The skin that we speak.* New York, NY: New Press. Essays by teachers concerning dialects in the classroom.

Derman-Sparks, L., & Phillips, C. B. (1997). *Teaching/learning anti-racism: A developmental approach.* New York, NY: Teachers College Press. A guide to fostering anti-racist identity, awareness, and behavior in the classroom.

Gay, G. (Ed.). (2003). *Becoming multicultural educators: Personal journey toward professional agency.* San Francisco, CA: Jossey-Bass. Fourteen authors from diverse backgrounds share their personal stories in advancing multicultural perspectives.

Gerald, A. (1999). Coping with misconduct in the college classroom: A practical model. Asheville, NC: College Administration Publications. Provides discussion, sources of, and advice for managing college students' inappropriate behavior in college classrooms.

Gurin, P., Nagda, B. (R). A., & Suniga, X. (2013). *Dialogue across difference: Practice, theory, and research on intergroup dialogue.* New York, NY: Russell Sage Foundation. The authors synthesize their scientifically based research (random assignment, with experimental and control groups) on intergroup dialogue and describe their courses focused on developing intergroup understandings.

Hickey, M. G., & Lanshan, B. K. (2012). *Even the janitor is white: Educating for cultural diversity in small colleges and universities.* New York, NY: Peter Lang. Focuses on challenges that teacher educators who are committed to diversity education frequently confront and shows how teaching practices may be enhanced to support diversity.

Howard, G. R. (2006). *We can't teach what we don't know: White teachers, multiracial schools.* New York, NY: Teachers College Press. Highlights what exemplary teachers believe, know, and do to support culturally responsive teaching.

Irvine, J. J. (2003). *Educating teachers for diversity: Seeing with a cultural eye.* New York, NY: Teachers College Press. Addresses how race and ethnicity, social class, and culture affect the educational process and provides suggestions for enhancing the teaching and learning process for all children.

Kissen, R. M. (2002). *Getting ready for Benjamin: Preparing teachers for sexual diversity in the classroom.* New York, NY: Rowman & Littlefield. These essays provide revealing analyses of school cultures and give insightful prescriptions for teacher education to further fair treatment of individual differences in ways that can create safe and democratic school learning environments.

Kottak, C., & Kozaitis, K. (2011). *On being different: Diversity and multiculturalism in the North American mainstream.* Whitby, Canada: McGraw-Hill Ryerson. Based on cross-cultural studies of human diversity, this text explores contemporary diversity in North America.

Ladson-Billings, G. (2009). *The dreamkeepers: Successful teachers of African American children* (2nd ed.). San Francisco, CA: Jossey-Bass. Highlights the importance and practices of exemplary teachers who foster academically rigorous and culturally relevant classrooms.

Landsman, J., & Lewis, C. W. (2006). *White teachers, diverse classrooms: A guide to building inclusive schools, promoting high expectations, and eliminating racism.* Sterling, VA: Stylus Publishing. Focuses on the importance of inclusive and equitable teaching to promote student success.

Martin, R. J. (1995). *Practicing what we teach: Confronting diversity in teacher education.* Albany: State University of New York Press. Martin describes the actual practices of teacher educators seriously addressing diversity in their classrooms.

Nieto, S., & Bode, P. (2011). *Affirming diversity: The sociopolitical context of multicultural education* (6th ed.). New York, NY: Pearson. Explains how personal, social, political, cultural, and educational factors affect the success or failure of students in today's classrooms.

Nieto, S. (1999). *The light in their eyes: Creating multicultural learning communities.* New York, NY: Teachers College Press. An account of what needs to occur to foster multicultural learning communities in schools and the role teachers play in changing students' lives.

Nieto, S. (2010). *Language, culture, and teaching: Cultural perspectives* (2nd ed.). New York, NY: Routledge. Text for teacher education (preservice and inservice); questions, classroom teaching activities, and community-based activities are provided to support readers' understanding of the concepts presented.

Noll, J. W. (Ed.). (1999). *Taking sides: Clashing views on controversial educational issues.* Guilford, CT: McGraw-Hill. Written in a debate-style format, this work is designed to inform the reader of major controversies in education.

Palfreyman, D., & McBride, D. L. (2007). *Learning and teaching across cultures in higher education.* New York, NY: Palgrave Macmillan. This theory-grounded text provides examples and resources to support understanding and action in situations in which learners and/or educators from different cultural backgrounds interact in educational settings.

Prentice, D. A. (1999). *Cultural divides: Understanding and overcoming group conflict.* New York, NY: Russell Sage Foundation. This edited volume provides a rich source for research and theory concerning cultural identity from psychological, historical, and sociological perspectives.

Richardson, S. M. (Ed.). (1999). *Promoting civility: A teaching challenge—New directions for teaching and learning, No. 77.* San Francisco, CA: Jossey-Bass. Offers creative, thoughtful strategies for promoting civil discourse and resolving conflict when it arises—both in the classroom and in the campus community at large.

Schoem, D. L., & Hurtado, S. (2001). *Intergroup dialogue: Deliberative democracy in school, college, community, and workplace*. Ann Arbor: University of Michigan Press. A thorough representation of research about and efforts aimed at developing intergroup dialogue about race in multiple types of educational settings.

Shulman, J. H., & Mesa-Bains, A. (Eds.). (1993). *Diversity in the classroom: A casebook for teachers and teacher educators*. Hillsdale, NJ: Lawrence Erlbaum. Based in practitioner knowledge and experiences, this text provides cases to inspire enthusiastic discussions concerning race, class, and cultures in the classroom.

Redman, G. L. (2007). *A casebook for exploring diversity in K–12 classrooms* (3rd ed.). Upper Saddle River, NJ: Merrill/Prentice Hall. Collection of teaching cases drawn from real classrooms; illustrates and provides concepts and questions for discussion concerning teaching all children. Support provided for writing new cases.

Scheurich, J. J., & Skria, L. (2003). *Leadership for equity and excellence: Creating high-achievement classrooms, schools, and districts*. Thousand Oaks, CA: Corwin Press. Designed for school administrators and teachers to consider ways to support equity and academic excellence.

Schniedewind, N., & Davidson, E. (2006). *Open minds to equality: A sourcebook of learning activities to affirm diversity and promote equity* (3rd ed.). Milwaukee, WI: Rethinking Schools. Sourcebook of activities to help students understand and change inequalities based on race, gender, class, age, language, sexual orientation, physical and mental ability, and religion. Activities designed to foster participatory, cooperative, and democratic classrooms.

Singleton, G. E., & Linton, C. (2006). *Courageous conversations about race: A field guide for achieving equity in schools*. Thousand Oaks, CA: Corwin Press. Focusing on policy and school reform, this text supports "conversations about race" via exercises and tools to support deep and powerful discussions.

Tatum, B. D. (2007). *Can we talk about race?* Boston, MA: Beacon Press. The author argues that schools have not become less segregated since *Brown v. Board of Education*, and offers an "ABC" approach—"Affirming Identity," "Building Community," and "Cultivating Leadership"—to address this problem.

Teel, K. M., & Obidah, J. E. (2008). *Building racial and cultural competence in the classroom: Strategies from urban educators*. New York, NY: Teachers College Press. A collection of essays by teacher educators and practicing teachers that utilize personal experience and knowledge to illuminate issues of diversity in the classroom and support the development of cultural competence.

Van Ausdale, D., & Feagin, J. (2001). *The first R: How children learn racism*. Lanham, MD: Rowman & Littlefield. The authors present their findings and theory of very young children's development of concepts of race, ethnicity, and racism in an urban nursery school.

Villegas, A. M., & Lucas, T. (2002). *Educating culturally responsive teachers: A coherent approach*. Albany: SUNY Press. Focuses on the preparation of culturally responsive teachers who are prepared to teach diverse racial and ethnic student populations.

Wall, V. A., & Evans, N. J. (Eds.). (2000). *Toward acceptance: Sexual orientation issues on campus*. Lanham, MD: University Press of America. Summary of the research concerning gay, lesbian, and bisexual students; promotion of awareness and counseling; and diversity among and within these groups. Includes resources for working with LGB students.

General Diversity: Journal Articles and Chapters

Akiba, M. (2011). Identifying program characteristics for preparing preservice teachers for diversity. *Teachers College Record, 113*(3), 658–697. Authors present findings of study examining preservice teachers' backgrounds, beliefs, and teacher education experiences; concludes with recommendations for program characteristics to successfully teach for diversity in education.

Anderson, J. A. (1999). Faculty responsibility for promoting conflict-free college classrooms. *New Directions for Teaching and Learning, 77*, 69–76. Examines the role both faculty and students play in fostering a positive, democratic learning environment.

Baldwin, R. G. (1997–1998). Academic civility begins in the classroom. *Essays on Teaching Excellence, 9*(8), 1–2. This article discusses the importance of civility in college classrooms and demonstrates ways to promote a civil classroom learning environment.

Boice, B. (1996). Classroom incivilities. *Research in Higher Education, 37*(4), 453–485. This article elaborates on the findings from a 5-year study on classroom incivilities.

Cockrell, K. S., Placier, P. L., Cockrell, D. H., & Middleton, J. N. (1999). Coming to terms with "diversity" and "multiculturalism" in teacher education: Learning about our students, changing our practice. *Teaching and Teacher Education, 15*, 352–366. Through a qualitative study of written assignments and dialogues, the authors identify categories of their students' beliefs about diversity and education in the United States.

Delany-Barmann, G., & Minner, S. (1996). Cross-cultural workshops and simulations for teachers. *The Teacher Educator, 32*(1), 37–47. doi:10.1080/. The varied activities provided by this article can be used to support teacher educators in fostering cross-cultural dialogue.

Frey, B. (2008). *Crowd control: Promoting civility in the classroom*. Retrieved from www.umfk.maine.edu/pdfs/facultystaff/civlitreview.pdf. This annotated list of publications on developing civil classroom communities is helpful for instructors seeking more information on developing and encouraging a collegial environment.

Gillette, M., & Boyle-Baise, M. (1996). Multicultural education at the graduate level: Assisting teachers in gaining multicultural understandings. *Theory & Research in Social Education, 24*(3), 273–293. The authors utilize reflective narrative based in course documents to explore how they supported graduate-level teachers in developing multicultural understandings.

Gonzales, V., & Lopez, E. (2001, April). The age of incivility: Countering disruptive behavior in the classroom. *AAHE Bulletin*, 3–6. Provides background and strategies for managing college classrooms in "the age of incivility."

Goodman, D. (1995). Difficult dialogues: Enhancing discussions about diversity. *College Teaching, 43*(2), 47–52. Using a social identity development model, this article provides ways to foster conversations on cultural diversity and oppression in the college classroom.

Johnson, D. W., & Johnson, R. T. (2009). Energizing learning: The instructional power of conflict. *Educational Researcher, 38*(1), 37–51. This article provides theory and the findings from the author's meta-analysis of research on constructive controversy.

Kelly-Woessner, A. K., & Woessner, M. C. (2013). My professor is a partisan hack: How perceptions of a professor's political views affect student course evaluations. *PS: Political Science and Politics, 39*(3), 495–501. Indicates that student evaluations of professors who challenge student beliefs can be lower than those of professors who do not; recommends that tenure and promotion committees take this finding into account.

Maude, S. P., Catlett, C., Moore, S., Sánchez, S. Y., Thorp, E., & Corso, R. (2010). *Infants & Young Children, 23*(2), 103–121. Infusing diversity constructs in preservice teacher preparation: The impact of a systematic faculty development strategy.

Morrisette, P. J. (2001). Reducing incivility in the university/college classroom. *International Electronic Journal for Leadership in Learning, 5*(4). Retrieved from iejll.synergiesprairies.ca/iejll/index.php/ijll/article/view/497/159. Addresses "uncivil" student behaviors directed at faculty in higher education; names factors contributing to such behaviors and provides strategies to avoid and manage them when they do occur.

Nilson, L. B., & Jackson, N. S. (2004, June). *Combating classroom misconduct (incivility) with bills of rights.* Paper presented at the 4th Conference of the International Consortium for Educational Development, Ottawa, Ontario, Canada. Retrieved from www.umfk.edu/pdfs/facultystaff/combatingmisconduct.pdf. Reviews strategies to prevent classroom misconduct from occurring and proposes two models of an original strategy in which the instructor and students agree upon a "bills of rights and responsibilities."

Singh, B. R. (2001). Dialogue across cultural and ethnic differences. *Educational Studies, 27*(3), 341–355. Singh suggests that "communicative relations" are more than conversation, but involve "communicative virtues," which author suggests how to foster.

Sue, D. W., Lin, A. I., Torino, G. C., Capodilupo, C. M., & Rivera, D. (2009). Racial microaggressions and difficult dialogues on race in the classroom. *Cultural Diversity and Ethnic Minority Psychology, 15*(2), 183–190. This qualitative study analyzes the role that microaggressions play in inspiring "difficult dialogues" that can, if inexpertly managed, lead to harm for students of color; implications and recommendations are provided. doi:10.1037/a0014191.

Watt, S. K. (Ed.). (2007). Difficult dialogues: Special issue. *College Student Affairs Journal, 6*(2). Retrieved from www.lib.odu.edu/ojs/index.php/csaj/issue/view/1. This special issue, presenting articles developed for student affairs professionals, aims to inspire conversations about diversity, social justice, and privilege. It also suggests strategies to support dialogues that are both difficult and productive.

Young, R. L., & Tran, M. T. (2001). What do you do when your students say "I don't believe in multicultural education"? *Multicultural Perspectives, 3*(3), 9–14. doi:10.1207/S15327892MCP0303_3. The authors offer ten suggestions to establish a classroom in which students learn to, among other things, recognize multicul-turalism as "contextual," and to respect and recognize all voices.

Zúñiga, X. (1998, Winter). Fostering intergroup dialogue on campus: Essential in-gredients. *Diversity Digest*. Retrieved from www.diversityweb.org/Digest/W98/fostering.html. This short, online text highlights the importance of and ways in which dialogues across group boundaries can be facilitated.

English Language Arts: Books

Boiarsky, C. (2003). *Academic literacy in the English classroom: Helping underprepared and working class students succeed in college*. Portsmouth, NH: Heinemann. This series of essays discusses content and socialization issues involved in "academic literacy." Offers activities and strategies teachers can use to help students acquire skills they need to read and write at the college level.

Christensen, L. (2000). *Reading, writing, and rising up: Teaching about social justice and the power of the written word*. Milwaukee, WI: Rethinking Schools. Essays, lesson plans, and powerful examples of student writing, all centered in "language arts teaching for justice."

Christensen, L. (2009). *Teaching for joy and justice: Reimagining the language arts classroom*. Milwaukee, WI: Rethinking Schools. Shares classroom-tested ideas for making writing instruction a central part of the curriculum by empowering stu-dents of all backgrounds and skill levels to write about their lives and experiences.

Fisher, D., Rothenberg, C., & Frey, N. (2007). *Language learners in the English classroom*. Urbana, IL: National Council of Teachers of English. Outlines purposeful and pow-erful lessons that accelerate the achievement of students who are learning English.

Tatum, A. W. (2005). *Teaching reading to Black adolescent males: Closing the achieve-ment gap*. Portland, OR: Stenhouse. Bridges the connections among theory, in-struction, and professional development to present practical suggestions for reading strategy instruction and assessment that is explicit, meaningful, and cul-turally responsive. Includes guidelines for selecting and discussing nonfiction and fiction texts with Black males.

Vásquez, A., Hansen, A. L., & Smith, P. C. (2013). *Teaching language arts to English language learners* (2nd ed.). New York, NY: Routledge. Provides readers with the comprehensive understanding of both the challenges that face ELLs and ways in which educators might address them in the language arts classroom. Offers prov-en techniques teachers can readily use to teach reading, writing, grammar, and vocabulary as well as speaking, listening, and viewing skills.

English Language Arts: Journal Articles and Chapters

Blackburn, M. V., & Smith, J. M. (2010). Moving beyond the inclusion of LGBT-themed literature in English language arts classrooms: Interrogating heteronor-mativity and exploring intersectionality. *Journal of Adolescent & Adult Literacy, 53*(8), 625–634. Focuses on the shortcomings of LGBT-inclusivity by concentrat-ing on the problem of heteronormativity and the promise of intersectionality with a deliberate focus on adolescents and adults engaging in literacy practices, construed broadly, in both in-school and out-of-school contexts.

Foreign Language: Books

hooks, b. (2010). *Teaching critical thinking: Practical wisdom.* New York, NY: Routledge. An essential text for understanding connections between critical pedagogy, mindfulness, and self-reflection.

Lippi-Green, R. (2012). *English with an accent.* New York, NY: Routledge. Perhaps one of the most accessible introductions to "American" language policy, language ideology, and contested notions of standardness and accent. (Original work published 1997)

Martinez, G. A. (2006). *Mexican Americans and language: Del dicho al hecho.* Tucson: University of Arizona Press. An introduction to critical bilingualism and the application of that idea to Mexican American language in the United States.

Pollock, M. (2008). *Everyday anti-racism: Getting real about race in school.* New York, NY: New Press. Pollock's edited resource is designed for teachers and teacher educators to identify racism and advocate for anti-racism inside and out of classrooms.

Valdés, G. (2001). *Learning and not learning English.* New York, NY: Teachers College Press. Subtractive language education, up close and personal.

Zentella, A. C. (2004). A Nuyorican's view of our history and language(s) in New York, 1945–1965. In G. Haslip-Viera, A. Falcón, & F. Matos Rodríguez, *Boricuas in Gotham: Puerto Ricans in the making of modern New York* (pp. 20–34). Princeton, NJ: Markus Weiner. A fantastic linguistic autoethnography on growing up bilingual and multicultural in New York City. Spanglish is introduced as identity, a way of life.

Mathematics: Books

Bresser, R., Melanese, K., & Sphar, C. (2008). *Supporting English language learners in math class, grades K–2.* Sausalito, CA: Math Solutions. This lesson-based book provides tools for meeting math content goals and language development goals simultaneously in grades K–2. Contents cover geometry, number sense, data analysis, algebra, and word problems.

Bresser, R., Melanese, K., & Sphar, C. (2008). *Supporting English language learners in math class, grades 3–5.* Sausalito, CA: Math Solutions. This lesson-based book provides tools for meeting math content goals and language development goals simultaneously in grades 3–5. Contents cover geometry, number sense, data analysis, algebra, and word problems.

Coggins, D., Kravin, D., Coates, G. D., & Caroll, M. D. (2007). *English language learners in the mathematics classroom.* Thousand Oaks, CA: Corwin Press. Describes ways to incorporate ELL supports and includes a wealth of strategies that connect standards-based mathematical concepts with language development.

Echevarria, J. J., Vogt, M. E., & Short, D. J. (2009). *The SIOP model for teaching mathematics to English learners.* Boston, MA: Allyn & Bacon. Addresses issues faced in teaching math to English learners (ELs) at each grade level (K–12) and provides educators with access to research-based, SIOP-tested techniques for lessons specifically for the mathematics classroom.

Kersaint, G., Thompson, D. R., & Petkova, M. (2012). *Teaching mathematics to English language learners* (2nd ed.). New York, NY: Routledge. Provides advice on how to teach mathematics to the ELLs in the classroom. Includes a fully annotated list of math web and print resources.

Melanese, K., Chung, L., & Forbes, C. (2011). *Supporting English language learners in math class, grades 6–8.* Sausalito, CA: Math Solutions. Includes lessons and strategies for modifying grades 6–8 instruction to meet the needs of ELLs. Each of the lessons addresses one or more of the Common Core State Standards for Mathematics.

Ortiz-Franco, L., Hernandez, N. G., & De La Cruz, Y. (Eds.). (1999). *Changing the faces of mathematics: Perspectives on Latinos.* Reston, VA: National Council of Teachers of Mathematics. Focuses on a number of salient research and practice issues in the teaching and learning of mathematics among Latinos, the second largest minority group in the United States.

Ramirez, N., & Celedon-Pattichis, S. (Eds.). (2012). *Beyond good teaching: Advancing mathematics education for ELLs.* Reston, VA: National Council of Teachers of Mathematics. Through guiding principles and instructional tools, together with classroom vignettes and video clips, shows how to support ELLs in learning challenging mathematics while developing language skills. Design is interactive and requires reader to move back and forth between chapters and online resources at nctm.org.

Mathematics: Journal Articles and Chapters

Bresser, R. (2003). Helping English language learners develop computational fluency. *Teaching Children Mathematics, 9*(6), 294–299. Describes ways to structure discussions to provide access to students with varying linguistic expertise. By using prompts, asking questions, and encouraging mathematics conversations, teachers can help ELLs with both English-language development and computational fluency.

Brown, C., Cady, J., & Taylor, P. M. (2009). Problem solving and the English language learner. *Mathematics Teaching in the Middle School, 14*(9), 532–539. Describes strategies that helped one ELL student understand mathematics concepts and increase his mathematics achievement. Urges teachers to explore how mathematics is language bound and how language acquisition is the biggest obstacle to learning mathematics for ELLs and to use strategies that will help ELLs both with language acquisition and with understanding mathematics concepts simultaneously.

Chval, K. B., & Chávez, Ó. (2011). Informing practice: Designing math lessons for English language learners. *Mathematics Teaching in the Middle School, 17*(5), 261–265. Describes a four-part process used to plan lessons and make enhancements to put research about teaching mathematics to English language learners into practice. Provides examples from classrooms and research to illustrate the four components and highlights research-based strategies to illustrate how research can be turned into practice.

Chval, K. B., Chávez, Ó., Pomerenke, S., & Reams, K. (2009). Enhancing mathematics lessons to support all students. In D. Y. White & J. S. Silva (Eds.), *Mathematics for every student: Responding to diversity PK-5* (pp. 43–52). Reston, VA: NCTM. Presents an example of how a 1st-grade teacher used research to enhance one lesson from the *Investigations* curriculum to meet the needs of all of her students as they were developing mathematical thinking, problem solving, and communication. Concludes with suggestions for enhancing K–2 mathematics lessons for ELLs.

Chval, K. B., & Khisty, L. (2009). Latino students, writing, and mathematics: A case study of successful teaching and learning. In R. Barwell (Ed.), *Multilingualism in mathematics classrooms: Global perspectives* (pp. 128–144). Clevedon, England: Multilingual Matters. Explains how a teacher promoted her ELLs' success in mathematics. Of particular interest is the way in which mathematical writing for both second language growth and content learning in mathematics was used.

Chval, K. B., & Pinnow, R. (2010). Preservice teachers' assumptions about Latino/a English language learners. *Journal of Teaching for Excellence and Equity in Mathematics, 2*(1), 6–12. Describes three critical misconceptions held by preservice teachers (differential treatment of ELLs based on country of origin, isolation rather than community, and outsourcing to meet ELL needs) and discusses implications for teacher preparation and professional development to better equip teachers to teach mathematics to Latino/a students.

Fernandez, A. (2012). Mathematics preservice teachers learning about English language learners through task-based interviews and noticing. *Mathematics Teacher Educator, 1*(1), 10–22. Describes an intervention in a mathematics content course designed to foster awareness among middle school mathematics PSTs of the challenges that ELL students face and the resources they draw on as they learn mathematics and communicate their thinking in English-only classrooms.

Garrison, L. (1997). Making the NCTM Standards work for emergent English speakers. *Teaching Children Mathematics, 4*(3), 133–138. Describes how teachers can include elements of bilingual instruction to bolster mathematics instruction and suggests that teachers do not need to learn a new set of instructional strategies especially for ELLs but to adapt the strong educational practices that they already possess so as to meet the needs of these learners.

Gómez, C., L. (2010). One lesson, many facets. *Mathematics Teaching in the Middle School, 16*(2), 110–114. Emphasizes the need for instruction tailored to the challenges of learning English and content simultaneously. Discusses how through effective Structured English Immersion (SEI) practices, middle school mathematics teachers can make subject matter comprehensible while promoting English language development.

Gómez, C. L., & Kurz, T. L. (2011). Using Bloom's taxonomy with English language learners. *Mathematics Teaching in the Middle School, 16*(7), 388–391. Examines how teachers can use Bloom's taxonomy to differentiate instruction for ELLs; exposes typical deficiencies in curriculum planning and understanding of the cognitive abilities of English language learners. Stresses the need to engage all students, including ELLs, in higher-level activities.

Khisty, L. L., & Chval, K. B. (2002). Pedagogic discourse and equity in mathematics: When teachers' talk matters. *Mathematics Education Research Journal, 14*(3), 154–168. Presents one teacher with a record of assisting her 5th-grade Latino students in making significant academic gains in mathematics, and examines the way she uses her talk in teaching and how students in her class develop control over the mathematics discourse.

Moschkovich, J. (1999). Supporting the participation of English language learners in mathematical discussions. *For the Learning of Mathematics, 19,* 11–19. Explores how teachers support ELLs in learning mathematics and how ELLs can participate in mathematics discussions. Suggests that determining the origin of an error is not as important as listening to the students and uncovering the mathematical content in what they are saying.

Murrey, D. (2008). Differentiating instruction in mathematics for the English language learner. *Mathematics Teaching in the Middle School, 14*(3), 146–153. Discusses how principles of language acquisition may provide a framework to support differentiating instruction in the mathematics classroom. Describes a classroom in which all students were engaged in meaningful problem-solving activities that lead to conceptual understanding of perimeter and area.

Perkins, I., & Flores, A. (2002). Mathematical notations and procedures of recent immigrant students. *Mathematics Teaching in the Middle School, 7*(6), 346–351. Challenges the idea that mathematics is a universal language by describing differences in mathematical notations and procedures that exist in different countries, particularly Latin American countries. Provides recommendations for using these differences for the advantage of their students.

Roberts, N. S., & Truxaw, M. P. (2013). For ELLs: Vocabulary beyond the definitions. *Mathematics Teacher, 107*(1), 28–34. Presents challenges of mathematics vocabulary for English language learners and suggests strategies for including mathematics vocabulary curriculum development.

Torres-Velásquez, D. (2004). Culturally responsive mathematics teaching and English language learners. *Teaching Children Mathematics, 11*(5), 249–255. Discusses and illustrates some strategies for using culturally responsive mathematics instruction with ELLs—strategies that help students perceive and describe their world, their community, and themselves and that connect to their world, their peers, and their teachers by using mathematics and language.

Weist, L. R. (2008). Problem-solving support for English language learners. *Teaching Children Mathematics, 14*(8), 479–484. Discusses how, with proper instructional support, a student-centered investigative approach to contextualized problem solving can benefit all students, including ELLs. Argues that this type of support is particularly important for ELLs since, although word problems pose greater language demands, they encourage more meaningful problem solving and mathematics understanding.

Wilburne, J. M., Marinak, B. A., & Strickland, M. J. (2011). Addressing cultural bias: A variety of approaches and strategies can help English language learners understand and solve mathematical word problems. *Mathematics Teaching in the Middle School, 16*(8), 460–465. Addresses the issue that while the language and context of many word problems are familiar to American students who speak English as a first language, they are often unfamiliar to ELLs. Discusses how to identify cultural bias in word problems and urge teachers to look beyond the obvious language problems that ELLs may have with the academic language and consider our cultural suppositions.

Zahner, W. C. (2012). ELLs and group work: It can be done well. *Mathematics Teaching in the Middle School, 18*(3), 156–164. Outlines four major elements to consider while using groups in linguistically diverse classrooms: selecting tasks, assigning students to groups, setting norms for interactions, and assessing group work. Elements are illustrated with a task about measurement and proportionality.

Exceptional Student Education: Books

Connor, D. J. (2007). *Urban narratives: Portraits in progress.* New York, NY: Peter Lang. This book shares the stories of eight young individuals of color who are labeled as disabled and explores their experiences of navigating the American urban education system.

Fadiman, A. (1998). *The spirit catches you and you fall down: A Hmong child, her American doctors, and a collision of two cultures.* New York, NY: Farrar, Straus, & Giroux. Explores how cultural expectations affected the treatment and care of Lia Lee, a Hmong child diagnosed with severe epilepsy.

Harry, B. (2008). *Melanie: Bird with a broken wing—A mother's story.* Bloomington, IN: Xlibris. The author shares her personal experiences in raising and losing a child with a severe physical disability.

Mooney, J. (2008). *The short bus: A journey beyond normal.* New York, NY: Henry Holt. This autobiography and biography explores Jonathan Mooney's school experiences as a student with disabilities who rode the "short bus," a derogatory term used against students with disabilities.

O'Brian, R. (2004). *Voices from the edge: Narratives about the Americans with Disabilities Act.* New York, NY: Oxford University Press. The author's intention is to provide a more in-depth review of the Americans with Disabilities Act (ADA) and determine how this law impacts the daily lives of individuals with disabilities.

Sacks, O. (1985). *The man who mistook his wife for a hat (and other clinical tales).* New York, NY: Simon & Schuster. Based on his medical case studies, Oliver Sacks discusses the adversities that many individuals with severe neurological impairments endure on a daily basis.

Sacks, O. (1995). *An anthropologist on Mars.* New York, NY: Vintage Books. Through the use of medical case studies, Oliver Sacks explores how individuals with various neurological conditions adapt to life's experiences and challenges.

Exceptional Student Education: Journal Articles and Chapters

McHatton, P. A., & Shaunessy, E. (2006, November 27). My child and me: Traversing the educational terrain. *Teachers College Record.* Retrieved from www.tcrecord.org. This article is based on a series of interviews with parents of children with disabilities regarding their experiences with the education system. The findings are provided as a succession of found poems that represent a composite of the experiences shared by the participants along with reflections from the two researchers.

Baglieri, S., & Knopf, J. (2004). Normalizing difference in inclusive teaching. *Journal of Learning Disabilities, 37*, 525–529. Explores the concept of inclusion and addresses the need for educators to view inclusion from a disabilities studies perspective in order to better serve their students with disabilities and to create a more inclusive environment.

Science: Books

Barba, Roberta H. (1997). *Science in the multicultural classroom: A guide to teaching and learning* (2nd ed.). Boston, MA: Allyn & Bacon. Methods text that supports reflective practice along with strategies for supporting the learning of all students. While still valuable for its approach, the text is not up-to-date with new national standards.

Roseberry, A. S., & Warren, B. (Eds.). (2008). *Teaching science to English language learners: Building on students' strengths.* National Science Teachers Association. Addresses, from teachers' perspectives, issues, and approaches for teaching science with students of cultural and linguistic backgrounds different from their teachers; grounded in teachers' learning from students.

Settlage, J., & Southerland, S. A. (2012). *Teaching science to every child: Using culture as a starting point* (2nd ed.). New York, NY: Routledge. Text for preservice elementary and middle school teachers provides teaching approaches to attract all students to science and help all students learn. Accompanying website provides links to supportive websites, PowerPoint files for methods instructor, and additional documents for methods courses. www.routledge.com/cw/settlage-9780415892582

ORGANIZATIONS

General Diversity

National Association for Multicultural Education (NAME) is a nonprofit organization working for equity and social justice via multicultural education. The website provides a digital clearinghouse of resources for teaching for equity and social justice. nameorg.org

Rethinking Schools publishes educational materials to support teaching for equity; it is dedicated to public education and its role in a democracy and focuses on urban settings and student diversity. www.rethinkingschools.org/index.shtml

English Language Arts

National Council of Teachers of English (NCTE). Provides position statements about working with English learners, non-White minorities, and culturally and linguistically diverse students. www.ncte.org

English for Speakers of Other Languages

National Association for Bilingual Education (NABE). This professional, national organization has affiliates in 20 states, and represents and provides support for bilingual and English-as-a-second-language educational practitioners at all levels. www.nabe.org

Exceptional Student Education

Council for Exceptional Children. This professional and international organization is dedicated to improving the educational success of individuals with disabilities and/or gifts and talents. Their website provides information and resources for effective instructional practices specific to the field of special education. www.cec.sped.org

Foreign Language Education

American Association for Applied Linguistics. Scholarly, multidisciplinary organization dedicated to a wide range of language-related issues, including language education. aaal.org

Critical Race Studies in Education Association (CRSEA). An association of teacher educators dedicated to "furthering social justice" in P–20 schools through scholarship and praxis. www.crseassoc.org

The International Organization for the Study of Spanish in Society publishes the journal *Spanish in Context* and focuses on theoretical and empirical studies of "the different varieties of Spanish that constitute Hispanic culture." www.southampton.ac.uk/sis

Linguistic Association of the Southwest (LASSO). This organization focuses on the scientific study of language, with an international membership; holds an annual meeting, publishes a newsletter and the *Southwest Journal of Linguistics.* clas.ucdenver.edu/lasso/index.html

Spanish in the US. This group publishes proceedings from its bi-yearly conferences. sius2013.wordpress.com

Mathematics

The Benjamin Banneker Association. A national nonprofit advocating for high-quality mathematics education for African American students, this organization offers professional development (among other things) for teachers to support this goal. www.bannekermath.org

The Center for the Mathematics Education of Latinos/as (CEMELA) is an interdisciplinary, multiuniversity consortium focused on the research and practice of the teaching and learning of mathematics with Latino students in the United States. CEMELA will be relevant not only to Latinos but also to other groups of linguistically and culturally diverse students. math.arizona.edu/~cemela/english/resources/links.php

TODOS: Mathematics for ALL advocates for an equitable and high-quality mathematics
   education for all students—in particular, Hispanic/Latino students—by increasing
   the equity awareness of educators and their ability to foster students' proficiency
   in rigorous and coherent mathematics. www.todos-math.org

Women and Mathematics Education. A chief task of this organization is to support
   and connect mathematics teacher educators in their efforts to teach about and for
   women and girls in mathematics education. www.wme-usa.org

Science

Association for Science Teacher Education. This organization focuses on educating science teachers; it publishes the *Journal of Science Teacher Education.* theaste.org

National Association for Research in Science Teaching. This research focused organization publishes the *Journal for Research in Science Teaching,* which for many years
   has regularly included the most recent studies on teaching science with diverse
   populations as well as teaching teachers to do the same.

National Science Teachers Association. Publishes journals for elementary, middle
   school, and high school teachers; provides a diversity position statement and oc-
   casional articles concerning teaching science (K–12) with culturally and linguistically diverse students. www.nsta.org

Social Studies

American Anthropological Association (AAA). Organization that embraces all those
   with an interest in the discipline; special webpage for teachers and one for students. www.aaanet.org

American Sociological Association (ASA). The ASA's webpage on "Teaching and Learning" offers many helpful resources for educators. www.asanet.org

National Council for Geographic Education (NCGE). International organization dedicated to supporting geography teaching at all levels. ncge.org

National Council for History Education (NCHE). Dedicated to both advocacy and professional development in the promotion of the importance of history to schools
   and society. www.nche.net

National Council for the Social Studies (NCSS). The umbrella organization for social
   studies teaching at all levels (including college); defines social studies as "the integrated study of the social sciences and humanities to promote civic competence."
   socialstudies.org

About the Contributors

Vonzell Agosto is assistant professor in the Department of Educational Leadership and Policy Studies at the University of South Florida. Her research interests are curriculum, instruction, and leadership preparation and practice. These interests are pursued through the lens of antioppressive education and the possibilities for realizing equitable excellence in teaching, learning, and leadership. Dr. Agosto has presented her research at major conferences, including the American Education Research Association, University Council for Educational Administration, Bergamo, and Critical Race Studies in Education. She has published in *Teachers College Record, Journal of School Leadership, Teacher Education & Practice*, and various handbooks.

Sylvia Celedón-Pattichis is professor of bilingual and mathematics education in the Department of Language, Literacy, and Sociocultural Studies at the University of New Mexico. Her research interests focus on promoting equity and studying linguistic and cultural influences on the teaching and learning of mathematics, particularly with English language learners. She also prepares preservice teachers to work with culturally and linguistically diverse students. She taught mathematics at Rio Grande City High School in Texas. She was a coprincipal investigator of the NSF-funded Center for the Mathematics Education of Latinos/as (CEMELA).

Kathryn B. Chval is the associate dean for academic affairs, an associate professor of mathematics education, and codirector of the Missouri Center for Mathematics and Science Teacher Education at the University of Missouri. Dr. Chval is also the principal investigator for the Facilitating Latinos' Success in Mathematics Project and coprincipal investigator for the Center for the Study of Mathematics Curriculum and the Researching Science and Mathematics Teacher Learning in Alternative Certification Models project, which are funded by the National Science Foundation. Prior to joining the University of Missouri, Dr. Chval was the acting section head for the Teacher Professional Continuum Program in the Division of Elementary, Secondary, and Informal Science at the National Science Foundation. Dr. Chval's research interests include the following: effective preparation models and support structures for

teachers across the professional continuum; effective elementary teaching of underserved populations, especially English language learners; and curriculum standards and policies.

Deirdre Cobb-Roberts is an associate professor in the Department of Psychological and Social Foundations at the University of South Florida and a former McKnight junior faculty fellow. She received her PhD from the University of Illinois at Urbana-Champaign. Her research focuses on the history of American higher education, teacher preparation with an emphasis on cultural diversity, and the role of social justice in culturally responsive and responsible pedagogy. She has presented her research at major conferences, including those of the American Educational Research Association, American Educational Studies Association, History of Education Society, and the Critical Race Studies in Education Association. Dr. Cobb-Roberts was coeditor (with Sherman Dorn and Barbara J. Shircliffe) of the book *Schools as Imagined Communities* and has published in a number of journals, including *History of Education Quarterly*; *American Educational Research Journal*; *Journal of Teacher Education*; *International Journal of Educational Policy*; *Research and Practice*; *Educational Considerations*; and *Negro Educational Review*.

Bárbara C. Cruz is professor of secondary education at the University of South Florida. Her teaching and research interests include the preparation of social studies teachers, diversity issues in education, and teaching about Latin America and the Caribbean. Recent work centers on English language learners in the social studies classroom, including her coauthored books, *Teaching Social Studies to English Language Learners* and *Gateway to Social Studies*. In addition to scholarly works, Dr. Cruz has published a number of young adult biographies of inspirational Hispanics (such as Frida Kahlo, José Clemente Orozco, and Rubén Blades). She is the author of *César Chávez: A Voice for Farm Workers* and *Multiethnic Teens and Cultural Identity*, for which she received the Carter G. Woodson Book Award.

Cheryl R. Ellerbrock is an assistant professor of middle grades/general education in the Secondary Education Department at the University of South Florida. She teaches a variety of courses, including Teaching the Adolescent Learner, Teaching the Young Adolescent Learner, Classroom Management for a Diverse School and Society, Middle Level Education, Middle School Trends and Issues, Care and Personalization in Secondary Education, and Collegiate Teaching in Secondary Education. In 2011, she received USF's Outstanding Undergraduate Teacher of the Year award. Her research specializes in supporting the developmental needs of young adolescent learners, including exploring how secondary school environments support their needs, investigating ways to foster a responsive middle-to-high-school transition, and developing responsive secondary educators. She has recently published in scholarly journals such as *Middle Grades Research Journal,* the *Journal of Educational Research, Middle School Journal,* and *Urban Education.*

Elaine V. Howes received her PhD in curriculum, teaching, and educational policy from Michigan State University. Her career in education includes 4 years of high school teaching and 16 years as a teacher educator and researcher at MSU; Teachers College, Columbia University; and the University of South Florida. Elaine wrote *Connecting Girls and Science: Feminism, Constructivism, and Science Education Reform* (Teachers College Press, 2002), a book based on her high school teaching and influenced by both feminist and constructivist science education perspectives. Elaine's work with preservice and inservice teachers has led to publications focusing on teachers' practices in working with English Language learners in science, elementary preservice students' visions of science and science teaching, and the challenges involved in developing environmentally and culturally relevant science curriculum for K–8 classrooms. She is on the faculty of an innovative master of art in teaching program at the American Museum of Natural History in New York City, helping to educate new Earth science teachers who will study and work in high-needs schools, thus continuing her established interest in working with teachers and students to develop teaching that supports all students in succeeding in science.

Zorka Karanxha is an associate professor in the Department of Educational Leadership and Policy Studies at the University of South Florida. Her research focuses on leadership for social justice preparation, charter schools, and education law. She has presented her research at major conferences, including American Education Research Association, University Council for Educational Administration, and the Education Law Association. Dr. Karanxha has published in journals such as *Action in Teacher Education, Educational Administration Quarterly,* and the *Journal of Research in Leadership Education.* She has coauthored a book, with Perry Zirkel, entitled *Student Teaching and the Law.* Dr. Karanxha teaches courses on ethics and leadership, organizational theory, and culturally relevant leadership. She serves as coeditor of *Journal of Cases in Educational Leadership.*

Deoksoon Kim is an associate professor of foreign language education and second language acquisition/instructional technology (SLA/IT) at the University of South Florida. Her research focuses on L2 reading and literacy, socioculturally diverse learners, and applications of instructional technologies in second language acquisition and ESOL teacher education. She teaches preservice teachers in ESOL education and language preservice teachers in foreign-language education. Notably, she was a recipient of the USF Outstanding Undergraduate Teacher Award in 2008 and the Sunshine State Outstanding Educator Award from the Florida TESOL Association in 2012.

Miyoun Lim is assistant professor of science education at Ewha Women's University in South Korea. Her current research focuses on issues of multicultural science education in South Korea. Drawing from pedagogy of place, her research explores ways to consider students' sense of place in science classrooms and support teachers in connected science education.

Patricia Alvarez McHatton is professor and chair of the Inclusive Education Department at Kennesaw State University. Her research interests include diversity in education, teacher preparation with an emphasis on preparing culturally competent educators, collaboration, and school experiences of diverse youth and families. Her work centers on school-university-community partnerships. A major emphasis of her work is engaging disenfranchised youth in participatory action research for social change and arts-based research as a method for making research findings accessible to the communities in which it is undertaken. She is active in several professional organizations, having served as president for both the Division for Culturally and Linguistically Diverse Exceptional Learners (DDEL) and the Teacher Education Division (TED) of the Council for Exceptional Children (CEC).

Adam Schwartz (PhD, University of Arizona) is an assistant professor of Spanish in the Department of World Languages at Oregon State University. His research specializes in Spanish language education in the United States and U.S.–Mexico borderlands, and constructions of culture, borders, foreignness, race, and privilege both in and outside textbook-centered classrooms. He has taught Spanish at the middle school, high school, and university levels. Schwartz has also worked with preservice teachers and undergraduates from across all disciplines as an instructor of educational foundations courses.

Roseanne K. Vallice is an assistant professor in the Department of Special Education at Mercy College in Dobbs Ferry, New York. Her current areas of research include teacher preparation with an emphasis on secondary education and examining the beginning teaching experiences of special education teachers. She also examines the effects of culturally responsive teaching and the overrepresentation of culturally and linguistically diverse students in special education. She obtained her PhD from the University of South Florida, her MEd from Long Island University, and her BA from New York University.

Anete Vásquez is an assistant professor of English language arts education in the Department of Secondary and Middle Grades Education at Kennesaw State University. Her research interests include the preparation of English language arts teachers, preparing teachers to teach diverse learners, and best practices in field experiences. She has published in The ALAN Review and recently co-authored the book Teaching Language Arts to English Language Learners. Dr. Vásquez was a classroom teacher for 12 years teaching language arts at both middle and high school levels, and she was a recipient of a 2001 Milken Educator Award as well as the University of South Florida's Outstanding Undergraduate Teaching Award. She is passionate about working with preservice and inservice teachers across disciplines preparing them to serve the needs of all learners.

Eugenia Vomvoridi-Ivanović is an assistant professor of mathematics education at the University of South Florida. She is also the mathematics education program coordinator and master's advisor. She has taught mathematics at the middle school, high school, and college level and is currently teaching mathematics education courses to undergraduate, master's, and doctoral students. Through her work with the Center of Mathematics Education for Latinas/os (CEMELA), she has gained experience in doing research, teacher preparation, and professional development via new models, all of which address issues of language and culture, particularly as they relate to the teaching and learning of mathematics for Latinas/os. Her areas of experience and interest in research and teaching focus on improving and advancing mathematics education for students from groups that are historically underrepresented and undereducated in the field of mathematics and whose linguistic and cultural backgrounds have not traditionally been recognized as being resources for academic learning. Specifically, she is interested in the roles of language, culture, identity, and power in mathematics education; the mathematics education of language minority students; mathematics teacher preparation for diverse student populations; teacher development in informal mathematics learning contexts; teaching mathematics for social justice; and culturally responsive mathematics teacher education.

Eric Williams currently serves as director of school improvement for the Hernando County School District in Brooksville, Florida. In this capacity he oversees assessment, professional development, federal programs, and strategic planning and school improvement planning processes. He also manages all aspects of Hernando County's federal Race to the Top grant. He started his career in public education in Hernando County in 1995 as a middle school language arts teacher. He taught high school English, journalism, and desktop publishing in Cody, Wyoming, for 8 years. He earned his master's degree in journalism and mass communication from the University of Nebraska in 2005 and taught communications courses full-time at the University of North Florida for 2 years.

Index

A letter *f* following a page number refers to figure